D0880925

About the Editors

IVOR AGYEMAN-DUAH is founder of the Centre for Intellectual Renewal in Ghana and has been Advisor to The Andrew Mellon Foundation of New York on its Africa programme, the Aluka Cultural Project. He has also been Head of Public Affairs at the Ghana Embassy in Washington, DC and Cultural and Communication Advisor at the Ghana High Commission in London. He has also been a Visiting Scholar-in-Residence at the College of Arts and Letters, California State University in Pomona and a Visiting Writer at the University of Nebraska. He is author of eight books based on his travel research interests: economic history, cultural and literary studies, and biographies on Africa, the Caribbean, East and South-East Asia. Apart from book chapters, his essays and reviews have also been published in such journals as *African Affairs*, *International Affairs*, and *African and Asian Studies Journal*.

Born in Kumasi in March 1966, Agyeman-Duah has held Research Fellowships at the W. E. B. Du Bois Research Institute, Harvard University, 1998 and a Hilary and Trinity Research scholar-in-residence at Exeter College, Oxford University in 2007.

CHRISTINE KELLY is from Surrey, England, worked with the Centre for Intellectual Renewal in Ghana in 2008 as a Development Trainee and has similar working experience with Oxford Development Abroad in Uganda. She graduated in Philosophy, Politics and Economics (PPE) from Exeter College, Oxford University in 2007.

AN ECONOMIC HISTORY OF GHANA

Reflections on a Half-Century
of Challenges & Progress

AN ECONOMIC HISTORY OF GHANA

Reflections on a Half-Century of Challenges & Progress

Foreword by Wole Soyinka
1986 Nobel Laureate

Edited by Ivor Agyeman-Duah
With assistance from Christine Kelly

ayebia

An Adinkra symbol meaning
Ntesie matemasie
A symbol of knowledge and wisdom

Ayebia Clarke Publishing Limited gratefully acknowledges Arts Council SE Funding

*For farmers of all classes
and shades in their delivery
and for sustaining the
post-independence economy
of Ghana.*

Contents

Acknowledgements

Several people have contributed to the creative input of this project from the conception of the TV series, *An Economic History of Ghana: Reflections on a Half-Century of Challenges and Progress*, to which this is a companion book. In 2007, I was awarded an academic Visiting Scholarship, a Hilary and Trinity term Research Scholar-in-Residence at Exeter College, Oxford University, where I worked extensively on this, as well as doing other economic history research on Africa, and also on East and South-East Asian economic relations. I must express gratitude to the Rector of the College, Frances Cairncross, herself a distinguished economist, for making this possible, and to Katrina Hancock, Development Officer of the College, who helped to arrange my accommodation at Stapledon House and dealt with other related matters.

It was through the College that I met Christine Kelly, who had previously graduated in Philosophy, Politics and Economics (PPE). She has since worked in Ghana with the Centre for Intellectual Renewal for close to a year and served as an editorial assistant to the TV series and also to this book. Also to be appreciated is Joseph Boateng, who had been previously engaged with the CIR's projects and initially worked with me as the liaison officer responsible for arranging most of the interviews during my many travels.

Again we are happy that Ayebia Clarke Publishing Limited in Oxfordshire, England is publishing this book. A mutual respect for historical preservation has established a strong bond between publishers Ayebia Clarke and the CIR. Apart from publishing two previous works of the CIR, there is the shared desire to promote literary production from Ghana and Africa. While this particular offering may be off the main staple of literature and serious cultural writings for which Nana Ayebia herself is noted, it is also the case that Literature and the Arts can also not expand properly if issues of economic growth and eventually development are not addressed in Africa. Declining economic growth since especially the 1970s has partly accounted for the great depression in reading. So by publishing this work, we are ironically addressing another important issue. We also want to acknowledge the work of Ayebia and their editorial team including especially her designer, Amanda Carroll. Their work is always of the highest quality.

Lastly, our thanks to all the people who agreed to participate in this project and granted the interviews. They are all very busy people and notwithstanding some of the frustrations we encountered before we "caught" them, it was eventually worth it.

IvorAgyeman-Duah, Oxford.

FOREWORD
Wole Soyinka

I sometimes refer to my generation as the "wasted generation" and by that I am referring in fact to the aspirations and the achievements in the postcolonial period – from Ghana's independence in March 1957 and beyond. In other words: the vision was there, the enthusiasm was there, in fact the confidence was there. I sometimes also refer to ourselves as the "renaissance people" because we felt there was absolutely no limit to the potential for rebirth of the African continent, and in some kind of false mystical, romantic way, we felt we were the generation to produce this. I often refer to my generation as the "wasted generation" because of that disparity between vision, aspiration and achievement.

Leadership was the main problem. Yes, of course a lot of blame must be placed on the shoulders of the former colonial powers who, never really left. That's why the term "neo-colonialism" was invented by the analysts of the African situation and the colonial experience, including I believe, Kwame Nkrumah. So that was there, but then, collaboration had to take place; collaboration from a perspective of very short-term advantages and a determination to build a personality cult around oneself. We must be frank and very objective about this. Kwame Nkrumah was also at fault in this respect, in which the personality cult became something that existed for itself and could be nurtured by either side of the ideological divide, West or East. So there was a process of a failure to carry people along as partners in the enterprise of decolonisation and genuine, total liberation. But of course some were far guiltier than others. You don't compare Nkrumah with somebody like Idi Amin. No way. It is a combination of that skewed perspective of leadership ego in contrast to an acceptance of being complete, total equal partners in the enterprise of true liberation.

Certainly some leaders have learned from the errors of the past. I would group among such people somebody like Julius Nyerere of Tanzania, who also had a very advanced, progressive ideological orientation, but whose resources and interpretation of the possibilities of the resources in the modern world did not actually match the reality. But you have to give people like Nyerere credit for remaining faithful to the vision right to the very end. And so you had experiments like Ujamaa, which were people-oriented but unfortunately didn't quite work out on account of the resources which were available, and also the somewhat artificial approach to the re-organisation of traditional community development and reproductive strategies.

For me, it was enough that these people were sufficiently motivated, had a vision, and pursued that vision, no matter the errors. And then of course you have the supreme, absolutely unmatchable example of leaders like Nelson Mandela, who mixed vision and practice in a unique way, which of course was embodied by his own personality, and recognised the realities of internal decolonisation, the apartheid.

He dismantled it with his colleagues – it was a collective effort – but it was very pragmatic. Leaders like Oliver Tambo, Desmond Tutu, and the new generation of activists within the African National Congress managed to find a formula which did not blow up. And this was very much on the cards: not blow up the entirety of South Africa, setting back the self-recovery of the African continent, as would have happened a couple of decades ago. So there are examples like that. There are other experiments in various areas: Thomas Sankara of Burkina Faso, for instance, tried the populist approach, but again geared towards the involvement of the people as partners in progress, to use a cliché. You have the economic experimentation of the Ivory Coast, which worked up to a certain point but failed politically because of the policy of Ivoirité, which was exclusionist and therefore led to the problems in the Ivory Coast. I am sorry that each time I try to point to a positive I have to point to a negative, but we have to be practical because we're writing also for the new generation and letting them understand that errors have been committed.

There are, however, structures like the New Partnership for Africa's Economic Development (NEPAD); not so much NEPAD as the Peer Review structure within the African Union, which is based on a recognition within the leadership that there is something seriously wrong with the leadership. That Peer Review Mechanism is an acknowledgement of that fact, which is the first step. It is no longer the Wole Soyinkas, the Chinua Achebes, the Ngugi wa Thiong'os saying it now; it is the leaders themselves who recognise that there is something desperately wrong, and so they set up this mechanism. But they have to make this mechanism open. I believe very much not just in accountability, but in openness, transparency. They have to let the people know that this kind of mechanism is serious and it's not just an anodyne to paper over the cracks.

You have all over the continent, with the failures admitted, a recognition of the fact that stepping into the shoes of the departing colonial masters, you're not allowed to dominate your own people, and to act towards them like internal colonisers doesn't work any longer. So that is a shift in thinking, and that bodes well. The development also of organisations like the Economic Community of West African States (ECOWAS); the former East Africa Economic Community; the Southern African Development Community (SADC), the Southern Africa partnership with some of the former front-line states; these are, for me, efforts at recognising the fact that we cannot continue to blame the former colonial masters and the international conglomerates and so on. We can stand up and just say, "Listen, we will dictate, or we will negotiate on an equal basis, the strategies and tactics of partnership."

That is needed, for, with a correct political leadership, there will be concentration on the economy – not only Ghana's but Africa's. Fortunately in Ghana, there is President John Kufuor who is one of the few African leaders not with slaves in their mouths.

Wole Soyinka, January 2007
Nobel Laureate in Literature, 1986
Elias Ghanem Professor of Creative Writing,
University of Nevada, Las Vegas
President's Marymount Institute Professor in Residence at Loyola
Marymount University, Los Angeles

Introduction

This book of reflections, *An Economic History of Ghana: Reflections on a Half- Century of Challenges and Progress*, is a companion to the television series of the same title produced in 2008. It attempts, as the series does but in greater detail, a review of how far things have changed but also at the same time stalled. After a half-century of postcolonial management of the Ghanaian economy (since independence in March 1957) it has transited under the rule of the first government, Kwame Nkrumah's. Much has happened in terms of which direction or ideological positions – command or state controlled, classical or social liberalism – the economy should take.

Many individuals and institutions (some dead and many still alive) have been involved in this half-century process of change and renewal. Not all of them were or are trained economists; in fact they did not and need not be. From time immemorial – before economics became a profession – socio-economic interpretation and analysis of human actions and reactions have always been conducted and it is these practices of centuries before that have evolved into the analyses of the modern global economy of the 21st century.

Adam Smith (1723–90), the father of modern economics, was a moral philosopher who spent time at the Universities of Oxford and Glasgow and interpreted the economy of his time based on his training as a philosopher and according to the social and political conditions in which he found himself. The same applies to others like David Hume (1711-76) and David Ricardo (1772-1823), who were scholars in the Age of Enlightenment. But hundreds of years on, Smith's *An Inquiry Into the Nature and Causes of the Wealth of Nations* can still be read as a classic that has anticipated social and economic conditions which are applicable to this day especially with its abiding universal principles.

It was not until after the Second World War in the 1940s and the establishment of global institutions such as Bretton Woods that economics started to take shape in all sense as a profession. The first critical mass of economists were employed at the World Bank and the International Monetary Fund.

Even with that establishment, economics did not cover all aspects and geographic areas of the world, as the global picture was still in the frame of the metropole of Europe and to some extent North America. The periphery economies of Asia, Africa, Latin America and the Caribbean were not seen as real spots for concentration, and if there was discussion of economic issues relating to these areas, it focused on how the maintenance of colonial empires in India and some parts of South–East Asia or Africa were affecting the domestic economy in London. Perhaps the only time when these economies were considered was the moment when the influential Cambridge and 20th century economist, John Maynard Keynes and others debated whether Britain should let go of its colonies and concentrate on re-building its own domestic economy or continue to witness the collapse of its economy in the "needless" prestige of colonial possession.

It took efforts by people of the periphery like W. Arthur Lewis from St. Lucia, who was later knighted and received the Nobel Prize in Economics (in 1979), to help advance Development Economics (economics not as interpreted in the living conditions of Europe but its colonies and "dark" parts), first at the London School of Economics and Political Science and later at the University of Manchester. This was before he became a UNDP advisor to the Kwame Nkrumah government in the 1950s.

The practical side or the reality of economic development as shaped by history does not have exclusive players from any one particular discipline. Policy formulation and implementation have several players and the absence of some could affect the eventual well-being of an economy. An engineer who works on feeder roads in Ghana or any part of Africa makes economic decisions every day; so does a medical officer or a nurse, a banker, a traditional ruler or person of authority, who has control over land and sometimes labour (as in Ghana where over 80 per cent of land is controlled by chiefs) and has to decide whether it is important or otherwise to sell land to government (for the construction of, for example, an inland port). The illiterate money lender in a village market, a lawyer, a court judge, a Member of

Parliament, or the headmaster of a primary or secondary school all make decisions which filter into defining growth or development in any economy, whether consciously or not.

Therefore, for the running of any government or economy, the contributors have different backgrounds but all work towards one goal. This is what is reflected in these interviews with a selection of economists, policy makers, politicians, financial analysts, bureaucrats, diplomats, academics and civil society leaders.

The different parts of the book are based on themes but also on the historical evolution of institutions, on policies and on individual expertise. The book begins, however, with a Foreword by a distinguished Africanist, Nigeria's Nobel Laureate in Literature (1986), Professor Wole Soyinka. Based on transcribed reflections with him in 2007 when he was in Ghana to launch an earlier book I wrote, the Foreword is partly based on Ghana's 50 years of postcolonial rule and how it generally helped with the decolonisation movement in Africa. He talks of the huge expectations of his generation in the 1960s and the renaissance that deluded them – the failure of politics and its consequences for the economy. But he also sees something new and good coming from Africa, such as the New Partnership for Africa's Economic Development (NEPAD).

In Part One: Structures and Institutions in a Postcolonial Economy, we look at the transition from the colonial to the postcolonial institutions like the Civil Service, and also the transition of policies, because the metropolitan British interest in running economies of the colonies was tailored to suit the economic anticipation of the metropole. But that after all was what empire, at least in the Marxist sense, was all about. The infrastructural development of railways and roads from the forest country to the coast, routes of transport for materials such as gold, timber, and cash crops for export and of the inadequate schools and hospitals for the indigenous people. A colonial reverse of this was when the Nkrumah government built more schools and other public facilities.

These transitions needed institutions of State and skilled personnel to manage. If they were managed well, it was because the British brought in tested bureaucrats to do so. The extent to which skills were imparted to the Ghanaians and Africans who inherited the Civil Service by 1960 (when Nkrumah had led the Africanisation of institutions) is hard to tell. But we know that British civil servants were posted to the Gold Coast long before the 1950s and 60s and worked as Education and Health officers, engineers and architects. Terms of recruitment were so good that 40 and more years after their return to Britain from the Gold Coast, these former civil servants are enjoying good retirement. In London in their seventies and eighties, they even have a charity called the Ghana School Aid, which supports development projects and encourages British volunteers to Ghana. They recently published a historical anthology of memoirs of their days in Ghana, *Gold Coast and Ghana Memories*, some of which elaborate on activities and institutions still defining development contours in the country.[1]

Ambassador Annan Cato joined the Ghana Civil Service and Foreign Ministry in 1964 and therefore saw how these institutions worked. He got to know how the transition from colonial to postcolonial rule ensued as a young officer serving both at home and abroad. He later rose to be Director of State Protocol and Secretary to the Cabinet. These, were respectable institutions, as he reflects in the first part of this book. Civil servants had influence not only in ensuring that policies were implemented, but also that should there be a change of government, they would be the lifelines for stability. Nkrumah even trusted on many occasions the opinions of civil servants more than those of his political colleagues.

So why is it that the institution has become weaker in the eyes of many decades after? Mrs Mary Chinery-Hesse also worked in the system from 1962 and through that joined the United Nations. She became the first woman to be Deputy Director-General of the International Labour Organisation in Geneva and the first African woman to attain a position equivalent to Under-Secretary General of the United Nations. In Part One, she explains the causes of this decline, especially the role of military intervention and the destruction of institutional memory and how it has affected economic development.

With this institutional premise set up, Dirk-Jan Omtzigt, a Dutch economist based at the University of Oxford, discusses why some of the economic policies of the Nkrumah era failed. Having completed a

1 *Gold Coast and Ghana Memories* is edited by Eric Cunningham, with assistance from Jennifer MacDougall, Alan Mayhew, and Michael Hammer and co., and was published by the Ghana School Aid Charity in England in 2007. The book could serve as precious data for writers and scholars who want to do detailed work on aspects of Gold Coast development, especially from the 1920s.

great deal of research work on Ghana during those years, he asserts that Nkrumah's socialist orientation was part of the problem, that he had a good chance to make Ghana great but failed.

This assertion, popular in some academic circles, is sharply rebuked by another economist, Nii Moi Thompson, Executive Director of both the Accra-based Development Policy Institute and the Centre for Budget Advocacy and spokesman on the economy for Nkrumah's still-existing Convention People's Party. Nkrumah, he contends, made some mistakes but improved the economy in all aspects including infra-structure, human capacity building, and a sense of national conscious-ness, which was unprecedented in the history of any emerging postcolonial state in sub-Saharan Africa. He believes that the factors that led to his overthrow: Omtzigt's view that he developed a person-ality cult, personalised the army, got the economic indicators wrong, and could not attract Foreign Direct Investment, were in fact political excuses. Commodity prices, especially of cocoa and gold on which the economy depended, had collapsed at the world markets and consequently the West, especially the British and Americans he argues, had ensured that, like Robert Mugabe in Zimbabwe today, enough domestic discontent was cultivated, with icing from the external, to see Nkrumah's overthrow in 1966.

If this is a familiar debate in the economic history of Ghana, it has its referee in Part One as a result of Professor Ernest Aryeetey's inter-vention. In a question posed about why all governments from Kwame Nkrumah to J. A. Kufuor can pinpoint specific development achieve-ments in all aspects, yet growth had never translated into a desired economy, Professor Aryeetey, who is also the Director of the leading institution, the Institute for Statistical, Social and Economic Research (ISSER) at Ghana's premier University of Ghana, Legon, says there has never been co-ordination and an integrated implementation of all the potentially good policies. Strategies like the Import Substitution Industrialisation introduced by the Nkrumah regime or the Rural Agricultural Development agenda of the second elected leader, Kofi Abrefa Busia, or the Operation Feed Yourself, a green revolution strand or food sufficient production concept by the Kutu Acheampong military government that overthrew Busia were never integral or continued with the several changes of government over the years. You cannot, he argues, treat one aspect of an ailing economy and expect that the others will respond automatically. The economic history as it is now lacks a multifaceted approach and solution and that also has to do with the fact that politicians and some analysts are too quick in claiming success and too quick in condemning others.

With Gareth Austin, a Reader in Economic History at the London School of Economics and Political Science, and certainly the foremost authority on Ghana there, the works of other scholars are reviewed: Tony Killick of the Overseas Development Institute in London, whose works on early postcolonial Ghana are instructive; Michael Roemer, previously affiliated with the Institute of International Development at Harvard University and whose writings on Ghana cover the 1950-80s; as well as Naomi Chazan (Jewish scholar and political scientist who formerly headed the Truman Research Institute for the Advancement of Peace at Hebrew University) whose work is as contemporary as the 1990s on the political economy of the second Jerry John Rawlings military rule which ended in 1991. These may be scholars looking in from the outside, but as it was with many academic disciplines that evolved on Africa, it took a while for decolonisation and the monopoly of academic interpretation from the outsiders – European and non-African scholars – to subside and for African analysts to have space, especially in the late 1960s and 70s. Different interpretations notwithstanding, models are always helpful to acknowledge base. If earlier economic histories on Ghana and Africa were specific in terms of periods, as is normally the case, J. H. Frimpong Ansah in his *The Vampire State in Africa: The Political Economy of Decline in Ghana* (1992) attempted, as with his later work, *Flexibility and Responsiveness to the Economy of Ghana* (1996), to bring a wider area for reflection on the present.

These earlier works, as the discussion with Gareth Austin shows, are still important; but as a scholar with his own research and with his own new findings previously unavailable, he interprets the present in his own terms, especially how the issues of labour, land and capital and also past indigenous systems shape the present. He also discusses public policy and leadership in Ghana's economic history.

Part Two: A Vampire Economy with a Silver Lining is more specific. From the biggest economic sector of Agriculture, which employs over 60 per cent of the work force but ironically contributes less to Gross Domestic Product, we look at what is being done especially by way of government policy in the last two decades to generate growth. The argument of Moses Asaga, former Deputy Minister of Finance and

Economic Planning from 1997-2000 and financial economist with working experience in Aberdeen, Scotland and South Korea, is that continuity of good policy is helping development in Ghana irrespective of change of government. The cost of discontinuity, he argues like Ernest Aryeetey before him, has been huge and retarded growth.

Ambassador D. K. Osei who, as Secretary to President J. A. Kufuor from 2001-2008, has seen and participated in many of these economic policy formulations as a member of the Economic Management Team, says that even on specific sectors of the economy, an ability to craft a foreign policy which is development-oriented and focused along with an ability to cultivate the trust of global leadership, especially of the G8 and more prosperous economies of East and South-East Asia, has a way of helping.

President Kufuor's first appointment to the Ministry of Finance and Economic Planning was Yaw Osafo Maafo, an experienced banker and Member of Parliament, who had as special assistant Dr Anthony Akoto-Osei. Akoto-Osei moved from the Centre of Policy Analysis as a Research Fellow and later became Deputy Minister of Finance before being made Minister of State in that same Finance Ministry. Together with others from the Bank of Ghana and elsewhere, an impressive core Economic Management Team was formed. The first phase of economic management from 2001-2005 saw the longest currency stabilisation in Ghana's financial history for decades and thus made business planning on the micro level easier and fiscal discipline manageable. When a Cabinet reshuffle occurred and the Minister of Local Government, Kwadwo Baah-Wiredu, replaced Osafo Maafo as Finance Minister, he worked with prompted Anthony Akoto-Osei. What they and other members of the team did, as Akoto-Osei comments, was to maintain the fiscal policy and discipline, enabling greater growth to occur.

But what kind of growth? Before he became the Vice-President of Ghana (1997–2001), John Evans Atta Mills was the Commissioner of Tax and had enjoyed a distinguished academic life as Professor of Tax Law at the University of Ghana, Legon. His area of interest had been Taxation and Economic Development. In this book, he challenges the basis of comparing the two economic records of the NDC and the NPP, saying that comparison would not show best performance for any because the difficulties the PNDC and NDC confronted during the economic reforms from 1983 to when it got out of power were not the same for the NPP.

He also discusses the role of Taxation in postcolonial rule, though ambivalent on the issue of whether Tax Policy had always been an unnecessary issue of political economy in Ghana.

Ambassador Isaac Osei, an economist, had previously worked at the Ministry of Finance in the 1970s before branching into the Private Sector to head the biggest intravenous company in West Africa at Koforidua in the Eastern region of Ghana. He was also High Commissioner to the United Kingdom. He discusses the importance of cocoa as Chief Executive of the Ghana Cocoa Board (appointed in 2006). The most critical commodity for economic growth even in the colonial economy of the 1940s and 1950s (though Francis Agbodeka in *An Economic History of Ghana: From the Earliest Times*[2] sets cocoa introduction in the pre-colonial economy to 1857), cocoa has had the tendency to create shocks and dislocate the economy in the world market frontier in terms of price fluctuation. Ghana as a result worked market and producer price payment under Nkrumah's government. Besides it could generate political shock as it did with the political movement, National Liberation Movement (1954-1957), which sought in the cocoa-producing Ashanti region to tear the emergent Ghana apart as differences based on producer price and world price played on the economy. Jean Marie Allman's work *The Quills of the Porcupine: Asante Nationalism in an Emergent Ghana*, shows more than any work yet how a commodity almost tore apart the formation of an emergent postcolonial state.[3]

Despite the inability for years to diversify the economy, but be dependent on cocoa and to a large extent gold (whose receipts go directly to governments, unlike those of cocoa which filter to layers of beneficiaries from the cocoa farmer to the village grocery store operator and licensed pharmacist, and therefore help with the micro-economic sector) as Isaac Osei discusses, such institutions as the Cocoa

---

2 *An Economic History of Ghana: From the Earliest Times* by Professor Francis Agbodeka, formerly of the University of Cape Coast in Ghana, was published in 1992 by the Ghana Universities Press in Accra. It deals extensively with the role of minerals and commodities for over two centuries.
3 Allman's book, published in 1993 by the University of Wisconsin Press, is a remarkable work and enjoys regular citations. It looks into the political economy of cocoa at the dawn of independence and the consequences it had on political party formation from 1954-1957.

Research Institute, the Seed Production Unit, and the Ghana Cocoa Marketing Board have been resilient and helped grow the industry. More scientific and technologically-driven means of financing cocoa growers, and cocoa purchase through syndicated fund-raising from the financial markets in Europe (a policy which is a continuation from the Rawlings government) makes the cocoa economy rise higher.

The policy of adding value to cocoa, with a goal of increasing domestic processing capacity to 40 per cent through strengthening of industrial growth and production of cocoa products, seeks to generate employment and more revenue for government.

The growth of cocoa is certainly part of agricultural benefits. But as Dr Richard Anane explains from the perspective of the work of the Transport and Road Sector, the construction of roads from the cocoa growing villages to the urban areas for eventual export as well as the development of other feeder and urban roads, all of which ensure that goods produced do not only get to their intended destination but on time, is of the essence.

It is what Joyce Aryee (in the same Part), Chief Executive of the Ghana Chamber of Mines, the first woman to hold such position in Africa, and previously Education and Information Minister in the Rawlings government advocates: forward linkage, making the sector integral to the general economic mainstream. It should not depend only on revenue from certain commodities – cocoa, gold, bauxite and others – but on their diversification within the sector to spur other forms of growth.

The role of Energy production in the development of any economy cannot be underestimated. Indeed when Nkrumah set up the Akosombo Hydroelectric Dam and created the Tema Industrial Township, they were seen as the twin-industrialisation of the postcolonial economy. Many years after, with the addition of thermal energy, Ghana is still not industralised and in fact has had mishaps, especially in 1983 and 2006-2007, with electricity supply for domestic and industrial uses. In 2007, for instance, Newmont Mining Company had to delay its operations in Ghana due to intermittent power shortage, not to talk of the decline in industrial production of several goods, partly because of the lack of policy review, tight State control of the Energy Sector with little Private Sector participation or input from independent energy producers, and of course the lack of capital to re-invest and maintain facilities.

When Dr Charles Wereko-Brobby returned to Ghana in 1988 after working as a Research Fellow at the Imperial College's School of Management and Science and as Energy and Environmental Planning Programme Chief at the Commonwealth Secretariat, he served as an Energy Advisor to the Provisional National Defence Council and was Executive Director of the National Energy Board. He and his team confronted not only policy issues but infrastructure development that targeted the electrification of districts and villages. Dr Brobby talks about these past issues and their repercussions for the present in terms of challenges as Ghana strives to be a middle income economy. But much has also happened since then. The crisis, especially of 2006-2007, did not only force government to increase interest in thermal production, a reluctant President Kufuor, with an aversion to nuclear energy, gave in and set up an Advisory Board headed by Professor Adzei Bekoe, a nuclear scientist and chairman of the Council of State, to look into options for the diversification of the country's energy needs. As part of other long term measures, the government, through an agreement with Sino Hydro, a Chinese construction company, undertook a 500 million dollar contract of the Bui Dam, a 400 mega-watt hydro-electric project which had been on the drawing board since the 1960s because of inability to raise funding. Though it has its own environmental concerns and critics have not spared the government, it has argued in return that the gains could outweigh the losses and that with modern technology, environmental impact assessment could even be easier.

If Kufuor was overjoyed with mobilising funding for Bui and indeed a great funfair accompanied the sod-cutting ceremony, he had the privilege to announce to the country in June 2007 that Ghana had found oil at the Cape Three Point in the Western Region. This was through its partner Tullow Oil of the UK. It was anticipated that the initial 600 million estimated barrels, and more millions later, would make Ghana a potential oil exporting country.

Again, even though the revenue from oil would be royalties calculated, if managed well, as all of those who answered questions relating to it in this book say, it would ensure that scare resources would not be used for petroleum import bills but for other sectors of the economy.

Kufuor's famous message to the world through the BBC on June 18, 2007, as he held in one hand a glass of oil and in the other champagne, was one of great joy: "Oil is money, and we need money to take care of schools, the roads and the hospitals. If you find oil, you manage it well, can you complain about that?"

"Even without oil, we are doing so well already. Now, with oil as a shot in the arm, we're going to fly."

With more money hopefully, but well managed, social services should improve to help alleviate poverty, especially in the rural areas and among the urban poor, as Dr Ellen Bortei-Doku Aryeetey, Head of the Centre for Social Policy at the University of Ghana and a Senior Research Fellow at ISSER, desires. For though there has been some improvement in the delivery of social services since independence and currently as they affect women and children through such interventions as the School Feeding Programme, the Capitation Grant, and recently the Livelihood Empowerment Against Poverty (LEAP), growth in the economy, Bortei-Doku Aryeetey says, would pay attention to a critical mass of people who need such intervention as well as strengthen institutions such as the Department of Social Welfare.

Jeffrey D. Sachs is a renowned economist of The Earth Institute at Columbia University. He is an advisor to the UN Secretary-General as well as a number of governments in developing economies. In his book *The End of Poverty: Economic Possibilities of Our Time*[4], he talks about clinical economics – his concept of completing a thorough diagnosis of ailments in poor economies before any attempt at healing. Three years later, in his BBC Reith Lecture, published as *Common Wealth: Economics for a Crowded Planet*[5], he had gone beyond the clinical diagnosis to what I will call prescriptive economics. It is even prophetic as it was released at the time of global food crisis, which led to unrest in Haiti and elsewhere by June 2008.

Jeffrey Sachs, like Ellen Bortei-Doku Aryeetey, is very hopeful of new initiatives in Ghana, including the School Feeding Programme and the Capitation Grant. The Feeding Programme has multiple effects—it helps the rural agricultural sector with its availability of markets whilst also eliminating, at least in its theoretic formulation, post-harvest losses. Sachs' hopes for Ghana, where he operates a Millennium

---

4   Sach's best-selling book was published in 2005 by The Penguin Press. For his analysis on Africa, see Chapter Ten: The Voiceless Dying: Africa and Disease, pp. 188–209.

5   Published in May 2008 by Penguin Books Ltd.

Village, are high. In Yokohama, Japan, where I spoke with him at the Tokyo International Conference on African Development (TICAD IV), he was looking forward to the oil economy Ghana was about to enter into and its hopeful management.

In Part Three: Crossing the Jordan: Stimulation and Innovation in the Economy, we look at people whose innovations have contributed to economic development over the years. We begin with leading political economist, Professor E. Gyimah-Boadi, whose Centre for Democratic Development has been (with others) at the core of civil society growth, playing an advocacy role and checking the role of governance in development. With civil society not long on the political scene, Professor Gyimah-Boadi, who also teaches at the University of Ghana, was involved in the Ghana work of the Africa Peer Review Mechanism of the Africa Union, for which Ghana set the pace by being the first country to subject itself to the scrutiny of its political, economic and social policies. The Centre played a role in this using all tools in analysis and diagnostics of governance and democracy. Ghana, he argues, should not be happy patting itself on the back because she has scored so well on African rankings – the African Peer Review Mechanism, the Mo Ibrahim index, Afrobarometer and others. For, good as they are for eventual growth, Ghana must see itself competing on a global scale.

Another individual in Part Three who has brought innovation in his area of operation is Ken Ofori-Atta, Executive Chairman of Databank Financial Services. Globalisation is an old phenomenon, but in the 21st century it has transformed economies that were very remote. Not since the discovery of sea routes to Asia and other parts of the world and British leadership of the industrial revolution that spread from England, have the world's economies integrated so tightly. Capital and labour are today exported through easy communication to anywhere it will multiply in the world; finance for development can be sourced from private quarters apart from the known multilateral institutions; in the domestic set-up, reforms in the financial sector have ensured the collapse of the foreign monopoly in banking that operated since Ghana's independence. Today, in the year 2008, there are 28 licensed banks with branches across the country and 129 rural banks (with a regional break-down of: Ashanti 22, Central 21, Eastern 21, Brong-Ahafo 20, Northern 6, Western 14, Volta- 11, Accra 6, Upper East 4, Upper West 4), making access to loans and security of business deposits safer in the districts and towns across the country. Apart from these, there are 44 non-banking financial institutions engaged in savings and loans with some operating as discount houses, brokerages, leasing and mortgage finance. There are many more ways to invest domestically – through the Stock Exchange and other instruments such as Databank's E-pack – than previously.

After graduating from Columbia and Yale universities, Ken Ofori-Atta worked in New York with Salomon Brothers and Morgan Stanley before he returned to Ghana and with his friend, Keli Gadzekpo, who had also worked with KPMG, Peat Marwick, and Stuart Petroleum in Washington, DC, became members of the revamped financial sector in Ghana. Ofori-Atta tells the humble story as it bears on financial development.

Of course, industrial growth in Ghana is not enviable. Capital has been an impediment but there are still smart businessmen and women who can turn things around. Mr Oteng-Gyasi, who graduated from the University of Ghana, is a successful businessman and President of the Association of Ghana Industries. To ensure that a certain level of business-like attitude informs public University Administration, Oteng-Gyasi was appointed by the government as Chairman of the University of Ghana Council.

In his contribution, he talks about Industry and Education and the policies underlining growth or otherwise.

All developing economies have some common features: relatively weak institutions and human capacity; revenue and growth below expenditure and thus dependency on other sources to finance development, such as receipts from export or international trade, domestic taxation including those from the transnational, and of course contracting of loans whether through treasury bills, bonds and others. And then Aid, which especially in the 1970s and 80s (when Ghana and many economies in Sub-Saharan Africa were in dire stress), was the dominant source of support. It cannot be avoided even in the 21st century, because half the budget expenditure of Ghana is still dependent on donor support. This support comes in many forms, for example the Multi-Donor Budget Support (MDBS) which, since 2003 when first signed with the development partners, has given an annual $300 million to the country as loans and grants. The non-reliability of Aid, and thus moves for the economy to be stimulated from other sectors, is encouraging, even if it would take a long time to achieve.

Donor support and multilateral assistance, as discussed at the end of
the book is one area where agreement as to its relevance is not disputed
by those who even think developing countries should have little to do
with it. And so this Introduction ends with a perspective of a former
Senior Professional of the World Bank, an institution which, as has
been debated in the following pages, has and will continue to play a
central role in Ghana's development.

Gobind Nankani, President of the Global Development Network, an
international development agency with offices in New Delhi; Giza,
Egypt; and Washington, DC, was formerly Vice-President for Africa at
the World Bank. Apart from his supervisory role of the African
programmes at the Bank, he has extensive living experience in Ghana,
where he is a national and also had his early education. It was whilst
at the Bank, and under the Presidency of James Wolfenson, that the
biggest grant to any traditional authority was ever given under the
Asanteman Traditional Authority project, which experimented with
using the institution of Chieftaincy in Ghana to promote community
and social development. Although some innovation did occur on other
levels for the African programme, Nankani in this book talks about the
general set-up of the Bank, the African Division, and its role in helping
to generate growth in economies.

We also discussed calls for reformation at the Bank, which by 2008
was being spear-headed by the Commonwealth, led by the British
Prime Minister, Gordon Brown. Interestingly, this is fifty years after
John Maynard Keynes, negotiating with the Americans on behalf of
Britain and the Allies after World War II, set up the Bretton Woods
institutions. Will the Bank be very relevant to Ghana's development in
the next two decades with international financial markets and capital
expanding fast, especially from private quarters? If civil society grows
in quantity and quality, will the policy and advocacy role they play in
Ghana make the technical advice of the Bretton Woods institutions less
attractive?

These are some of the questions with which we end the book and
Gobind Nankani provides some interesting perspectives.

Ivor Agyeman-Duah
Stapledon House, Oxford.
May 2008

PART ONE

Structures and Institutions in a Postcolonial Economy

Ambassador Annan Arkyin Cato

His Excellency Mr Annan Arkyin Cato is a Career Diplomat and current High Commissioner to the United Kingdom. He joined the Ghana Foreign Service in 1964 and has served in different capacities in Ghana's Diplomatic Missions abroad for 44 years, in Addis Ababa, Rome, New York (United Nations), Geneva, Ottawa, and London. In London, he was Deputy High Commissioner and, between 1985 and 1987, Acting High Commissioner. He assumed his current post in 2006. From 1976–1986, Mr Cato worked as Chairman of the United Nations Ad Hoc Working Group of Experts on Southern Africa. He was High Commissioner to Canada for five years from 1992.

Mr Cato has also held several important posts in the Ghana Civil Service. At the Ministry of Foreign Affairs, he served at the Africa Division and as Chief of Protocol, the latter between 1978 and 1981. From 1987–1992, he was seconded to the Office of the President as Director of State Protocol. On completion of his assignment in Canada in 1997, he was appointed Chief Director at the Ministry of Foreign Affairs, a position he occupied until 2001, when he became Secretary to the Cabinet, retiring in 2005.

Mr Cato is the recipient of many prestigious awards among them the State award of Companion of the Order of the Volta, as well as The Freedom of the City of London Award for exemplary leadership and contribution to Ghana-UK relations, presented by the Mayor of London.

Mr Cato attended Achimota Secondary School before proceeding to the University of Ghana, Legon, where he earned a BA (Hons) degree in History in 1963. He continued his studies at the Ghana Institute of Management and Public Administration (GIMPA) and obtained a Diploma in Public Administration and International Affairs in 1964. He has three children and two grandchildren.

I

Ivor Agyeman-Duah: What was the nature of the Gold Coast Civil Service at the close of colonial rule in 1957?

Ambassador Annan Cato: It is a painful truth which one must accept that the whole rationale of colonialism seemed to be that the African was incapable of governing himself, and therefore that you needed an authority to direct the life of the African. The colonial administration was one that was staffed, certainly at the top level, exclusively by British citizens. Their duty and focus was to ensure that there was law and order and total respect for the administration under which we came, and also to make sure that they administered the colonies to the benefit of the colonial power. That was the nature of the colonial service.

IA-D: What was the nature of the Civil Service as inherited by Kwame Nkrumah? Had there been any change by the time he took over?

AC: Well I think that essentially that's what it was, and from the information that we have, the records do indicate that from the time of Ghana achieving internal self-government up to 1957, and even in the period immediately following Ghana's independence, the colonial Civil Service was reluctant to operate under an African government, and therefore their loyalty was suspect. It is this attitude that I was describing: basically the belief that the African was just not capable of administering the kind of administrative set-up that we were inheriting.

The evidence would show that, not only were the colonial civil servants reluctant to do this, but that also, during the period of internal self-government, many records were hidden away from the government that Nkrumah led. So, here you are in 1953, you have a group of people forming the Legislative Council and Nkrumah's internal self-government, and records of what was going on in the various ministries were unavailable to the Government. Even the records that were available were anything but useful. Two, you had top officials who did not feel that they should serve loyally under an African government and to help the government to succeed.

IA-D: So what were the objectives of Nkrumah in terms of the role of the civil servant in Ghana's development?

AC: Naturally, Nkrumah was quick to recognise that the government could not be successful, could not deliver on its commitments, without an efficient and loyal Civil Service, because the Civil Service is the Secretariat of Government. The responsibility of the political establishment essentially is to think through policies, to formulate policies, taking political factors into account. Once that is done, then you need to have a calibre of men and women who are not only knowledgeable, but also who have a commitment to government, who have a commitment to make sure that the policies the government formulates are implemented expeditiously and faithfully.

Now it took some time for Nkrumah to achieve that objective. You will remember that one of the objectives that Nkrumah gave for Ghana becoming independent was to demonstrate that we as Africans were as capable as any people anywhere of managing our own affairs and of governing ourselves, and also of attaining the heights that others had attained. So it would have been unusual for Kwame Nkrumah, after Ghana had become independent, to retain intact the kind of Civil Service that he had inherited. Of course you will have to remember, as I have said, that the Civil Service was anything but loyal to the African government, and so one of the things that Nkrumah tried to do quickly, and succeeded in doing, was to *Africanise* the Civil Service, to bring in as quickly as possible Ghanaians who had worked in the system for some time and who were capable, given the chance of a challenge, of helping the Nkrumah government to succeed.

So that was the beginning of what has come to be known as the Africanisation of the Civil Service. Certainly, everything we know about that service would indicate that, at that time, it was the best Civil Service in Africa – forget about South Africa. The Ghana Civil Service had become the best, both in knowledge application and commitment, and therefore the early gains and the major strides that were made in infrastructural development, in education, healthcare delivery, agricultural expansion – the whole gamut of activities of the State where Ghana made phenomenal successes – could not have been possible without the efficiency of the Civil Service that took over from the colonial administration.

IA-D: Who were some of the pioneers of that period?

AC: Many, many, many, many. I cannot mention all of them, or remember all of them immediately, and so you'll forgive me if I leave some of them out. Certainly, I think that if you are talking about those who have made their name in the Civil Service of Ghana, then you cannot leave out names such as Chapman Nyaho, A. L. Adu, Apaloo, Nathan Quao, Mintah, S. E. Arthur. When I joined the Diplomatic Service at the African Affairs Secretariat in the Office of the President in 1964, the civil servants who had constituted the colossuses of the Civil Service Administration were Enoch Okoh, T. K. Impraim, Michael Dei-Anang, Osah Mills. You cannot talk about the restructuring of the Civil Service without talking about Osah Mills. Let me tell you a story about Osah Mills. Apparently he had earned a reputation for his knowledge about the Civil Service and regulations, and when a petition was submitted to him, his first reaction would be to say "no" before he has had time to examine it. But these names that I mentioned, in my time were really solid people and we were privileged to have served under them.

Now I know that there was always the suspicion that all was not well between the politicians and civil servants. Where you have this suspicion, it bodes ill for the administration of any country, and, yes, when I came into the Service it was generally believed that Kwame Nkrumah did not place enough trust in the Civil Service. But this perception was not what I saw, because the advisors who were closest to President Nkrumah were E. K. Okoh as Secretary to the Cabinet and Michael Dei-Anang of the African Affairs Secretariat, and it used to be said that even after Cabinet had met and taken decisions, Osagyefo Kwame Nkrumah would sit down with these great people and analyse the consequences and repercussions of decisions on the basis that, yes, the politicians have a certain objective that they want to achieve, but that the civil servants are those that are in the field and ought to be able to guide the Government in appreciating what is achievable and what is not achievable. There were many issues that had financial implications and so on, and so the President would sit down with these people and, as I said, go through decisions, and as often as necessary he would override Cabinet decisions on the basis of the advice the civil servants would give to him. I know that even as a young man, occasionally you would hear Nkrumah say, "Ah, this thing has financial implications. Have you talked to T. K. Impraim? If Impraim has not agreed, I dare not say yes to you." It showed the kind of synergy that existed between the Government and the Civil Service, on the basis that the Government itself did recognise fully that although it was a very strong political administration, equally it needed a Civil Service that was strong in whom the Government had implicit trust. And I think that did exist at that time.

IA-D: People don't talk about the Civil Service in this fond way the way it is now. What do you think accounted for the so-called weakness in the Service today?

AC: The Civil Service has suffered from the vicissitudes that have visited our country. I think that every time you have had the military intervening, you have weakened the Civil Service. Let me explain this. To be an effective civil servant, you need to understand the boss under whom you work. Your duty is to advise. Your duty is to advise your minister as faithfully as you can. To be able to do this, a certain chemistry must develop between you and your political boss, and therefore when that happens and the military intervenes, the tendency is that they will say, "Ah, you are identified with this political party or with this minister and so on, so these are your marching orders, off you go". Alternatively, your wings would be clipped to the extent that you would be kicked about, moved from one ministry to another, not given the opportunity to offer your services. I think that anybody facing that kind of situation loses confidence and trust, and therefore successively, when there had been interventions, the Civil Service had become weaker and weaker.

There has been more than one moment where the whole top brass of the Civil Service – Senior Principal Secretaries – by public announcement were dismissed from office. When that happens, then even those who step into the shoes of those who have been dismissed do not feel adequately encouraged to do what is expected of them: to be loyal and to advise, and to give advice even when the advice that you are giving is unpalatable. It is almost criminal for a civil servant to encourage a minister to continue prosecuting policies that are doomed to fail, policies that are not likely to serve the needs of the public. I think it is criminal, and to some extent the perturbations have come about because, in trying to please ministers, some officers have not felt bold enough to tell them the truth on the ground.

IA-D: Nkrumah had a big ideological position in African politics: Pan-Africanism. Civil servants were to work within this framework. Did this compromise the neutrality of the Service in any way?

AC: I have tried to explain my own observations of the kind of synergy that existed between Nkrumah and the Civil Service that I was sworn into. Yes, Nkrumah had a very strong commitment to African liberation, and to a continental government for Africa, and he pushed this by every means possible, but it was also very clear that those that Nkrumah used in prosecuting this strident policy were largely not the politicians, but the civil servants. Even when the Ministers of Foreign Affairs were sent out on missions, Nkrumah made sure that he had civil servants always accompanying them.

I will give you an example that I myself was privy to. As a young officer, we were told to go to Sierra Leone. I didn't know what the purpose was all about; I was too young to understand, except that I was going to become the Secretary to this Committee which was being led by Mr. Wellbeck, but which also had on the delegation my Principal Secretary Mr Harry Amonoo, and so on. It just happened to be the case that Prime Minister Margai's government of Sierra Leone was alleging that Nkrumah's government was interfering in the affairs of Sierra Leone, and even trying to undermine the government. After considerable difficulties we were admitted into the Prime Minister's office. He had showcases – about three or four – in his office. The Prime Minister, after welcoming us, said, "Well what is it that brings you here?" and the minister then said, "Osagyefo sent us to assure you that he would never do anything to harm your government."

Then the Prime Minister said, "That's well enough, but I want you to go around, to look at these showcases, to look at the letters on display and tell me whether what you're telling me is something I should accept." We did. We looked around and there were some letters that had been written by a number of Ghanaian officials – I shouldn't be mentioning their names now – promising Siaka Stevens, who was the leader of the Opposition, their cooperation and assistance. One of the letters made reference to the Ghana High Commissioner then, saying "You keep in touch through him and we'll be routing support and so forth through the High Commissioner". The evidence seemed to be foolproof.

Then Harry Amonoo looked at me, looked at the ministers, and then whispered to the ministers, "You know, in these letters, there is nowhere that you can see any reference to the President's own involvement, and that should be our line. To begin with, we are in no position to attest to the authenticity of these letters. Secondly, there is nothing to suggest that Osagyefo had authorised these letters to be issued. Therefore I think this is the line we should pursue."

Truly, that's exactly the position we took. When we went back to talk to the Prime Minister, the minister then explained that, yes, these letters seem to have come from some officials that we were aware of, although we were in no position to certify Osagyefo Kwame Nkrumah knew about these so-called plots; he would never contemplate harming a government that it considered as being friendly. So you can understand, we did have a lifeline, and so after the exchange of pleasantries we were able to go back to Flagstaff House in Accra and to report dutifully. The import of what I have just said is simply this: ministers must think on their feet, but civil servants who accompany ministers in whatever situation must do a lot more thinking, and be able in all situations and all circumstances to help the political leadership to achieve what they have set out to accomplish.

So, to your question about the stridency of Nkrumah's policies: the successes were chalked in leading this continent first of all to freedom, in fighting against Apartheid, in championing the cause of Africa on the world stage at every opportunity. Ghana played a role in international affairs much larger than our economic circumstances, the size of our country, or any military might would have made possible. That we were able to achieve what we did, I think, is tribute to Nkrumah himself, the strong leadership he gave, but also to a very strong, knowledgeable, and focused civil service.

IA-D: So how was the Diplomatic Service involved in economic development? Was there a specific economic policy mandate?

AC: The Diplomatic Service of course was to protect Ghana's interests, however you define those interests, and to create an image about the country that would be sufficiently attractive for investors to look at Ghana. We had a small budget, our resources were limited, but we had to open our country to the foreign community. These days, you are talking about instant communication. Forty or fifty years ago, the situation was totally different. Those prejudices that we still see about Africa – those prejudices have not disappeared – were deeper at that time because the African was a phenomenon outside Africa: who are these people? All the more remarkable was that you had an African government. Even in the Caribbean, largely populated by people like Africans, people of African heritage, their minds had been conditioned to believe in our own inferiority. I am told that, in 1957, when the news made the rounds that a Black country had become independent and that you had a Black government, they couldn't believe it! Was it possible that you had somewhere in the world a government that was headed by Black people? But once they came to accept it, we had started breaking free from the bonds and chains that had shackled us for centuries and centuries.

So that was part of the responsibility of the Ghana Diplomatic Service, to say that yes indeed there was an African government; there was a new African that had emerged, and that new African was reflected in us and the work we did, interacting not only with our host countries, but with other diplomatic missions, and talking the kind of language that they could also understand. If you're talking about the prejudices, the prejudices did manifest themselves in many horrible ways. We're talking about a new dispensation, a new world order. When we talk to the present generation about what was, it is difficult for them to understand. We did that: get the world to understand what was happening in Africa, to understand why the African was fighting liberation wars and freeing itself, and to prove that we, too, were born free with rights and responsibilities.

IA-D: So you think the international respect Ghana had at the time was far more than the expenditure that it incurred in terms of its promotion?

AC: Enormously so. You cannot quantify the contribution of the Diplomatic Service in cedis and pesewas, in pounds and cents and dollars. In fact, in one of Dr Nkrumah's speeches, he had spoken about Ghana's contribution to Africa, and had made the point that that contribution couldn't be quantified; it was richer than the monies involved. So, yes, I do believe that the Diplomatic Service did help Ghana to have the kind of recognition which we've had, and fortunately we still do have.

II

IA-D: What is the job of a Secretary to the Cabinet?

AC: One cannot talk about the job of a Secretary to the Cabinet without talking about what the Cabinet exists to do. You will know that our Constitution confers on the President the responsibility to exercise the Executive functions of State, and the Constitution provides that, in carrying out the Executive functions of State, he or she would be assisted by a Cabinet. The Cabinet is made up of not more than 19 persons, the majority of whom must be elected from within Parliament, including the Vice-President as well. So in brief, the Cabinet exists to help the President to administer the country, to formulate policies, and to ensure that the policies are carried out.

The work of the Secretary to the Cabinet is essentially as the designation says: the Secretary to the Cabinet serves the Secretariat of the Cabinet. He coordinates the work of Cabinet. First of all, he establishes guidelines that must govern the preparation of, for example, memoranda, information papers, and things of that kind. He also schedules Cabinet meetings; draws up an agenda, in consultation with the President; screens memoranda that are intended for the Cabinet to make sure that they conform to a certain format that every member of the Cabinet recognises easily and can understand, and is likely to facilitate the work of the Cabinet; and ensures that every other aspect that contributes to making Cabinet effective is carried out. The Cabinet Secretary sits in Cabinet and has responsibility for recording the work of Cabinet. No machines are allowed, no recorders are allowed, so the Cabinet Secretary has to listen carefully to the deliberations and so on.

The work of Cabinet varies from country to country. In a country like Britain, Cabinet is not a deliberative body: Cabinet meets for specific periods, ratifies decisions, and out they go. Our President, John Agyekum Kufuor, because it was a new experience for many of the Cabinet ministers at the time when I was Cabinet Secretary, decided to make the Cabinet a deliberative body – in other words, to allow Cabinet to debate issues. And the President said to me, "That way, when decisions are taken, nobody will be justified in saying Ah, if I had been allowed to speak, I might not have agreed to this." Now one factor of Cabinet that needs to be emphasised is its collegiate nature, because the moment you have ministers saying, "I did not agree with this, or I agreed with that and he did not", you have chaos reigning – hence the process of deliberating, arguing, discussing issues. And, in the final analysis, agreeing on decisions enables ministers to feel bound by decisions that are taken.

So the Cabinet Secretary records decisions, keeps records of meetings and so on, and circulates these to ministers in time for the subsequent meeting of Cabinet. That way, if ministers are not comfortable with a decision that has been taken, or they feel that the Cabinet Secretary may not have captured a particular decision properly; there is the opportunity to effect corrections. Then comes perhaps the most important part of it: implementation. True, the Cabinet Secretary by himself does not carry the burden of ensuring that decisions are implemented – there is another department within the Office of the President that does that – but certainly what the Cabinet Secretary does is act as the memory of Cabinet. Therefore, now and then, the Cabinet Secretary has the responsibility to remind ministers about certain decisions in respect of which Cabinet is expecting the minister to report further. The Cabinet Secretary also has responsibility for records keeping. He keeps records of the work of Cabinet, and therefore at any time, any minister can come to the Cabinet Secretary and ask to see a record of a particular issue at a particular time.

The work of Cabinet is not executed solely at Cabinet meetings. Cabinet also has four Committees: Political and Security, Economic committee, Social committee, and Infrastructure Committee, each of which has a minister chairing it. A good deal of the technical work of Cabinet is executed through the Committees, because at the Committees, ministers are allowed to come in with the Chief Directors, or, in some of the more technical ministries and departments, to come with the people who have the technical know-how, not to be full participants in the meeting as such, but to be available to provide information that enables the Committee to make suitable recommendations to the Cabinet. Then of course the Chief Director works with the Office of the Head of the Civil Service in making certain decisions available to the Head of the Civil Service, and in also being available to help the Head of the Civil Service or, for that matter, any Chief Director, in having an understanding of any issue that might need clarification.

IA-D: In your opinion, how does the Civil Service contribute to economic development?

AC: When decisions are taken, the civil servant, the Chief Director, has a responsibility to analyse and to look at the implementation in the context of any budget allocations that might become necessary, and so to be able to advise the minister. I already indicated that sometimes, perhaps due to over-zealousness, a minister might want to move a particular decision further than it ought to be moved. It is a duty of the civil servant to be able to advise. In the revenue-collection departments, the government policies are implemented on the basis of the monies that accrue into the Consolidated Fund, and therefore integrity, knowledge, commitment, not bending the rules, being aware of what is expected, are all necessary – in effect, everything for the Civil Service to function efficiently, effectively, loyally, and with integrity. I think that it is when you have the totality of all this at play that the government will be better able to push its economic and social development programmes.

IA-D: Final question: you have seen a lot, you have passed through a lot. How does Ghana's future look in an economic sense?

AC: Very bright. First of all, we have put in place all the institutional sinews that are necessary for growth and stability: good governance, freedoms of our people, a free judiciary, freedoms of association, a very vibrant Parliament that oversees certain aspects of the work of the Executive. I think that Ghana is on course. In the last couple of years we have demonstrated that, with prudent management, we can achieve maximum outcomes. The Ghanaian economy is growing. Ghana has attracted the confidence of international financial institutions and the financial sector. The evidence is of course the number of companies that are now taking interest in Ghana. When last year government floated bonds on the London market, they were looking for $750 million. We had over $3 billion being subscribed to – this is a mark of confidence in the economy. The infrastructure of the country is growing. That is our basic responsibility; we have to establish an infrastructure that will make it possible for the Private Sector to function. Information Communication Technology (ICT) is absolutely necessary, as is agricultural expansion. Schools: you have to have an educational system that caters for an effective, strong polytechnic, so people can acquire skills; apprenticeship systems too, because the Private Sector will need the graduates of these institutions.

Now of course we are blessed with an additional resource, that is oil. From early 2008, the attention of government has been concentrated on consultations – a public forum was held on oil and on gas – identifying the areas that we needed to pinpoint in order to formulate a regulatory framework for the management of our oil resources. Remember also the help that we are getting from friendly countries. Ghana is ahead of the Millennium Development Goals in terms of poverty alleviation and the achievement of other goals spelt out under the Millennium Development Objectives. We are making progress towards the country becoming middle income in 2015. There are many challenges – admittedly, the issue of poverty is still too high. We need to address it. We need to bring in greater discipline in the way that we do things in the country. We can also work harder than we are doing.

We have gentlemen of the highest calibre now seeking the highest positions in our country in the December 2008 election. I think that, at the end of the day, whoever of them is elected will be capable of providing the kind of leadership that Ghana needs to continue to soar. The foundations have been laid by President Kufuor's government, and I think that that government will be leaving office proud of its legacy. It will be the responsibility of the successor administration to build on it, and to push the parameters of our country's development even further. It is in consideration of all this that I feel emboldened to say that I am very confident of the country's future.

IA-D: Thank you very much.

AC: Thank you.

March 2008

Mrs Mary Chinery-Hesse

Mrs Mary Chinery-Hesse is the Chief Advisor to the President of the Republic of Ghana, John Agyekum Kufuor, where she plays an important role in overseeing the implementation of government programmes. She is also the Vice-Chairperson of the National Development Planning Commission of Ghana, a member of the Board of the Centre for Policy Analysis of Ghana (CEPA), and a member of the Council of the University of Ghana. In recognition of her contributions to the country, Mrs Chinery-Hesse received the highest national award of the Republic of Ghana, the Order of the Star of Ghana.

Her career began in the Ghana civil service in 1962, where, among other posts, she served as Principal Secretary (Chief Director) in the Ministry of Finance and Economic Planning. Mrs. Chinery-Hesse joined the United Nations in 1981 and subsequently served in New York, Sierra Leone, Tanzania, The Seychelles, and Uganda. She was appointed the first ever African woman Resident Coordinator of the United Nations System, and the Resident Representative of UNDP. In 1989, she was named the first ever woman Deputy Director-General of the International Labour Organisation (ILO) in Geneva, Switzerland since its founding in 1919. She was also the first African woman to attain a position equivalent to Under Secretary-General of the United Nations.

Mrs Chinery-Hesse has served on a number of important Advisory panels, including the United Nations Blue Ribbon Panel of Eminent Persons on Global Security and Reform of the United Nations, the Panel of Eminent Persons on Financing for Development, and the Eminent Persons Advisory Panel of the African Union.

She was educated at Wesley Girls' High School, Mfantsipim School, and the University of Ghana, before proceeding to Trinity College, University of Dublin, Ireland, and the Economic Development Institute of the World Bank, Washington, DC, USA. Her academic credentials span the disciplines of Sociology, Economics, and Development Studies.

Ivor Agyeman-Duah: What is the role of the Chief Advisor to the President in terms of the day-to-day running of the office?

Mrs Mary Chinery-Hesse: The position of Chief Advisor is really new in terms of the administrative structures of government. It is a position that was created by President Kufuor recently – only a year ago. For his first term he did not work with anybody in that position so I guess what I am doing here was shared among what other people were doing within the context of the Presidency. Largely, it was the Chief-of-Staff who had this double bed. At some point I guess the President realised it was necessary to get what I like to call a *driver*, to ensure the implementation of government programmes: there would be somebody who had responsibility basically for helping him to think through issues, but also to follow things up within the context of government machinery.

If one looks at the conditions of service which were given to me, a sort of job description, he appointed me senior enough of Cabinet rank – not a Cabinet minister, but having the rank of a Cabinet minister – able to deal with people at the most senior levels of government machinery to cover all sectors of the economy, and then all government business. In other words, in terms of the work of day-to-day, I have the responsibility as Chief Advisor to track and make sure that everybody is doing what they have to do. Basically this is it – it is very varied. The advantage is one is able to use the full weight of the Presidency to ensure that people do what they have to do.

I work very closely with staff in the Presidency. I work a lot with the Chief-of- Staff, I work a lot with the Secretary to the President, with the Secretary to the Cabinet, and also with the Chief Director of the Presidency, but the one who I work closest to is of course the President. I do not think I have a being in the context of the Presidency outside of the President. This confidence means that on a day-to-day basis we manage to work as a team, also with the Chief-of-Staff and the Secretary to the President, to make sure that we deliver. Delivery is the name of the game.

IA-D: So is there a formal structure in terms of a policy unit within the Presidency?

MC-H: Yes, there has always been a policy unit, which is a very important part of the work of the Presidency. We have the unit manned by professionals; all of them are consultants who have worked in other places and bring a lot of experience to the work of the Presidency. They monitor, they evaluate, they track, and they also give policy advice. I would say that in terms of a Secretariat to support the policy work I do, the policy unit would be my Secretariat, but of course they do other things as well. They support the whole Presidency.

IA-D: How does this unit relate to the Ministry of Finance and Economic Planning? I guess they all should have policy units within them.

MC-H: Basically, the Presidency is the nerve-centre of government. In terms of programmes, projects, etc., it is very important that what is translated after it has gone through the process of Cabinet approval, or even within the context of the Budget, would continue to reflect the persona of the President. He therefore uses the unit to ensure that there are relations not only with the Ministry of Finance, but with other ministries. Indeed, all ministries are supposed to have policy monitoring and evaluation units – they do have them. The Presidency requests that they make submissions on a quarterly basis as to how they are performing, and of course the Ministry of Finance and Economic Planning, which has responsibility for the Budget, is then a very important ally as we try to make sure we interpret the Budget into implementation as it is intended.

In my personal capacity, I work very closely with the Ministry of Finance and Economic Planning. Indeed the Minister of State and the Deputy Minister for Finance are constantly here because the President worries about ensuring that there is not a roll-back in terms of the macro successes that have been chalked during his administration. We therefore think a lot together, and also with the Governor of the Central Bank. It is an advantage that I have worked in these areas for so long. I have been Chief Director of the Ministry of Finance of course in the 1970s, but I was Chief Director for over seven years before I joined the United Nations and before that time I was working with

Development Planning so, having managed this economy before when I was much younger, I have come back and I have the advantage of seeing how things were done in the past, how they are being done now, and to try to plug holes, but reflect also on what we have lost because of our turbulent history.

IA-D: Before you went into the international circles, you were working in the Ministry of Finance and Economic Planning, and now you're back. As you said, you have at least mastered the processes. Some attribute under-development to some degree to lack of efficiency in the Public Sector. Do you think this is the case?

MC-H: Yes. I would say that for a country like Ghana, which has selected the Private Sector as the engine of growth, the role of the Public Sector becomes even more important. It is an important facilitator for everything that happens within the economy. Even as government disengages from doing business and being directly involved in carrying out large chunks of activity within the economy, the Public Sector is expected to be an important facilitator to make sure that they make doing business easy, to make sure that there are controls in place. The Private Sector works with predictability; it works with institutions which guarantee that things will be done in a speedy manner, that whatever happens, things will be facilitated. Access to information, etc. – these are important roles for the Public Sector and unless it is in a position to back the Private Sector up, it is useless.

Within the context of the normal work of government, it is the Civil Service which supports ministers. It is very important that they feel the same sense of commitment that we had when I was a civil servant. It was a very privileged position and truly we could be relied on to go the extra mile to ensure that the business of the country was managed effectively. Of course, politicians come and politicians go, but public service tends to be abiding. They have an important repository role. They really have to be custodians of the institutional memory. As we grow in our democracy, one expects that we will have a track which will mean that we are not always starting from scratch, as happened in the past, but that we have incremental steps. As new administrations come in, they need somebody to tell them where the nation has got to so that they can build on it. That is the role of the Public Service and that has become extremely important. Whether they are performing it very well now, I think the jury is still out.

IA-D: Why was it different in your time to what it is like now?

MC-H: As I say, we have had a turbulent history. People forget that at one time, on the radio, the top Civil Service was creamed off. As many as 46 senior Principal Secretaries were made to leave during the 31st December revolution in the 1980s, and they left at a time when those who were coming up had not been fully groomed to step into their shoes. I think it has been so difficult to recover what was lost at that time. There have been many attempts, but it is not easy. It is not easy at all to take off so many experienced people and expect that the recovery will not be difficult. We will get there one day. We will get there one day because succeeding governments since then have been trying to restore the situation to previous levels.

IA-D: In which areas did the loss of civil servants critically affect economic development?

MC-H: In all aspects. I was in Ghana at the time, and the top went away with all the skills for managing the Public Service which had been garnered since colonial days. It affected all aspects of our lives, not only within the context of development. It was a sad move, but these things happened. Because of the weaknesses which resulted, of course people also lost confidence in the civil service, which meant that they were set aside. These are some of the things that President Kufuor has been trying to correct. For the first time, he has set up a Ministry for Public Sector Reform with its own minister. That shows the importance he attaches to getting things back on track. We have made great strides since the Ministry was established. I think we will get there – the building blocks are there.

IA-D: Why is it that the reforms have not worked?

MC-H: Because you see, you need a sort of knowledge base to be able to build on, and since all of it nearly disappeared, there has been a lot of experimentation. The reforms have tried to introduce things which are not quite Ghanaian. We have tried to learn from best practices, but they have been foreign. The current attempt is trying to be all-inclusive. There is a lot of consultation as the various elements of public sector reform are put in place, and because of that we are going to get a Ghanaian product which we hope will guarantee better success.

IA-D: What has been the relationship between this government and our development partners on a bilateral and multilateral basis – that is, with countries and also the World Bank institutions, the EU, and others?

MC-H: For the moment, I would say we have a very solid relationship. As countries go, especially African countries, we have had situations where we felt talked-down at, especially during the period of structural adjustment. We felt that a lot of the prescriptions that were being proposed by these Bretton Woods institutions, and also backed very much by our development partners because they tend to line up behind them, were not necessarily in our interests. But we had a capacity issue. I have worked globally, and I know that in countries where there was the ability to get one's act together so you have your own solutions to problems, when these institutions have come to talk to you it has been possible to dialogue. In many African countries, they have walked into a vacuum: you object to what they are proposing but you do not have an alternative. I would say that right now in Ghana, after all our difficulties, we have enough institutional capacity that we manage to get respected and to be treated as equals. We have a proper dialogue and we are able to convince each other and in the end what comes out is something that really belongs to the government, because the government is not just accepting any prescriptions.

Because the country is doing very well, we have had the best relations with our development partners since President Kufuor took over, and it continues but from a position of strength. Now, as a country, we have moved to a point where we can source money outside of Aid. As you know we actually went on a road show and we have launched a sovereign bond, which was absolutely oversubscribed. This means we have the capacity to look for other sources of funds than to go along with things we don't believe in just to get money, and I think our situation is much improved. We are a good model for other countries, in Africa especially.

IA-D: What do you think will be the legacy of Kufuor's administration in the economic sense?

MC-H: The stability. We have got all the building blocks in place for a massive take-off. If you look at the financial environment, it is cleaned up. When the President took over, interest rates were going through the roof at more than 40 per cent; inflation, the same. The money supply situation was terrible. We had a terrible budget deficit, etc., etc. In terms of the macroeconomic framework, I think there has been so much stability that we have become a normal country. The cedi was being devalued on a daily basis – sometimes we said it was falling like a stone, but we don't say that anymore. Ghanaians used to love to see dollars and pounds sterling and other strong currencies. Now we like people to like seeing the cedi, which is happening. If you ask somebody, "Should I give you one pound or the equivalent in cedis?" they will say, "Cedis, why not?"

Things have been put in place – that is number one – but that is not the only thing. There was a time we had a hungry season in Ghana. It was normal that we would have a period of plenty during the harvest but Agriculture would not guarantee that 365 days a year you would have food. Now, the hunger period is gone; it means we have 365 days of Agriculture. It has been managed in such a manner that we do not suffer from famine during any particular period.

That is Agriculture, let's turn to Health. We have looked at the statistics – you try to measure various indicators – and for me, the spread of Public Health facilities has been very impressive. I mean the distance it takes somebody to reach a health facility has been drastically reduced. The difficulty was people being able to afford the services. President Kufuor introduced a National Health Insurance Scheme. With payment of a little money, a person's family is covered to a point that you are looked after free and you also get free medication for many conditions.

You turn to education; it is the same thing, especially for the girl child. As you know, if a family cannot afford to keep all children in school, there is a preference to send the boys. Come time to drop out, it is the girl child who suffers. Now there is a Capitation Grant, which virtually ensures free education. I think this is fantastic, and there is no excuse for not sending children to school. In addition, as part of the Education Reform, in Africa for the first time, children can go to kindergarten free as part of the normal cycle of education. Of course we have teething problems, but I think as a concept and what we have managed to do has been fantastic, and others have commented on it. Of course as Ghanaians, we do not have the basis for comparison; we do not know what is happening in other countries, so people are not aware that this has happened.

I could go on – wherever you turn, whichever sector you touch. You look at the road sector, it has been truly fantastic. The amount of money that the government has put into the energy sector is really phenomenal. People only remember the blackouts, but Ghanaians have short memories so even that is receding. The amount of investment that has been put into energy to make sure that we never again face a deficit is truly encouraging. Turn to telecommunications and look at the explosion in the use of the mobile phone. This is going to get even better. The way the backbone is being put in, it is going to be very interesting in the telecommunications sector.

Part of the reason we have had this situation is the stability we enjoy – good governance. We enjoy stability and therefore others are willing to put their money into Ghana. We are really attracting a lot of foreign investment. We have a lot of foreign Private Sector enterprises coming to establish themselves here, and it can only get better, but we have to maintain the stability.

IA-D: We have women like you in very influential positions. For the first time, the Chief Advisor to the sitting President is a woman; we have for the first time a woman who is Chief Justice – all from Wesley Girls' High School of course?

MC-H: Yes, naturally!

IA-D: Do you think this will in any way serve as an incentive to others – that is, girls growing up? In the near future, do we hope to see a drastic reduction in under-development as it affects women?

MC-H: We say that a woman's voice is necessary. I have had discussions with the President since I started working with him, and after some time his comment was that our people were very wise that they always said when they had difficulties, "Let me go and consult the old lady", because wisdom resides in the bosom of a woman in Africa. We bring a certain calmness to situations, the kind of calm which will make everybody think deeply, without emotion, on certain issues. We soften the ground for sensible decision-making. I say that the more we involve women in decision-making, the more as a country we will do well. Right now, we have the same capabilities as men. I say that when God distributed talents, as a fair God, he did not say, "I give all the talents to the men and nothing to the women". I say he tossed the talents up and some went into women, so any country that does not take advantage of its womenfolk will never make it because in doing so you short-change the country up to 50 per cent.

Over time, we have had very strong women; we really have women from all walks of life, most of them from Wesley Girls' High School of course! Everywhere you turn – you turn to the scientific field, we are there; you turn to academia, etc., etc. Within the context of the Civil Service, since President Kufuor took over, you would be surprised at the number of Chief Directors who have been appointed and who are women. There were only one or two before he took office. Now there are more like ten – a third of the Chief Directors are women. And he has had the courage to appoint a woman Chief Justice – very good. We have a Ministry for Women and Children's Affairs – for the first time again – working very hard to put women in their rightful place and to let society appreciate their work.

As for development, without the woman no country will make it, especially in Africa. Even when we turn to agriculture, who farms? It is the woman. Who looks after the home? Who knows how to manage money in the interest of the family? It is the woman. And now within the modern sector, as they have seen people like the Chief Justice (but there are others – too many to mention), the girl child knows that she can make it. She can make it to the highest level. The importance of women like myself is to be role-models so people know that women can do everything.

But we have an additional responsibility: in the highest councils, we speak for women; we draw attention to the role of women in whatever situation; we make sure that everything is engendered, that a woman's component is not forgotten. We also act as mentors. We have accepted the role of mentor, and we play this role at all levels, starting from the schools, even within the context of selection of subjects for the entrance to university and so on. We strengthen them, we make them have self-esteem. I think the more women are put in such situations, the better it will be.

In my life, I have always broken some frontier: in the United Nations, as the first African woman Resident Coordinator in the United Nations system; in the ILO as the first woman Deputy Director General in its long history; the first African woman to get to the rank of Undersecretary General, etc. It has made a difference – you open doors for other women to also be allowed to come in. The responsibility you have is to really tell yourself you have to work harder and to perform better than your male colleagues, because you are always fighting to be noticed. But now we are noticed.

IA-D: Now that there is a balance of positions, what do you think is the future of our country?

MC-H: What the President has established is for us to get to middle income status by the year 2015. Then of course we have the Millennium Development Goals, with the targets set for 2015. In certain areas, we have already achieved the goals. We keep saying that the Millennium Development Goals are the lowest minimum denominators, that as a country, looking at the speed with which we are growing, we should set our targets higher. So we will achieve the Millennium Development Goals, but we will do much better. Fortunately we have struck oil. As a country, we have become extremely credit-worthy because the future, as we say, is bright. I think that within the next ten years, nobody will recognise this economy. There are great things which are going to happen in terms of development. President Kufuor's legacy is to have put in place all the building blocks and the future can only be bright.

IA-D: Thank you very much.

MC-H: Thank you.

December 2007

Dr Dirk-Jan Omtzigt

Dr Dirk-Jan Omtzigt is a Dutch economist currently specialising in International Macroeconomics, Labour Economics, and Development Economics. For four months from February 2008 he served as International Lead Economist for Adam Smith International in Kigali, conducting an economic review of the zero fleet policy for the Rwandan government. Concurrently, he undertook a consultancy study for the European Union on the effectiveness of EU policy and budget in achieving social inclusion and cohesion. He has in this capacity engaged in high level interaction with eminent policy makers and academics, including Professor Amartya Sen. From November 2007, Dr Omtzigt consulted for the Emerging Africa Infrastructure Fund, examining the constraints on infrastructure investment in Africa. Previously, he has worked for Macquarie Bank, Goldman Sachs, and Lehman Brothers in London.

Dr Omtzigt also has extensive teaching experience. He was a Tutor in Economic Theory at Lady Margaret Hall, University of Oxford, before becoming Stipendiary Lecturer in Economics at St. Catherine's College, University of Oxford, where the majority of his students earned distinctions in their examinations. As part of a Departmental Doctoral Studentship, he taught Mathematics and Statistics at the Economics Department, University of Oxford. He was also a Lecturer at the Goldman Sachs Financial Analysts University, London, and an economics teacher RC Lyceum De Grundel, The Netherlands.

Dr Omtzigt has a number of publications to his credit, including interviews with Nobel laureates Professors Amartya Sen and Joseph Stiglitz. The former is forthcoming and the latter appears in *Oxonomics* (2006), a journal of which he was the founding Editor. He has also presented papers on the topic of Ageing at the Public Economics UK Workshop at IFS and at HM Treasury in London. In 2006, he was a referee for *Oxford Economic Papers*.

Dr Omtzigt recently received a DPhil Economics from the University of Oxford, where his thesis investigated the issues of demographic change, individual decision making, and policy options. He holds an MPhil in Economics from Oxford; a BA Honours in Mathematics from, Oxford; and a BA Joint Honours in Mathematics and History from University of Durham, UK, where his undergraduate dissertation addressed the economic history of Ghana since independence. Dr Omtzigt spent one year as the Auditor of the University College of Education of Winneba, Ghana.

Ivor Agyeman-Duah: The colonial economy before 1957 was definitely different from the postcolonial economy in the 1960s and 1970s – I mean the one that Nkrumah inherited. How did this transition affect the economic development of Ghana in the post-independence era?

Dr Dirk-Jan Omtzigt: I think the post-independence era, and firstly the Nkrumah period, gave a set of institutions, beliefs, and productive capacity that was going to burden and slow down the economic growth of Ghana in the 1960s and 70s. Maybe it is good to just go back one step and see what exactly happened. Prior to independence, Ghana was a mono-cultural economy, primarily dependent on cocoa. As W.A. Lewis told the Ghanaian government in 1952, there were not enough skilled people, but Nkrumah went ahead with a development effort whereby the government was at the centre, so government expanded very rapidly. It actually expanded into productive activities, so it started factories, enterprises, etc.

First of all, the belief that the government is responsible for economic development firmly took root, and that was taken up by all the heads in the 1960s and 70s. They didn't fundamentally change their beliefs in that regard. Secondly, what you've seen is that, because the economic development of Ghana did not go as Nkrumah wanted it to, he more and more relied upon a client-patronage network whereby he gave out import quotas to those who supported him. When that failed, he resorted to coercion and force. At a certain point he didn't even trust the Army anymore and he actually set up his own Presidential Guard. It was when they didn't get paid – because the government was so constrained that even they had to suffer cutbacks – that they overthrew him. This idea about what the power-base was, shifted from democracy all the way through to the Army. The idea that the State was the prime actor in economic development, that the Military played a big role in your route to power, and the whole set of state enterprises – that is what actually was going to hold back economic development in the 1960s and 70s in Ghana.

IA-D: So what was so unique about that period then, the immediate post-independence era in the 1960s and 70s?

D-JO: A number of things struck me, first of all the number of coups: five coups during that period, which is extraordinary, but actually if you look through West African history, it is almost the average. In that sense it is both unique and interesting. Secondly, if you look at the time-span of democratic rule, it became shorter and shorter. In fact, no one until Kufuor was legitimately re-elected in a fair and open election since Nkrumah. That is extremely interesting. Thirdly, the sheer decline in GDP per capita: between 1971 and 1981 GDP per capita declined by round-about 35–40 per cent. That is an extraordinary drop! It is very interesting from an intellectual point of view, but the human tragedy is just extraordinary in that period.

IA-D: The State under Nkrumah was obviously a command economy, and it was also the period of the Cold War. What were the side-effects of this?

D-JO: What happened was the State took centre stage in development. Often we think about African countries as Third World countries, and the term Third World is to kind of denote non-alignment – non-alignment to the West, non-alignment to the communist countries. Actually, the opposite was the case in terms of political ideology, and Nkrumah aligned himself very much towards the socialist camp, and then later on, when Rawlings came to power, it switched over to the IMF/World Bank type of ideology. What happened was a huge expansion of state enterprises, so by 1966 we had about 53 state enterprises, and about 12 public boards, so we saw massive expansion there. Correspondingly, we saw an increase in the number of publicly-paid employees, from about 98,000 to about 250,000 over the Nkrumah period, so the State really expanded very rapidly. What we also saw was an increase of investment in the economy to about 19–25 per cent, so there was a very high level of investment in the economy.

The problem was there weren't enough domestic savings, so there was a gap. That gap could be filled in three ways: by Aid, by Foreign Direct Investment, or by Borrowing. Now the problem was that Nkrumah used a lot of anti-colonial, anti-capitalist rhetoric, so there was no Aid forthcoming from the western countries. Similarly, the emphasis on the State as the main actor really put off a lot of Private Sector investment. So Aid and Private Sector Foreign Direct Investment was about 10 per cent of the requirement. The third solution was borrowing. The problem was that most of the capital was tied up with western countries, not countries that might have been friendly to the Nkrumah regime, so they had to resort to A, putting import restrictions on various goods, so there were a lot of import tariffs, and, B, to the printing of money.

What was the result? We saw that, first of all, by putting import restrictions, even the most basic ingredients for production weren't available. The gold mining company didn't have enough fuel and explosives to actually mine the gold. A bamboo manufacturer spent about 80 times as much on wages than on imported input. So clearly what you saw were very low utilisation rates of these companies. For example, the nationalised footwear company had a utilisation rate of about 24 per cent, so really productivity was very low. At the same time, the government was printing money, so what did you get? You got high inflation: during the last three years of the Nkrumah regime we had double-digit inflation. It was a vicious circle: there is not enough foreign capital, so we have import quotas, so companies can't buy the inputs to produce what they actually want to produce, so there aren't enough exports – it was a vicious circle going down. The results were high inflation, negative GDP per capita growth, and part of it was financed by borrowing and the debt-service ratio actually exceeded 50 per cent when Nkrumah left power. On all accounts, this really left the State on the verge of bankruptcy.

IA-D: So what were the economic dimensions of this? Did it for instance contribute to his overthrow in 1966?

D-JO: It clearly had a role to play, but I think there is a broader critical economy argument here. What happened is that Nkrumah derived his power because he was credited with the independence of Ghana. That was his first level of support. Secondly, he raised expectations that

Ghana would be the shining example of Africa within ten years. Now that was not going to happen, so the vicious circle of economic decline meant that people lost faith and he lost popular support. But another thing to note about the downward spiral is that there were more and more price controls. Therefore, more and more quotas could be allocated to supporters, so it actually gave the ingredients to set up a patronage network, but at a certain point even that didn't work.

Nkrumah was granted extraordinary powers in a kind of phoney referendum in 1964, and he created his own Presidential Guard because he didn't trust the Army. When that level of support, or that way of staying in power, no longer helped, he totally fell back on his Presidential Guard, and when even their benefits were cut, that was really the straw that broke the camel's back and chucked him out of power. Yes, the economic decline was instrumental in it, but it was really when he lost the support of even his own Presidential Guard that he could no longer stay in power.

IA-D: Ghana became a member of the World Bank in 1957, over 50 years ago, and the first major reform of the economy took place in 1983 or thereabouts – the Economic Recovery Programme and the Structural Adjustment Programme. What were the features of this programme, and what did it do to the economy of Ghana in the 1990s and early part of the 21st century?

D-JO: OK, let me answer that question in four parts. First of all, let's just look at the background to why Rawlings suddenly turned to the World Bank and the international institutions; secondly, what they were trying to do; thirdly, what they achieved; and fourthly, what they did not achieve. I think that is probably the most useful way of looking at this.

First of all the background: when Rawlings came to power, he did not see the economic set-up as a problem, but just the implementation, so he advocated strict adherence to price controls. He didn't believe that the price controls themselves were the major problem. The result was, with a quite heavy-handedness, they adhered to the price controls, and what happened was that massive shortage arose because no one was willing to provide at the prevailing price on the market. A second problem, almost a continuation of the first, was a lack of materials. Thirdly, there was a deterioration of the terms of trade, so, as in the previous administrations, there was a huge lack of foreign reserves. The foreign reserves had gone down to about 1 to 2 per cent of GDP, so Rawlings went on a mission to the Soviet Union to ask for money. The problem was, at the time the Soviet Union didn't have any money at all and they advised him to go the IMF to get support, but to keep the fire of the revolution, as he called it, still alive. He was in a very difficult position because remember, at the time one million Ghanaians were expelled from Nigeria, the terms of trade were deteriorating fast, and the Soviet Union wasn't able to give him any financial assistance. Those three reasons really drove him into the hands of the World Bank and the IMF.

The Structural Adjustment Programme had four features. First of all was getting the right incentives – that means devaluing the currency from 2.75 cedis to the dollar to 25 cedis to the dollar, slowly abolishing price controls and import and export quotas. Second was the attempt to attract foreign capital by really first of all taking care of energy resources. Thirdly, there was in one of the documents a re-definition of the role of the State, whereby the State really had to recognise its limits and really look at its core role, and not try to expand and set up companies and enterprises. Fourth was solid monetary and fiscal policy, so balance the book both internally and externally and don't resort to printing money. So what was the result?

First of all, you saw this devaluation of the cedi, which really gave a boost to exports. If you look at both gold and timber, you saw, in volume terms, a massive increase in exports. The problem with cocoa is, cocoa has a lead time of about five to seven years from when you plant it to when you harvest it so there was no immediate big spike increase in cocoa production. Fiscal balance was restored, and that is rather a major achievement. Because of the changes the government made, it was able to attract quite a number of concessional loans from international institutions and other Aid agencies. As a result, what you see is, in the first three or four years, an expansion in the manufacturing part of the economy from about 8.5 per cent to about 10 per cent. So indeed you see the first signs of economic development, and clearly there was positive GDP per capital growth.

So what didn't go well? The problem was that, although there was a massive increase in volume terms of exports, in terms of value they didn't do very well because there was a massive decrease in the terms of trade. If you index it, it was about a fourth of 60 per cent in that period. So volume increased but value did not – that was the first problem. Secondly, there were social problems. To actually get to a fiscal balance, the government cut expenditure on Health, expenditure on Education, and this created civil unrest. They had this conference called PAMSCAD – the Programme to Mitigate the Social Cost of Adjustment – whereby they actually looked at ways to alleviate these consequences of the economic restructuring programme. Thirdly, because it could now borrow from abroad, the government really racked up quite a lot of debt. Yes, it got concessional loans, but its outstanding debt also increased therefore from $1.3 billion to $3.1 billion. It also became very dependent on Aid. The only way to balance its book was to become the poster child of a lot of these development agencies, but then inherent in that is how fragile this recovery was and how dependent it was on Aid. Lastly, one of the aims was, as was outlined, to attract foreign capital. That did not happen, certainly not to the extent that they had hoped. The reasons were many-fold.

First of all, there was uncertainly as to how sincere Rawlings was in changing his mind. He seemed to be very opportunistic because he only changed his mind when the Soviet Union could not give him any finance, so there was a problem there. Secondly, part of the restructuring and the re-definition of the role of the State was to get rid of a lot of the state-owned enterprises. That process was really slow, so this created an environment of uncertainty. Thirdly, there was still very high inflation within the economy, so that again gave another level of uncertainty. All these contributed to that part of the goal of the Structural Adjustment Programme not being achieved.

IA-D: In comparative economic analyses of Africa and Asia, more frequently between Africa and South-East Asia, people cite policy formulation and implementation as being critical in the development of East Asia as compared to Africa. Do you share this view?

D-JO: That is a very interesting question, because a lot of these South-East Asian countries had fairly comparable living standards with African countries at the time of Ghana's independence. There was a very interesting paper in 1994 that actually looked at comparing Ghana to South Korea, because on the date of independence they had almost identical GDP per capita, and Korea also had similar problems. It suffered quite badly during the Second World War, then you had the

Korean War, so you can't say that their circumstances were really different or that they had a massive advantage. So this is a really interesting question.

Now, I think it is both the policies that have been proposed that have contributed to Africa, and Ghana in particular, lagging behind, and also their implementation. First of all, the speed at which the Ghanaian economy tried to develop was too high; they really thought they could do it overnight. Secondly, the time-span of most of these development plans was really long, considering the uncertainty. Thirdly, there was no attention – I think in Nkrumah's first plan there were two paragraphs – devoted to cocoa production, which was the major earner of foreign currency. There was no attention paid to that at all. Fourthly, and this is quite crucial, Ghana didn't take advantage of its comparative advantage. Its comparative advantage was lots of fairly cheap labour, but most of the industries that the State went into were very capital-intensive, so it was very dependent on capital equipment imports, and there was no comparative advantage there.

So the set-up was already part of the problem, but there were additional problems in its implementation. For example, the fiscal balance that was proposed, contrary to the plan, wasn't kept. Contrary to the plans, foreign currency reserves were totally run down. There were really good provisions on screening investments by the Ministry of Finance on viability, but they were totally ignored and most of the projects weren't actually screened at all. Fourthly, due to popular pressure to enter into certain sectors or not, there was total over-engineering of certain enterprises. For example, there was a mango canning factory that was set up by the State to provide employment, but no one actually looked at it very carefully, so that it had the capacity to supply a number of times the world demand for canned mangos. It was never going to be profitable! So, both in terms of policy and in terms of implementation, you can see the problems.

IA-D: But in the East Asia-Africa debate, there are those who also talk of the contribution of Japan, for instance, to Korea, and they also talk of the huge investments the United States made to Korea, investments that, even if we add all the amounts that they gave to African countries from 1950 to 1980, don't come anywhere near what was given to Korea alone. Don't you think this might have also contributed to the growth of South Korea?

D-JO: That is a very difficult question, because a lot of the assistance and investment in Korea has been military...

IA-D: I just wanted to play devil's advocate and present a different viewpoint. So how is the economy of Ghana doing in the early years of the twenty-first century from where you are?

D-JO: There are a number of observations. First of all, you see that the economy has really taken off. You can almost see a structural break in economic growth since 2000 and really that has increased quite remarkably. I think 2005-6 was about 6.5 per cent growth, so really there is solid economic growth. That is not just coincidental. The World Bank publishes a report every year called the *Doing Business* report, and they rank all the countries on how easy it is to do business, and Ghana in the last two years running has been in the Top 10 in terms of the quickest rises. Lots of restrictions on doing business have been abolished, so it becomes much easier. That is part of the answer. Yes, Ghana is doing very well.

Going forwards, it is interesting to see where it is going to go with the find of oil – 1.3 billion barrels of oil. Often you see oil being a curse more than anything, but having spoken to a number of people, I've got quite a lot of faith that the revenues will be used properly; they will not fall victim to Dutch disease, which means that, because oil is a foreign currency earner, your currency will appreciate, which makes it harder for other exporters to do business. But you can neutralise this, and there has been a debate already as to how to properly do that. So the way that oil is used, both in terms of making sure that Dutch disease doesn't happen and also in terms of making sure that there is technological spill-over – that this is not an enclave economy offshore that has no technological spill-over with the mainland. If you can actually achieve that; if you can do something value-added with the oil, that would be very good, and I've already heard people talking about that.

I also think, and this is probably the most important thing, the conundrum as to whether development and democracy can go hand in hand has been solved. It almost looked for twenty or thirty years as if you couldn't be a democratic country and develop. Each time, we had Busia or whoever thrown out of power and the military taking power. Now, we have had a really good handover of power in 2000, and

Kufuor being re-elected in 2004 was the first person to be properly re-elected. So, yes, democracy and development can go hand in hand, and I've got great hope for Ghana.

IA-D: Thank you.

November 2007

Dr Nii Moi Thompson

Dr Nii Moi Thompson is an economist and currently the Executive Director of the Development Policy Institute, which he founded. He is also an Associate Fellow at the Centre for Budget Advocacy, Accra, as well as the economic spokesman for the Convention People's Party. He has extensive experience in economic development and policy analysis stretching from his days as a Budget Analyst at the Office of Management and Budget in Pittsburgh, Pennsylvania, in the United States, to his position as Senior Economist at New York State's Bureau of Fiscal and Economic Analysis in New York City, also in the United States.

As an independent consultant, he has worked extensively in both Ghana and other parts of Africa. He has been an Advisor to Ghana's National Development Planning Commission and the erstwhile Ministry of Economic Planning and Regional Integration. As a member of the Transition Team on the Economy in 2001, he wrote his Sub-Group's report on "fiscal discipline and macroeconomic stability". He has consulted for many international organisations, including the British Department for International Development, the Ethiopian Development Research Institute at the Office of the Ethiopian Prime Minister, and the World Bank. In addition to providing regular critiques for the Bank's *Doing Business in Ghana* report, he also was recently the lead consultant on the Bank's study of Local Economic Development (LED) and its contribution to national growth and later, through the Bank, as a consultant to the Ghana Statistical Service on the Fifth Ghana Living Standards Survey. He is currently part of an international team examining patterns and trends in Agriculture Expenditures in Ghana and how they can be improved.

He is a regular contributor to radio, television, and newspaper discussions on national development, with his most recent crusade being against increases in utility tariffs without corresponding improvements in service delivery.

Nii Moi Thompson was born on April 19, 1960, in Kumasi but grew up in various parts of the country, including Nkwawie and Agona Swedru. Having run away from home at age 16, he first moved to Liberia in 1976 and shortly afterwards to Sierra Leone, where he secured a job as a reporter on one of the leading newspapers at the time, *We Yone*. He worked there from December 1977 to December 1978 and then returned to Liberia where he worked on a few weekly papers. In 1980, he applied to work as a reporter on the newly established *Daily Observer* newspaper but was offered the position of Sub-Editor instead. As an Editor he interacted extensively with policy-makers at all levels in the Liberian government and in the Diplomatic Community. He migrated to the United States in 1983 to study journalism but "defected", in his own words, to economics because he found "classroom journalism" to be boring.

Dr Thompson holds a PhD in Development Economics and Public Policy from the University of Pittsburgh; an MA in International Economics from the State University of New York; and a BA in Economics from the City University of New York, all in the United States.

Ivor Agyeman-Duah: How would you assess Nkrumah's postcolonial economic policies and the foundations these might have laid for economic development from 1957?

Dr Nii Moi Thompson: We had, as you know, a prelude to 1957, which was the 1951-57 period, so that's a kind of pre-independence Convention People's Party (CPP) period and Nkrumah himself was particular about including that in his history. We're talking about the limited government period when he was the Leader of Government Business in 1951. They inherited in 1951 a Ten-Year Development Plan from the British, but they clearly thought that there was such urgency that they didn't have time to spread it over ten years, and they squeezed that into five years. What was also remarkable about that was, it was the first time we had an all-African Cabinet so to speak, with a few exceptions like Defence and Finance. But they took over and squeezed this ten-year programme into five years, and actually increased the Budget for it, and went ahead and laid the foundation for independence.

During this period, we had rapid growth in some key social areas: primary schools, middle schools, teacher training colleges, universities – unbelievable growth. These were areas that had been experiencing very limited growth, very timid growth because of obvious colonial policies. Nkrumah said, "No, we're going to change this".

So from 1957 then, we had almost complete control, because Ghana was still part of the Commonwealth – it wasn't until 1960 that it became a Republic and therefore moved away from the influence of the Queen – but we were pretty much in charge. The objective was to industrialise Ghana in the shortest time possible. And it's interesting sometimes when you look at the kinds of policies, the structure of the policies, which were to have these special development plans. If you look at the orientation of these plans, they're actually almost identical to what South Korea right around the same time also adopted, which was to produce consumer goods using imported machinery.

What they did was to do surveys and find out what Ghanaians used most. They found, for instance, that we used a lot of matches because we had to light charcoal and so forth and so on, and we were buying a lot of matches and importing them. The government went ahead and set up the Kade Match Factory. And they realised that we also needed sugar for our *koko* so they established a Sugar Factory. And then we had to wear shoes, so the Kumasi Shoe Factory was set up. It was this rapid, integrated approach to development, calling for massive investments, which Nkrumah made.

People are often heard saying that he squandered huge amounts of money that he inherited from the British, which is all false. What really happened was that, at the time of independence in 1957, Nkrumah said "Wait a minute, you guys owe us two hundred million pounds". This was money that the British forcibly took from us during the Second World War. They took it actually from cocoa proceeds: as we exported the cocoa, they took the money along with some minimal interest that they set, which is actually quite a good deal: you borrow the money on your own terms, which was what they did. And they used that to support the pound at the end of the Second World War when the pound had more or less collapsed. So Nkrumah said "Give us our money". And they did. The question is: what did he use the money for?

You look at the Akosombo Dam, which was then 70 million pounds. We paid half of that. He was willing to pay all of it, but for obvious strategic reasons the Americans, the World Bank, and the British insisted on paying the remaining half. The Tema Harbour, and the entire Tema township, was raised partly from that money, as was the Motorway, which originally was supposed to run from Tema to Kumasi, the Boankra inland port, and then to Paga in the North. All of these things came from him. So the money wasn't even adequate to begin with, given the scale of projects and ambition and vision that he had for Ghana.

Come 1965 you had the collapse in cocoa prices, which then subverted the plan. It brought all the hardships which rather unfortunately served as the basis for a military coup in 1966, and we haven't recovered from it yet.

IA-D: That means that, from the start, we were not able to diversify the economy. We were depending virtually on cocoa and gold.

NMT: Yes, in the initial stages, and this was informed by economic theory, as Nkrumah was advised by a lot of the top economists from around the world, including Sir Arthur Lewis, who later went on to win the Nobel Prize. The theory was that, in the early stages of development, when industries are low, you necessarily have to finance expansion of Industry, or the non-Agricultural sector, with the surplus from Agriculture. So at that point we really had no choice but to use the surplus from Agriculture to expand the Industrial Sector. If you look at the first development plan, expenditures were 11.2 per cent for Agriculture and Industry. And Agriculture wasn't just primary Agriculture; we also wanted secondary Agriculture, or Processing, so that it added value and therefore created employment.

So in the first plan they had 11.2 per cent. The second plan was 20.3 per cent. By the third plan, it had risen to 37.3 per cent. The ultimate objective was to reduce our dependence on cocoa, which was very volatile then – gold didn't really feature that much at that time – and then create this industrial base where we would manufacture imported things, export some, and then set the price. So, yes, it was part of his strategy. It wasn't the *end* of everything.

IA-D: But Arthur Lewis left because of disagreements with Nkrumah on the policy front.

NMT: Yes, because Arthur Lewis was more of a technocrat; Nkrumah was a visionary at heart: "Thank you for giving your advice, but this is what we're going to do". Thailand's experiences have shown that experts are not always right. Sometimes you just have to go with your gut instinct, and also be able to read the political terrain.

I'm sure you've recently heard about Malawi, how they initially took World Bank advice on disengaging the State from Agriculture. In the end, they actually went begging for food. This was a country that was producing enough and feeding itself before it took this quote-unquote "expert" advice. So after they found themselves in this humiliating position they said, "To Hell with World Bank policies", and just a few years back they went back to their old ways and now they're producing a surplus again. So the experts do not always get it right. It's good to listen to them, get some technical insights and whatnot, but ultimately these are also political processes and political decisions, not just technocratic decisions. If we had listened to some of these people, we wouldn't have made the kind of progress that we made.

IA-D: What about the role of the State in economic development and, in the case of Nkrumah, the role of the party? Because one of the disagreements that Arthur Lewis had with him was the role of the CPP in the economic management of the country, where cocoa contracts were given to members of the party, which he thought affected the smooth running of the economy.

NMT: Certainly there was some malfeasance there, but we should also bear in mind that Nkrumah was facing two objectives, or at least aimed at two objectives, both of which required institution-building. One was nation-building: he faced the task of holding together what were effectively four different political parties. We had the Gold Coast; we had Ashanti, which at the time included Brong-Ahafo; we had Trans-Volta; and we had the Northern Territories. Suddenly we had independence and we had to hold these things together against the centrifugal forces that were working at the time. Secondly, while holding the country together he also had to promote social and economic development. And the process of getting that required that you had the institutions that would be dedicated to this progress.

Unfortunately, we came into independence with these fragment-ations, because we also had a situation where political loyalties tended to coincide with tribal or even ethnic loyalties. These days everyone keeps citing PDA – the Preventive Detention Act – but no one talks about other laws that Nkrumah implemented that eventually helped to create the single Ghana which we enjoy today, for example the Avoidance of Discrimination Act, which was that there were to be no political parties using ethnic names or religious names. And that, ironically, was what led to the creation of the UP – the United Party – because once he passed that law, groups in Accra, the Ashanti group, the Trans-Volta, the Northern People's Party couldn't stay in that particular mode because that would have been against the law, so if anything it united them.

That decision to go one-party and concentrate so much in the hands of one particular political group was informed by the social and political conditions of the period. I believe that if things had been allowed to proceed, if our political destiny had been allowed to follow its own course, over time we would have gained traction and seen what heights our nation would have ascended to. Sometimes we watch the Black Stars play soccer, and everyone is standing there singing, all lost in the national anthem. At that particular moment, no one is thinking of themselves as Ga, Fante, or Hausa: we are all Ghanaians. That's the kind of sense of nationhood, oneness—that Nkrumah wanted. We all take Ghana for granted, but during that period it was quite a challenge.

IA-D: The growth pattern in the early years of postcolonial rule was very visible in the structure of development – schools and things like that. But something must have gone amiss because in the course of all this the economic indicators started declining; by 1966 some of the indicators were very low. What happened?

NMT: As I said, there was a collapse in cocoa prices. When you do a plan, the plan typically comprises programmes and projects, and then costed activities to give expression to these projects and programmes. But you have sources of funding for that. In this case, cocoa was our single largest source of funding, and cocoa prices collapsed between 24 and 30 per cent or thereabouts. In fact, there was a sequential decline in cocoa prices in the early 1960s, and they were actually in the process of trying to diversify the sources of funding, including by an increase in the Domestic Savings Rate. That itself raised a lot of opposition, but Nkrumah said, "At some point we have to finance these things." So he faced this problem, and suddenly this wonderful vision that he had was facing severe challenges in the form of financing, which came about in 1965.

Now, at this point he was also more or less at loggerheads with the Americans, which I thought, looking back now, was somewhat tactless on his part. When you face adversaries like that you use your wits as opposed to trying to flex your muscles. So he was going through this period where he had these disagreements with the Americans. Even when Ghana qualified during this period for some kind of assistance from the IMF and the World Bank, the Americans were pulling the strings in the background. If you read the declassified Central Intelligence Agency (CIA) documents, the Americans said: "Let's hold back. Let's not give him these funds to tide him over. Let's hold back the funds and create desperate conditions that will lead to desperate actions on his part and therefore create the pretext for a military coup."

The frightening thing is that is precisely what is being done in Zimbabwe today. Let's not go there now, but the similarities are quite striking, because in the case of Zimbabwe they also said, "OK let's impose these quote-unquote "smart" sanctions" – which for them included businesses that were owned by Zimbabwean government officials. But these businessmen don't produce for themselves, they produce for the public, so if you put sanctions on them that leads to scarcity in goods and services, which we are seeing in Zimbabwe now. We saw some of that in Ghana in 1965. That created the conditions, and then the coup came.

Even then, some of the key indicators have still not been bested yet. For example, as I speak with you, our biggest desire in this country is to be a middle income country with $1000 per capita, which really isn't anything – sometimes I wonder if our leaders actually think through these things before they talk – but if you adjust for inflation and look at our per capita income in 1963, it's actually far higher than $1000, so by today's standards we were a middle income country despite the problems. And it's important to emphasise that all economies go through difficulties. As you know, the United States economy is wobbling now, but no one is going to advocate a military coup just because George W. Bush and his people have gone through a rough patch. Europe goes through it. Japan for almost a decade was stuck in a recession. So these are natural parts of the general cycle of economic development, but for Nkrumah people used it as an excuse, as a pretext, to subvert that whole Great March Forward.

IA-D: The problem with commodity prices collapsing under Nkrumah, especially cocoa, is that countries like Ivory Coast, countries like Indonesia, were also affected but still their growth rates were maintained. And in the case of Nkrumah, critics also use his pursuit of Pan-Africanism as an ideology – the unification of Africa, opening up of embassies around Africa and other places where we were getting very little in terms of returns – as the source of some bad investments that he made. Did this, in your view, affect economic development?

NMT: First of all, the nature of investments, whether by Nkrumah or anybody, is that for a brief period after the major investment you don't make any profits. Typically you even run at a loss, until you reach break-even point and then you begin to make profits. So that is one issue, and I don't think it can be used against him; people try to use it as an after-the-fact accusation of Nkrumah.

Secondly, the monies we spent to help promote the liberation of Africa weren't that huge. They were simply fractions of our total expenditures. People sometimes make reference to the loan given to Guinea, but it was a *loan*. It wasn't a free grant. And in any case, let's go back further and remember what Nkrumah said in his Independence Day declaration, that the independence of Ghana was meaningless unless it was linked up with the total liberation of the African continent. He didn't just say it; he went on to try and live it out, and looked to other parts of Africa where they needed help to decolonise as the first step towards creating a continental African Union. Because really, part of the reason we are suffering in Africa now is the lack of unity, the lack of a continental political, economic, and social unit. We are still fragmented all over the place. So, it was well-spent. If that experiment had been allowed to follow its course, we wouldn't be in the mess that we are in today. And guess who had an interest in not seeing a united Africa? Those who were colonising Africa, either directly or indirectly. And so Nkrumah trying to remove them from Africa then naturally became a threat.

Nkrumah was heavily Garveyist in orientation. If you read his autobiography, he says, and I quote: "Of all the books that I read, none did so much to fire my imagination than *The Philosophy and Opinions of Marcus Garvey*". It's a very powerful book, and it fired him up. So a lot of his approaches were Garveyist in orientation. I recently read in the *Graphic* an article by someone who said that we should change "Black Star" because the word "Black" stood for too many negative things. But that's because of ignorance; Marcus Garvey, who actually travelled throughout the Caribbean and the Americas and elsewhere, realised a common thread. He found that Blacks, whether they were in the majority or the minority were always at the bottom of the economic ladder. And at that point, he said and I quote: "I shall not rest until I make Africa the Black Star among the constellation of nations." So that was the first time the term "Black Star" was actually used, and Marcus Garvey went on to create the Black Star Line company in New York. And when Nkrumah later on led Ghana to independence he even adopted the name and the whole African personality thing. Garveyist philosophy was to inspire the African. It was to build in you some kind of confidence, which we didn't have before. If you listen to Nkrumah's speech on the day of independence, he referred to all these things, except he didn't use the word "Garvey". But it was basically Garveyist in orientation. And it was worth it. There's nothing whatsoever wrong with you dipping into your pocket to help your brothers achieve their aims.

IA-D: We are in the twenty-first century. Would you, for economic management's sake, say that we can still adopt some of the economic philosophies of Nkrumah – like state control of the economy, which in many places is taking second position to liberal markets?

NMT: Part of the problem of pigeon-holing ourselves without looking at our historical conditions is that we are then likely to make all the wrong decisions, and we keep doing that. Talking about state controls, what is happening in the UK now? They are trying to buy back some of these private companies that are falling on hard times. The US just bailed out Bear Stearns to another company. The Japanese government actually bought back a few firms. So the extent of state involvement in the economy should be determined by the history of a given country. There shouldn't be a global ideology, where a team of technocrats just get on a plane from Washington DC, having first heard of Ghana when they went into a tourist shop and bought a book about the country, and come in and prescribe these cookie-cutter kinds of prescriptions. They have been to Tanzania, and what worked in Tanzania must work in Ghana and must work in Uganda – we must avoid those things.

Secondly, the degree of state intervention even in Nkrumah's time was not total. If you read the Seven-Year Development Plan, which was supposed to run from 1964-70, it makes a lot of provisions for the role of the Private Sector because even they realised that the State, however well-intentioned it was, could not provide all the resources to finance our development agenda. However, it also reserved the right of the State to step into certain areas of the economy where private enterprise may not take any ready interest. A good example is the creation of the Agricultural Development Bank. Because of the risky nature of Agriculture – you have floods, you have drought, and you lose everything – the commercial banks at the time were not willing to engage in the concerns of farmers, so the State stepped in and set up what was originally called the Agriculture and Credit Cooperative, which was meant to cater for them. So that was a very good, justifiable position for the State to take.

These days we definitely do not want the State going into production of everything, but it can certainly provide other types of involvement, such as extension services, which we are not doing enough of, and which accounts for the reason why we are not food sufficient yet. As we speak, we import $200 million of fish every year despite the fact that we have one of the longest coastlines in the world. That is because the State has neglected its role under structural adjustment that you should leave everything to market forces. But sometimes market forces can be evil forces. The only force that can work against those evil forces is the power of the State. It's a collaborative thing: you cannot have a situation where the Private Sector runs everything, nor can you have a situation where the State runs everything. That never was the case, and it certainly is not the case now. I do not see that being the case in the foreseeable future.

IA-D: The Agricultural GDP does not match the number of people in the Agricultural sector. This has been so for a very long time. What has accounted for this?

NMT: Low productivity. Agriculture provides something like 60 per cent of the labour force, and yet it accounts for just under 40 per cent of GDP. So that means you have too many people out there producing too little. We have low productivity for a whole host of reasons. I just came from an agricultural community in the Eastern Region, and we sat down and talked to them, we saw their problems. They are so basic! It is just that the political will to deal with these problems is not there. And what are some of the problems? I just mentioned extension services. It is a major problem. They need these services to first understand what they are doing. I came back to Accra with a huge sack of oranges, even though I pleaded with them not to give them to me. But they told me that they were just going to go to waste because they had developed some disease. They had asked the local agricultural extension officers to help them, but they cannot help them because they have not received the resources from Accra. So all the money they used in planting the oranges then goes to waste.

Access to credit remains a problem; access to markets too. I talked to people who had been given micro-credit to raise pigs and other animals, but there is no market: they are in the middle of nowhere in the forest. No one has thought to plan these things all because we said we should stay out and let the markets take over. But I don't know any place in the world where everything is determined by the market. I always remind people that when you walk into a typical supermarket in America, you might think that everything is market-determined, but there are actually federal price floors. There are certain levels below which supermarkets are not allowed to sell certain things as a way of both protecting farmers and also protecting small "Mom and Pop" stores, as they call them. So even there, there is a degree of State involvement in guiding the economy.

Where we went wrong was the clumsy nature of state involvement. It became an end in itself, rather than being a means to achieve something. The soldiers could tell you: "Hey, price control: you bought this thing for three cedis, you must sell it for one cedi", which does not make sense. But the concept that the State must play a role in the economy is a time-honoured thing. Nkrumah himself was informed largely after the Second World War or, for that matter after the First World War, when the State in Europe took a major role in their economies. These social democrats and whatnot came out of that philosophical milieu. The US Social Security system, Medicare – these are all state interventions, but for some reason when we decide to do that here, they tell us that we should leave the State out, which I think is unfair. A major problem that we face in Ghana and Africa now is that we lack the capacity to even understand our problems and advance solutions or counter-proposals to what those in Washington give us.

IA-D: We've been talking about these problems for many years – state farms, post-harvest losses – and governments come and go. We haven't seen Agriculture being the centre of a policy programme. Why is it that we keep talking about these issues and the problems remain the same?

NMT: I've come to the conclusion that we have three types of poverty in Africa. Unfortunately we only focus on one, which is material poverty: one dollar a day, two dollars a day, and the rest of it. But there are two other types of poverty that are even more debilitating than the material one. We have poverty of vision, and then poverty of common sense. This is what is plaguing us. You might have read that the government has approved tens of millions of dollars to buy a Presidential jet. In fact, they are buying two: a main one and a supplementary one (with Parliamentary approval). And if you look through the 2008 Budget, about 63 or 64 per cent – let's just say 60 – of our budget for Agriculture this year is expected to come from abroad. But we have money to buy Presidential jets. This is the poverty of vision, the poverty of common sense that I'm talking about.

As I speak with you, if you are lucky and turn on the tap the water will run. If you are not lucky, it will not run. Yet our leaders spend so much money on themselves and try to find all sorts of justifications for it. The latest justification for buying the jet and building the Presidential Palace is that it will raise their prestige. You have a Presidential Palace, you have a Presidential jet, and you can't feed yourself or provide water for your people, and that's supposed to lead to prestige? I think it will rather lead to ridicule. So we have this poverty of leadership that is really crippling Africa, and the question is often asked: what is the solution? We just have to keep extracting good leadership from them and we have to let them know.

Sometimes they also tend to prey on the...I don't want to say ignorance, but lack of awareness of the public. One of the Presidential candidates for the December 2008 elections recently launched his campaign and the statistics he had in there were just flat-out false! It just didn't make sense; they actually indict his government! But no one questioned it. The main opposition party didn't question it. The media, well they are somewhere else. Anything you give them they will publish. No one has a critical mind as to say "Wait a minute, these numbers don't make sense". How could the other government have spent $320 million on manufacturing – and back then manufacturing constituted 9 per cent of GDP – while these people are telling us that they have spent over $2 billion and meanwhile manufacturing has declined? Either someone is lying, or the government has been grossly inefficient. They spend $2 billion in a sector and the sector declines, while someone spends $320 million and the sector actually rises. There is something fundamentally wrong!

IA-D: What were the main economic problems, challenges and prospects when we had gone in for the Structural Adjustment Programme in 1983? What was the landscape of the economy?

NMT: In 1983, we were in the doldrums, we were in the gutter. We had three successive years of negative economic growth, largely as a result of factors beyond our control for that period. We had drought and then we had the bushfires. The economy basically collapsed. We were experiencing negative growth for the first time in so many years. Of course there had also been a systematic institutional decay, starting from 1966. For example, after the coup, some of the projects and programmes that we had that were meant to raise and move us forward were abolished. Some of the state-owned enterprises were simply shut down and neglected.

So what we saw between 1980 and 1983 was the culmination of this steady decline. Once they launched the Structural Adjustment Programme, it was a *quid pro quo*: you have to do these kinds of things before we give you money. Don't forget that industry had ground to a halt because we didn't have the foreign exchange to import the spare parts, and the IMF is telling you, "If you do this and this and this and this, we'll give you the money to import the spare parts." Some of the policies they did undertake under structural adjustment were actually good. For instance, the dismantling of price control, because it had become this behemoth that no one could control. It is funny to read through some of the old Budgets and see that the government actually used to tell you how much you should charge for a piece of soap or a box of matches. These days, all of these things are gone, but that was the madness of the period.

It was followed by a period of stabilisation. It's like taking a patient into an emergency ward: you have to stabilise the patient and then begin to work on him. Unfortunately they were using the same policies they used for stabilisation to try and promote growth, and it simply didn't make sense. By raising interest rates, you are simply suppressing industrial expansion. They had reckless, populist liberalisation of the economy without preparing the domestic economy for what was coming. Over time, industry started declining. Manufacturing used to be about 16 per cent of GDP, it is now 8 per cent – it has gone down. Services have expanded, but they are low-value services: people selling in the streets and in traffic and so on. But after the stabilisation phase... It's like driving a vehicle: you put it in first, you take off. You cannot go on in first gear or you will ruin your engine. You need to change gears according to how fast you want to go. We haven't done that yet. Unfortunately, the New Patriotic Party government has also done the same thing. Every year when you go through the Budget they say we are poised for high growth. To be fair to them, we've actually moved in terms of the pace of growth from 3.7 per cent in 2000 to about 6.4 per cent last year. But this was mostly in particular areas, namely mining, which is not job-creating growth. You have high growth but low employment, so that is "jobless growth" as we call it. And then you have some of it coming from cocoa, and cocoa has a paradox where, at least in contemporary Ghana, some of the poorest areas in Ghana are also cocoa-growing areas. So you go to a place like Juabeso-Bia in the Western Region – very fertile, very productive for cocoa, but it has been designated one of the poorest areas in Ghana. You have growth there but somehow the monies disappear, and then when you track them down you realise that they are in Accra to be used at will by the political elite.

IA-D: Are the economic indicators good now compared to ten years ago?

NMT: They are not good compared to ten years ago if you look at living conditions of the people. There are two ways you can measure performance – you can measure it from an economic standpoint...

IA-D: I'm talking about 6 per cent GDP growth, inflation approaching single digits...

NMT: "Approaching" – that's a good word. It's been elusive for the past six years! There are two ways of measuring success. You can measure success horizontally or you can measure it vertically. The two are not mutually exclusive. If you measure it horizontally, it means you are measuring success relative to where you came from, which is fine. It is acceptable. So the inflation rate is down: well it went from 25 per cent in 2000 to 33 per cent in 2001 and since then it has declined to just over 10 per cent, and now it's picking up again to around 13 per cent or so. So historically you've done well, if you measure success horizontally.

But if you compare yourself at a fixed point in time with others, our inflation rate is still very high compared to – let's say – our rate of depreciation, which is less than one per cent. What that means is that your currency is overvalued and your exports, therefore, are no longer competitive, which explains why, if you look at the statistics, exports as a share of GDP have actually been declining since 2001. Manufacturing itself, which constitutes the bulk of exports besides cocoa, has also been suffering. The recent construction as a result of the CAN 2008 (Africa Cup of Nations competition) also helped push growth a little bit.

The bigger picture is that this growth has not really translated into improved living conditions for the people. The ultimate objective in development is the living conditions of the people. You can have very fancy, very perfumed macroeconomic statistics, but if the living conditions of the people haven't improved then you really haven't done anything. Our UNDP Human Development Index actually declined in 2005, and this was the first time it has declined since the UN started keeping records in 1975. So that tells you that there is something wrong there. You only have to look around: we are drowning in filth, we have a sanitation crisis, in addition to a water crisis. We just barely came out of an electricity crisis last year, and we're still suffering from it. Personal safety is now an issue. Main highways in Ghana are dead at night. Drivers don't want to use them because they will be hijacked by armed robbers, possibly killed. So the quality of life in Ghana has actually declined despite the positive growth, and the increase in the rate of growth.

This is a paradox that we have to resolve. That is, is growth an end in itself or should it be a means to improving the living conditions of the people? If you have high growth but the living conditions are declining, it is time you paused to consider the relevance or the quality of that growth. Who is profiting from it? As I speak with you, we have three-bedroom apartments here that go for $360,000, and these apartments have been sold out. The government's own report has shown that inequality has increased by 15 per cent. So it's not all well.

I notice also from anecdotal evidence that people are leaving, especially professionals. I wish they wouldn't leave, but I can understand why they do. It becomes very frustrating when you are working so hard, you are paying your taxes, you are doing everything, and then some leaders here in Accra just hijack the resources and use them for themselves and their family members. So people are better off going to Sweden, or the UK, the US, wherever, and they leave. It is not always about salaries, that they pay low salaries here and people will earn more in the US. No, it is not always like that.

IA-D: What has been the role of the multilateral institutions – the World Bank, the IMF, and the others? Can we do without them?

NMT: For now, no. Their involvement, especially the World Bank, has been a sort of mixed blessing all because of the lackadaisical leadership that we have here. For example, the decision to publish our inflation report on a monthly basis was a World Bank conditionality. You ask yourself: why must someone get on a plane from Washington to come and tell you to publish your inflation rate every month? The decision to reduce the number of days cheques clear in Accra to three days from something like seven or eight days was a conditionality from the World Bank. So there these instances where, operationally at least, their involvement has been beneficial.

Where it has been harmful is where their involvement has been more ideological than practical. So they insist on removing the State without even looking at our objective, peculiar conditions all because someone in Washington has decided that the State shouldn't have any particular business in this area. But you'll notice that their own state involvement is informed by their particular history. The US is now trying to bail out Bear Stearns. Who am I or you to go to Washington and tell them not to get involved? They are doing those things on the basis of what they think is good for them. We, on the other hand, have to look outside. Part of the reason, as I said earlier, is that we simply lack the capacity to do the kind of policy analysis that we can then counter them with.

When they come in and say "Do this", we can say, "No we're not going to do this, and these are the reasons why".

Even the basic information for analysis and planning doesn't exist. If I were to call a ministry now and ask for expenditure data dating just back to the year 2000, they would scratch their heads and give me long stories as to why they cannot give it to me. The most they can do for me, now that we are in 2008, is probably 2005-2006; 2007 is out of the question. So when you have such paucity of information to make decisions, those who have better capacity always dominate you. They throw all these fancy terminologies at you, and you buckle. You think they are actually making sense. In point of fact, they are not. They are just bull-shitting you and you fall for it.

IA-D: Have there been instances in other countries where their policies have been counted and the results have been given – that is, with indigenous knowledge and indigenous people?

NMT: Yes, yes, yes! Malaysia did that during the 1997 financial crisis. Malaysia in fact was the only country that said, "We will not take your prescriptions. We will go about it the Malaysian way." In less than a year they were vindicated. The IMF had to admit that they were wrong in Malaysia and the Malaysians were right. That's because the Malaysians had built the capacity. Every now and again I visit the Malaysian Prime Minister's website to see how they are doing. It is up-to-date. I was recently at the website of our Castle and the most recent item they had was from 2006! When I was on radio I talked about it and a few hours later someone updated the website.

There is some value system that is dysfunctional, where we don't treasure excellence or the need to even pursue excellence. Everything is just material possessions. As long as we live in big homes surrounded by barbed wire fences, we view that as progress. In fact, it is a symbol of retrogression because 20 or 30 years ago, people had just ordinary windows. Here we are, with barbed wires and security fences and iron bars, and we're still sleeping with one eye open. There is something wrong.

IA-D: What have been the most significant achievements as a country, not as a government or as a party, over the last 25 years and what are the prospects for the future?

NMT: It is interesting you should ask that, because I was listening to radio and the Speaker had been sworn in by the Chief Justice as Acting President for three days. It struck me that this was a sign of progress, at least in terms of institution-building. We've come a long way. It wasn't very long ago – during my own generation – when the military Head of State, Kutu Acheampong for instance, could not travel outside of Ghana. The whole time he was in power, the farthest he went was Togo, and he came back the same day for fear of getting overthrown. We've reached a stage where both the President and the Vice- President can travel and the Speaker acts as President for three days. I think it is remarkable progress, and we need to find every means possible to protect and defend that.

Despite all the flaws of the government – and there are plenty of them – these kinds of institutions must be protected at all costs. And this is where our worry lies now, given the fact that we are now going into elections. You have some intemperate statements being made on radio airwaves, and there doesn't seem to be any concerted effort being made to counter that. Whenever I go on radio or talk to journalists, I remind them that they have a professional responsibility and a patriotic duty to ensure that this democratic infrastructure is actually preserved by watching or editing the kind of language people use. I tell them they need to avoid things like "This is a do or die election". There is nothing to die for here. When they had the disputed elections in Kenya, right around the same time they had the disputed elections in Georgia. You didn't hear about anyone there taking a cutlass and cutting people and so on. Africans think somehow that you should always spill blood just to show how savage you can be, but we don't have to be that way. They just did a re-count in New York for the primaries for the Democrats, and it turned out that in areas where they said Obama got zero he actually got something like 126. You don't hear about Obama's supporters going around with cutlasses either. In other words, you have to build institutions to address these things. And one way of doing that is to get people to think in a rational way.

Of course, I mentioned the fact that the Budget doesn't have to be read on some radio station at night by some soldier anymore – it is read in the normal sense, and we have the debates, and so on. No one is telling you how much you should sell your things for. I remember in the 1970s in Kumasi, the soldiers used to go around and beat up people like crazy all because they were selling things above control prices.

We've moved away from that. So from that point of view I think we've come a long way, and we ought to be proud of that. There is still a long way to go yet, for instance decentralising government so that things go down to a local level and that we don't just sit in Accra.

IA-D: Do you believe in Ghana's future in the coming years?

NMT: I more than believe in Ghana. I believe we have everything except good leadership. The vision is simply lacking. One of the biggest legacies of Nkrumah is to get us to think of ourselves as Ghanaians, and we've managed to keep that unitary sense of nationhood. I hope we continue to retain that. That will probably depend on the extent to which we allow politicians to manipulate our emotions and our beliefs. I, for instance, am a Pan-Africanist and so for me my race is more important than my tribe. My tribe must necessarily be subordinate to my race. And that was the Nkrumah vision. Unfortunately, we haven't bought into that yet, so we have politicians who, come election time, will go and play on people's emotions. The irony and the tragedy of it all is that if you look at it closely the whole business of tribe is so superficial. It's what the Marxists call reification – we reify something abstract and give it a life. But when you step back and look at it, what does it mean to be a Ga, Fante, or Hausa? People use tribe for social organisation. But if you were to take a child born of Ga parents and ask a group of Ghanaians to tell you the tribe of that child, they wouldn't be able to tell you. They can of course tell you that this is a Black child, an African. That's it. The tribe of that person becomes a social construction. If you can take that same child and give it to a Dagomba family to raise him or her, he or she will grow up to be a Dagomba, despite being born of Ga parents.

Somehow we manage to create this emotional attachment to tribe and our politicians then exploit that. During elections they will come and tell you: "Vote for me, we speak the same language, we're from the same village". But the second he wins, who are the people who profit? We need to purge the minds of the people of this tribal myth. People come to me with tribal agendas all the time. I tell them that I am a Garveyist: Race first, and then tribe becomes secondary, if at all it features. In fact, tribe for me is third: African, Ghanaian, and then tribe third. But it will take a while for people to move away from this irrational attachment to tribe. If you bring a Martian who could provide water 24 hours a day, trust me I would vote for him over even my father or my mother.

IA-D: Thank you very much.

NMT: You are most welcome.

March 2008

Professor Ernest Aryeetey

Professor Ernest Aryeetey is the Director of the Institute of Statistical, Social and Economic Research (ISSER) of the University of Ghana, Legon. He has been on the Research Faculty of ISSER since 1986. He has also been Temporary Lecturer at the School of Oriental and African Studies, University of London (1993); Visiting Professor at Yale University Department of Economics (1999); and the Cornell Visiting Professor, Department of Economics at Swarthmore College (2001–2002).

Professor Aryeetey's research work focuses on the economics of development, with interest in institutions and their role in development, regional integration, economic reforms, financial systems in support of development, and small enterprise development. He is very well known for his work on informal finance and microfinance in Africa and has consulted for various international agencies on a number of development and political economy subjects. He has presented seminar papers at Departments of Economics and Planning in such universities as Ohio State University, the University of Manchester, Oxford University, Harvard University, New York University, University of Copenhagen, University of California, Los Angeles, Georgetown University, and Sophia University, Tokyo.

Professor Aryeetey has published 3 books, 5 edited volumes, 32 journal articles and many working and discussion papers. Among his publications are *Financial Integration and Development in Sub-Saharan Africa* (Routledge 1998), *Economic Reforms in Ghana: The Miracle and the Mirage* (James Currey 2000) and *Testing Global Interdependence* (Edward Elgar 2007). He was the second recipient of the Michael Bruno award of the World Bank to become a Visiting Scholar for May-October 1998.

Professor Aryeetey was the President of the Ghana Institute of

Planners (1998-2000) and is a current member of the American Economics Association. He is also a member of the Boards of the United Nations University World Institute for Development Economics Research (UNU-WIDER) and the Global Development Network. He is a Member of the Programme Committee and Resource Person of the African Economic Research Consortium, Nairobi. He was a Managing Editor of the *Journal of African Economies* and is the Acting Editor of the *New Legon Observer*.

Professor Aryeetey studied Economics at the University of Ghana, where he obtained a BA (Hons). He then earned an MSc in Development Planning from the University of Science and Technology in Kumasi, Ghana, and a PhD in Political Economy from the University of Dortmund, Germany in 1985. He is married with two children.

Ivor Agyeman-Duah: Professor Aryeetey, looking at the principal sectors of the economy – that is, the manufacturing sector, services, and the agricultural sector – what has been the trend since 1957 when we got our independence from colonial rule? How have these sectors performed?

Professor Ernest Aryeetey: Well Ghana began its new life after independence as an Agricultural economy. At the time, about 70 per cent of all output came from Agriculture, which also employed about 75 per cent of the entire labour force. The dominance of that sector has always been very significant. Today, its share in the economy is down to about 45 per cent. It fluctuates between 40 and 45 per cent – that is what it has been doing over the last decade. The most important question we need to address in this regard is whether the change in share of Agriculture is necessarily a change in the structure of the economy. I am not sure it is; indeed, I do not believe it is. In that period, we have seen the share of industry and also the share of services come up somewhat, but the improvements in their shares have not been very steady, and that for us is an indication that Agriculture may have declined but we have not seen a major structural shift in the composition of the economy. Therefore, contrary to what one would have expected levels of economic growth and development to be – more of output coming from Industry and services with time – this is not happening. Indeed the worst performer in the period had been Manufacturing within Industry, so most of the improvements in

Industry have come not from manufacturing but from things like Construction and from Mining, and that is not a good indication of the type of changes in structure that one would look for in a fast-growing economy.

That is the situation with the structural composition. What is very interesting is that in the last few years, when you take annual growth of the economy, you find that in periods when Agriculture has done well you also see more rapid growth in the economy. A good example is what we saw two years ago, in 2006, when Agriculture, driven largely by improvements in cocoa production, saw a more than 30 per cent improvement in its growth in one year, and that also pushed up the performance of the economy in terms of growth. Clearly, it is a good thing that cocoa is able to provide that kind of impetus to an economy that has not been very consistent, but again the fact that you literally put all your eggs in one basket is something that one has to be very careful about. What it really means is that in years when cocoa does very well, our economy also does very well, and in the years that cocoa does badly, the performance of the economy becomes quite shaky. These are not good signs. For every economy, you want to diversify as much as possible the sources of growth. That has been the biggest challenge that we have not been able to overcome in the years since independence.

We would like ideally to have an economy in which a lot of the growth is coming from Manufacturing, and a lot of it is coming from services. Why do we talk about Manufacturing as a major sector for pursuing growth? It is largely through Manufacturing that you are going to create more productive employment. It is through Manufacturing that you are going to add value to the various inputs that you have in the system, and it is through that that our people earn higher incomes. So if you want to have a much more productive economy, an economy in which our growth is driven by improvements in total factor productivity, then we want one in which the dominance of Manufacturing is supreme. It is in everybody's interest really to have more and more of our output coming from the Manufacturing sector instead of low-productivity Agriculture. That is how we will create jobs. That is how incomes will rise for large numbers of people. That is how we will then deal with the poverty issues that confront our economy.

It does not mean at all that Agriculture is not good for us. By all means, Agriculture is still the largest single sector in the economy, and therefore it is in our interest for that sector to do well, but I think in the long term our position should be that Agriculture will do well with fewer resources – less labour, more capital, and bigger output for each unit of input that we put into Agriculture. That is why today you hear more and more people talking about the need for modernising Agriculture. That is why modernising Agriculture today is a major part of the Ghana Poverty Reduction Strategy (GPRS) and it is also a major part of the medium-term development plan being put into place by the National Development Planning Commission. Modernising Agriculture in order to use fewer resources, making it generate higher returns for those involved in Agriculture; diversifying so that Manufacturing becomes a major part of the economy; and then moving from there to Services later is what I have always advocated to be the right approach to bringing this economy forward.

IA-D: Why is it that over the years the Manufacturing sector has not performed as we expected?

EA: Manufacturing has not done very well for one most important reason: we have not directed enough investment into Manufacturing. In the first few years after independence, the government of Ghana took it upon itself to bring about the sort of structural change that I talked about earlier. It sought to make Manufacturing the bedrock of the economy, so you will find that in the early- to mid-1960s the Kwame Nkrumah government pursued what they called the Import Substitution Industrialisation programme – ISI for short. The ISI programme was premised on the need to diversify the economy. So it was the government that invested in the production of bottles, it was the government that invested in the production of tomatoes, in the various juices, in the textile industry, and so many other areas with a view to making Manufacturing a major part of the economy. The argument at the time was that we did not have a strong enough Private Sector that would carry out the necessary investments. That was the argument the Nkrumah government made.

Interestingly, since the ISI programme or approach ended in the late 1960s, after the overthrow of the Nkrumah government, we have not really seen a substitution of the public investments with private investment in Manufacturing. We have not seen a major middle-class of entrepreneurs going into Manufacturing. Yes, there are private entrepreneurs involved in Manufacturing in Ghana. The unfortunate thing in my view is that the needed investments have not been reflected in the type of investment that we have seen. Most of those who have attempted to do Manufacturing have done so on a very small scale; have done so with very little investment in technology. As a consequence, we have not been able to enhance the productivity of Manufacturing, so for many of those who today would call themselves manufacturers or entrepreneurs – whatever name you choose to attach to their endeavours – you will find that the investments they make are actually quite small compared to let's say what you find in Asian economies.

In many economies, one would then turn to Foreign Direct Investment; one would then turn to foreigners who may want to put something into Manufacturing. For some strange reason, we in Ghana, as in many other African countries, have never been able to attract significant Foreign Direct Investment into Manufacturing. That is a source of worry. There have been many explanations for the difficulty, and I am not sure that all of them will hold for a country like Ghana. A typical one that you will find in the literature is the absence of the appropriate macroeconomic environment, but we have tried to deal with that in the last 20 years. We have tried very hard to improve the Investment Code. We have tried very hard to enhance the performance of the economy through macroeconomic reforms, yet we have not seen much improvement when it comes to attracting Foreign Direct Investment into Manufacturing.

Some have argued that a reason why we have not been able to do this is the absence of the appropriate or the right institutions – things like property rights not being properly in place. We have seen some reform effort being put in place in that regard. As to whether they have had some impact or not, I tend to be of the view that the response to all these initiatives has been much less than anticipated. Indeed, the flow of Foreign Direct Investment into our economy has been far less than expected. Most of what you have seen in the last ten years has gone into things like Mining and also in some service activities – far less into Manufacturing than is desirable.

IA-D: Each political regime starting from Nkrumah has laid claim to specific economic projects, infrastructure for example. They pinpoint

these to say "Well there was some amount of growth during our period; this was done, this was done." Why, then, hasn't Ghana progressed further if each regime can point to certain development achievements? Why are we still talking of lack of growth?

EA: My position on that particular question is that yes, indeed there are many things that we can credit almost every government we have had with. The major difficulty, however, has been that we have not seen over the years much consistency in the approach. The example I gave you earlier, about Nkrumah pursuing the Import Substitution Industrialisation approach, is one many of us still remember. We followed that with the first military government in 1966 not having any particular orientation in terms of where to move the economy, even though they continued with the dominance of state enterprises. You will find that despite the rhetoric, the number of state enterprises increased in the military regime that followed Nkrumah, and also continued to increase under the first civilian regime that followed it – namely the Busia government of the Progress Party until its overthrow in 1972.

What is interesting about the Busia government was the emphasis on Rural Development. To the credit of the Busia government, you will find that emphasis on things like rural roads, or what we call feeder roads, really took off. Rural electrification took off; rural water programmes took off under the Busia government. Unfortunately, not much effort was made to link all these rural development initiatives with the bigger picture of enhancing employment, enhancing production at the aggregate level. Yes, we developed rural roads, we developed rural electrification and we developed rural water, but made no effort to relate them to production in a serious manner. Here is a situation where an earlier government had put a lot of emphasis on production without developing adequately the desired infrastructure, then another government comes and puts most of its efforts into infrastructure, forgetting in relative terms the direct manufacturing, or production of the goods and services.

If you look at the Acheampong military government (from 1972 to 1978) that replaced the Busia government, they of course were very concerned about the distribution of the goods and services being produced. The Acheampong government, for example, in its first few years put a lot of emphasis on Operation Feed Yourself and Operation Feed Your Industries. It is not much different from what you may call self-reliance, the whole idea being that instead of importing things that we consume or inputs we use for our industries, let's produce them here. That principle, or the motive, is not really different from what Kwame Nkrumah was trying to do with his Import Substitution Industrialisation programme.

Clearly, you will see from this that all governments, at least up to that stage, had been very much bent on Ghana being self-sufficient. That was what motivated them, but they went on to set up what they called the Regional Development Corporations – EREDEC in Eastern region, BARDEC in Brong-Ahafo region, and others. So we have had these different approaches, all meant to enhance production within the Ghanaian economy.

The most radical change came with the Jerry John Rawlings military revolution of the Provisional National Defence Council (PNDC) in 1983 and the reforms that were strongly supported by the Bretton Woods institutions. There, attention was for the first time moved to having macroeconomic reforms, the idea being that once the reforms took place and the economy stabilised, structural improvements would follow. We have seen in these past 25 years that it is important to have these macro reforms and it is important to have macro stability, but they cannot be enough. There are many other direct interventions that must take place to ensure that the macro reforms and the stabilisation package actually do deliver investments, and do deliver employment, and therefore do deliver higher incomes to households. So, yes, we have tried many different things, but in my view we have not had a very comprehensive programme that takes into account what government must do, or what the Public Sector must do, and what the Private Sector can do to complement it.

The production of goods and services everywhere done productively requires a very active and engaged Private Sector. We have not in my view developed properly that Private Sector, and it is the weakness of the Private Sector really that has led to a less-than-impressive performance of the economy. If you have a Private Sector that is not able to deliver for whatever reason – the reasons do not have to be of its own making – so long as it remains weak, governments have to do more than they should be doing, and governments have not been the most efficient producers of goods and services. Therefore, if you have a situation where the economy is dominated by the government, you will always have problems.

If you take this economy for example, if you look at the different sectors that facilitate or aid the production of goods and services, you will find that most of those who are able to borrow adequate amounts for investment in their businesses are those that have government contracts, either for manufacturing, or for construction, or for the delivery of some particular service. You get a government contract today and tomorrow a bank will lend you money to undertake that business. If you don't have a government contract, the chances of getting a good enough long-term loan from any bank in Ghana are very low. It is the dominance of the Public Sector that is the problem, but that dominance is there largely because you have a weak Private Sector. The challenge for us is how to develop a strong and effective Private Sector capable of doing the investments that are required, capable of creating employment, capable of transforming the structure of this economy.

IA-D: Is there a situation where we can get all of this together? So far what you have said is that all these governments have had a particular interest and have been able to do a particular thing, but is there a situation where we can bring all these production aspects together to make an integrated whole to bring the economy forward?

EA: I believe increasingly that many people see the need for that. That is why today you see civil society groups calling for greater dialogue in the development of policy; that is why you find that in the discussion with the development partners, for example, the language used is changing into one that allows for more flexibility in the choice of policy actions. For example, the advent of the multi-donor Budget support is intended to give government greater flexibility to determine what it wants to do with the support it receives from donors. Increasingly, I think people are becoming aware of the need for the comprehensive approach in managing and planning the economy.

There was a time when the word "planning" was seen very negatively; everybody assumed that planning meant the government dictating what had to be produced and consumed. Today there is much more understanding of the fact that planning within a liberal economy is possible; planning for a comprehensive delivery of goods and services is possible in which you outline the roles of the private sector and the public sector and indeed what role can be left for civil society in terms of contributing to policy-making, contributing to the dialogue and the debates that would ensure that all the things we have talked about do come to happen.

This comprehensive approach is, I believe, beginning to manifest itself in the preparation of the medium-term plan by the Development Planning Commission that I mentioned earlier. There you will find there is discussion for what should be done for Industry, there is discussion of how Industry should be linked to Agriculture, and there is discussion of how these two sectors should be facilitated by the right human capital. What type of education do we need in Ghana? What kind of health system should we have in place in Ghana? How should these two facilitate the generation of employment? What type of employment is most appropriate for Ghana and how will this provide the skills that are needed for Industry and for Agriculture? That is the type of orientation.

Indeed also in the development plan there is a strong focus on what should be happening in human settlements. Over the years we have watched Accra, and to some extent Kumasi, become the only places where you could find modern employment. They have become also the only places where you can find access to significant modern services, whether it is Health or Education or other social or economic services. Now, there is discussion of how to ensure that the various towns of Ghana – middle-level towns, small-level towns, which largely will be the district capitals – can become major centres for generating employment and therefore growth. This can only happen when you have a very comprehensive approach.

If you look at the economic reforms that we undertook over the 1980s and 1990s, there was very little attention paid to the settlements where the production would take place. Everybody took it for granted that if the economy was doing well, people would go and manufacture things in places like Techiman, Koforidua, Kintampo and so on. It has not happened. Today we know that government has to have a clear programme for making it happen. That is the sense in which I get the impression that things are beginning to change, albeit too slowly. If there is any way in which we as Ghanaians can help speed up that process then that would be very helpful.

IA-D: You have done some comparative studies in Africa and Asia's economic development. What were the findings?

EA: Back in the 1980s, many of us were being made to understand the so-called East Asian "miracle". It was the consequence of simply adopting and implementing what I would call orthodox policies – the type of free-market policies that we have associated with the Washington consensus for a long time. Today, we have learned that there was not one single approach that led to the East Asian success, that indeed true pragmatism can help deliver good results. By this "true pragmatism", what I mean is: in many countries – I am talking about Korea, I am talking about Malaysia, I am talking about Thailand, I am talking about Taiwan, and today even China – they took fairly orthodox policies and adapted and amended them to fit their own socio-cultural setting. In doing that, they brought about changes to these orthodox policies that were unique to their own economies. The role that the State played was immense and quite defensible.

What you will find in Asia is that the State was not a passive one that simply sat there and watched the Private Sector do things. Rather, the State actively tried to engage the Private Sector to do what it desired. That role, which is unique in the Korean sense, is something that every country has to think about. In what way, for example for a country like Ghana, can the State be made an active participant without pushing aside the Private Sector? What kind of support should the State give to the Private Sector? What kinds of partnerships should there be between the two? What kind of environment fosters that kind of partnership? These are things that every country has to work out for itself. There is a tendency in these parts of the world – namely Africa – for us to look outside for the answer. My suggestion has always been: when you look outside, don't go and take what they did and say "Now I'm going to do it". Take what they did, learn from it, and ask yourself in what way can you adapt aspects of it for your own economy, your own society, your own culture, in order to lead to similar outcomes without destroying your basic structures?

That is what I have learned from working on Asia; I have learned that I cannot walk into Malaysia and copy everything that they are doing. I have learned, however, that if I want to be like Malaysia, I have to apply more common sense to the way I manage my economy. I have to look at my economy and say, "This is appropriate for freeing the Private Sector", but in doing so I must know the abilities of my Private Sector. That is the only way in which we can become like Malaysia, or like Korea, or like Thailand – being very sensible in the way we use external ideas.

IA-D: Do you think that the multilateral institutions – the World Bank, the IMF, and others – have been very helpful in the running of our economy? Some think that they hijack economies and others think that they try to do good things for those who can't manage economies for themselves.

EA: There has never been any doubt in my mind that for a country that has come to our stage in development, you would need these development partners. There is no doubt in my mind about that. What has never been clear in the development literature is how that relationship should be structured. In my view, it should be a relationship that allows mutual respect; it should be a relationship that allows for innovation in economies; it should be a relationship that allows for the governments that are receiving support to be able to experiment with things, based on their own histories. We have not seen that yet. Now, there is more talk of pursuing that angle.

In the relationship of the past 20 years, there has been far too much domination, not because, in my view, the World Bank or the IMF wanted to dominate these economies, but because we ourselves had not done enough of the homework that was required. Therefore, we left ourselves open to too many ideas being suggested from outside. Now, I think with all the capacity-building initiatives that have taken place over the past two decades, it is time to assert ourselves by determining what development paths we want to pursue, what policies are most appropriate and most meaningful for our development, and then pursue and negotiate these with our development partners. It is when we go to the World Bank with good programmes that we can encourage them and put pressure on them to support these good programmes.

Therefore, there is a role for them to play in our economy and in our economic development, but we have to structure that relationship properly – one that leads to mutual respect and mutual benefit. There is no doubt that the World Bank benefits considerably from involvement with developing countries, but we have to ensure that that benefit is mutual and also leads to considerable capacity for production and productivity enhancement in our country.

IA-D: What specific role does the Institute of Statistical, Social, and Economic Research (ISSER) play in the economic development of

Ghana? What kind of research are you engaged in and have you engaged in over the years, and with what impact on economic development?

EA: It is very interesting that you ask that question because ISSER was more or less the creation of the University of Ghana and the Ministry of Finance. The whole idea back in the mid-1960s was to set up a Policy Research Institute that would carry out research that was deemed to be meaningful for the Ministry for developing policy in Ghana. In this regard, right from the beginning ISSER was expected to link up with all the different arms of government and contribute to policy debates by bringing out the Ministry research material that would inform those debates. I think ISSER has played that role quite well under the circumstances. By "under the circumstances" I mean, considering the kind of resources that have been made available to it by the State.

Back in the 1970s, for example, ISSER was very much involved in the development of policy towards the Cocoa Sector. ISSER did a very extensive study of the Cocoa Sector, which led to a number of publications that were shared with the government. That was largely because cocoa was the main sector of the economy, and it still is today. That is an example of how relevant ISSER research was even in the old days. In the 1980s, ISSER was the first institution around here that did studies on poverty. In those days, everybody took poverty for granted. People just assumed that poverty in a developing country was nothing strange – that we were born to live with poverty and that it would only eventually be overcome as a result of a slow change. ISSER did poverty studies back in the late-1970s and 1980s that showed very clearly how the poor lived their lives, and how things like inequality in our society were worsening. That was what had happened.

Throughout the 1990s and over the past few years, ISSER began producing annually what we call *The State of the Economy* report. This happened at a time when there were no other publications that documented on yearly basis how the economy was doing. This was the result of good research being done by ISSER. It means, for example, there were people at ISSER working on Trade, working on Industry, working on Agriculture, working on Social Services, and so on. We were able to summarise all of these into a document that reflected the performance of the economy over the previous twelve months. That has been one of the most informative documents you will find anywhere on the economy of Ghana. Today, you will find that different arms of government are beginning to document the performance of different sectors of the economy much more than they did before, but you will not find in those reports as much commentary as we provide on the performance of the economy.

Last year, we finished a major study on Land in Ghana, looking at the possibility for Land Tenure Reform. The three-year programme that we carried out with the support of the US Agency for International Development, USAID, brought out over 20 different documents on the way the Land sector in Ghana has been performing and what prospects there were for reforming that. Today, we are embarking on a major programme on Trade, and the link between Trade and Poverty. Is it possible to move an economy like Ghana's out of Poverty on the back of enhanced International Trade? That is something that we are looking at. Right now, there are about 35 different projects going on at ISSER that look at different things in the social and economic sectors. All of these have been primarily designed to ensure that ISSER contributes effectively to policy debate on each of these things. Whether it is Poverty, Industrialisation, Urbanisation, Agricultural Development, Irrigation, somebody here is doing work on it.

IA-D: Economic indicators are always a source of controversy – rate of inflation, GDP growth, interest rates, and so on. Are our indicators indicative enough of actual economic development?

EA: There are a number of ways in which we can look at that question. A good example is that we have had fairly decent growth over the past decade, and indeed most significantly in the last five years. By all standards, for example, when you have had more than 6 per cent growth, as we had a year ago, you would expect a very obvious reflection of that in the way goods and services are produced. When an economy has been growing at more than 5 per cent for close to two decades, you would expect that the stock of goods and services available would more than double in that period. We have not seen that, and therefore it takes us to the question: what does it mean for an economy like Ghana's to grow at 5 per cent? It means that 5 per cent for our economy is fairly meaningless. It is these kinds of situation that lead to questioning of figures that we receive from public sources.

On inflation, currently I don't think there is much dispute about the accuracy of the figures. The source of contention that I see – and I am part of that debate – is whether the pursuit of single-digit inflation is the most appropriate, or the most desirable, for an economy in our situation. I have argued quite strongly that I have nothing against low inflation, but there can be lots of discussion about what really is "low" for an economy like this. Who is it that can say in a very convincing manner that 11 per cent inflation that leads to very significant growth is by all means worse than 9 per cent inflation that leads to a slowdown in growth? It is an empirical question, and unfortunately I don't think our economic managers are very much interested in these empirical questions, the kinds of discussions that must take place, and the kind of debates that must inform these, which will then inform in the longer run policies that we can put in place. There is too much of a rush to claim success over the problems that we have in this economy, and in that rush to claim success we then overlook the bigger picture; we then overlook the long-term requirements for growth and development because we are anxious to score early success.

IA-D: Looking to the foreseeable future, and given Ghana's current economic performance, will we reach the middle-income status that we are talking about within the next decade?

EA: I believe we can. We *can* and we *will* are different things. I believe we can if we put in place the right policies, structures, and institutions. We do have policies in place that are not necessarily intended to speed up the delivery of goods and services. We do have policies – let's say in the area of education – that in my view are not supportive of improvements in quality. While we have put a lot of emphasis on increasing enrolment in our schools, we have undermined that whole programme by not paying attention to the quality of education. Somebody clearly has to sit back and say, "How do we achieve both?", because it is not only about getting all the kids in school, but also ensuring that the kids in school acquire skills that will lead to higher incomes for them, because that is how we are going to reduce poverty. If they do not have skills, their incomes will not go up, and if their incomes do not go up, achieving the goals on poverty will be more difficult.

Government has to sit back and say "Let's put in place a programme of action that would deal with each of the eight Millennium Development Goals." Unfortunately I think we have relied far too much on very orthodox sets of interventions, which have been driven to a very large extent by what are interests in relation to donors have been. Too many of our social services are driven by what donors are willing to support, so if there is something we want to do, we are doing it because donors are interested. If donors think that something is not the most important thing, even if Ghanaians are convinced that it is the most desirable thing, then we don't do it. A good example is employment generation.

Many donors do not believe that employment generation is the result of direct action taken by government in relation to the Private Sector. They believe that simply by having in place a sound macro environment, the Private Sector will respond appropriately. Therefore, because it has not received support from donors, we as a people have not engaged with the question of how we secure larger numbers of employed, productive people. We have to. It is in our interest to do it. For a long time, we didn't have anything like an Industrial Policy and why was this? Within the World Bank, the whole idea of an Industrial Policy was seen to be unnecessary.

IA-D: Thank you very much.

EA: You are most welcome.

March 2008

Dr Gareth Austin

Dr Gareth Austin is a Reader in Economic History at the London School of Economics, having previously served as Senior Lecturer and Lecturer at the same institution. From 1986–88 he was an Economic and Social Research Council (ESRC) Post-Doctoral Research Fellow at the Institute of Commonwealth Studies, University of London, before which he lectured on the Economic and Social History of West Africa for two years at the University of Birmingham in the UK, and for three years at the University of Ghana, Legon (1982-85). More recently, Dr Austin was a Global Economic History Network (GEIN) Fellow at Kyoto University and a Guest Lecturer at the Department of History at the University of Cape Town. He is the current President of the European Network in Universal and Global History.

Dr Austin's research and teaching interests are in African and Comparative Economic History. In this vein, he is working to complete a book on *Markets, States and Production in West Africa* and a co-edited volume (with Kaoru Sugihara, Kyoto) on *Labour-Intensive Industrialization in Global History*. Among many other published works, he is the author of *Labour, Land and Capital in Ghana: From Slavery to Free Labour in Asante, 1807–1956* (University of Rochester Press, 2005). At the London School of Economics, Dr Austin teaches several courses relating to Africa and Economic History, one of which included a primary-source based special subject on, The Political Economy of Ghana, 1951-92. He has given invited presentations at a number of other universities, including Harvard, Stanford, Kyoto, and Oxford. He is a former Editor of the *Journal of African History*.

Dr Austin holds a BA in History from the University of Cambridge and a PhD in Economic History from the University of Birmingham (1984).

Ivor Agyeman-Duah: In *The Vampire State in Africa – The Political Economy of Decline in Ghana,* J. H. Frimpong Ansah has as one of his theses that on the eve of decolonisation there were already identifiable weaknesses in the Ghanaian economy. To what extent was this a danger to the postcolonial economy?

Dr Gareth Austin: I think almost everybody today would agree that that was true. It's also a point made by Douglas Rimmer in his book *Staying Poor,* on postcolonial economic history. The most obvious sense in which it was true was dependence on foreign trade for government revenue and for foreign exchange. For example, at the time of independence Ghana had what seemed to be a substantial foreign exchange reserve, but actually it was quite vulnerable to any change in the price of cocoa, and also to the fact that, as a newly independent government, irrespective of political party they were under great pressure to spend a lot of money – to spend the reserves, particularly in promoting Education and Health within the country. But if we look at it in a slightly longer-term perspective, there are both strengths and weaknesses.

Ghana's great opportunity economically in the late-19th and the 20th century could be said to have been land-extensive agriculture: land-extensive because population was relatively light in relation to land, so almost everybody had access to land and, in the South at least, most of that land was fertile. But it had to be *extensive* not *intensive* because the fertility of the soil was quite fragile, so you needed to allow enough time for it to fallow to maintain fertility.[6] In a way, the Ghanaian farmers of the late 19th and early 20th centuries did absolutely the right thing in adopting cocoa. Tetteh Quarshie, I hope is still famous and known to every Ghanaian, because what he did was actually very important. The adoption of cocoa made Ghana relatively prosperous – the most prosperous of the colonies in tropical Africa. But that came with the risks that the price of cocoa could go down as well as up and also the fact that in the long term, as the population of Ghana rose, the number of cocoa beans per head – even if you had a major growth in output as we've seen in the last few years – is not going to keep pace with population, and the price of cocoa doesn't rise

---

6   'Extensive' cultivation meaning a relatively low ratio of inputs (of capital or labour) to land.

all that much when incomes in the buying countries rise. So in the very long term, it is obvious that Ghana not only needs to find insurance against falls in world commodity prices, but also needs to find a more lucrative way of making a living in the world economy.

IA-D: Would you say that there were smart public policies to combat this?

GA: "Smart" of course depends on what your objectives were, and governments always have political as well as economic objectives. They also operate, as we all do, in the context of their time. The CPP government was given advice from some of the most prominent economists of the day, and I suppose you could say that they were selective in the extent to which they responded to it. But W. A. Lewis, the West Indian economist who won the Nobel Prize, wrote a famous report on Industrialisation in the Gold Coast in 1953, where he advised the Ghana government that it was too early to adopt a policy of Import-Substitution Industrialisation, even though he himself was about to publish what became a famous model on how you could industrialise using cheap labour. He thought Ghana's labour was not cheap because the population was relatively light in terms of the available land, so he could not see a way of going for Industrialisation early. In a sense, the Ghana government followed that policy for a few years and then in 1961 adopted a more radical policy with much more government intervention, and tried to achieve Import-Substitution Industrialisation. Lewis might say that they were too impatient. In retrospect, probably Lewis was right: to be a bit more patient would have been a more effective policy. But at the time, that policy change that Kwame Nkrumah made was in line with what many other leading economists of the time were saying, which was that government had to lead in economic development. So at the time it would have seemed smart to many people.

IA-D: One of the arguments that Robert Bates[7] has also made has to do with institutions and shortfalls within the ruling party, the CPP,

---

7   Robert H. Bates, famous for his rational choice institutional economic arguments and for his book *Markets and States in Tropical Africa* (London, 1981, 2005), has done extensive research on postcolonial production of cocoa and its affiliated marketing institutions and the extent to which they were obstacles to growth in the Ghana economy.

with respect to governance. **What was the nature of the political economy at the time, because it looked like Nkrumah was more interested in the politics and ideology of his time than in the economy? The same applied to his response to Arthur Lewis' advice: he was first and foremost a politician before any other thing.**

GA: Yes, of course Kwame Nkrumah famously believed that politics could change economics. A very important event in shaping postcolonial Ghana was the conflict between the CPP and the National Liberation Movement (NLM), the federalist movement centred in Ashanti, in the following sense: what in retrospect would have been a policy that probably would have delivered higher incomes for Ghanaians, in the 1960s and 70s anyway, would have been a policy of allowing the producers to keep a higher share of their income, and that was the policy that the NLM advocated. I won't make any other comment on the difference between the two but I think, strictly from an economic point of view, the NLM's policy, favouring their own constituency, actually would have worked out better from the point of view of the country as a whole.

In that sense, the decisive defeat of the NLM in the 1956 election, just before independence, was a very important event, and I think Ghanaian policy in many ways shows a lot of continuity from then until the Structural Adjustment in 1983, even though you had changes of regime. The military government of 1966, and then the K.A. Busia government, did not altogether reverse Kwame Nkrumah's policies; they modified them a bit but on the whole there is a lot of continuity. Then of course in the Acheampong era it went disastrously wrong.

IA-D: **So from your own work, especially** *Labour, Land and Capital in Ghana: From Slavery to Free Labour in Asante*, **would you say that indigenous systems and policies as related to land, labour, and capital would have evolved smoothly but for colonial intervention?**

GA: As far as Land Tenure is concerned, yes. The colonial government didn't intervene very much in it, if we consider it from the angle of security of Tenure. This is what economists say you need above all: that if you're investing in the creation of a cocoa farm for example, you want to know that you will receive the benefit of it – that nobody is going to take it away from you. And here the Akan distinction – or the traditional distinction if you like – between ownership of land itself and ownership of property created on the land, was very important. This is because it meant that even though there was a lot of uncertainty as to which stool owned a particular area of land, and therefore about whether this farm should pay rent or not, if it was in Ashanti for example, the principle that what the farmer had created, be it buildings or trees, was not in doubt. That was the existing pre-colonial custom, and the colonial government enforced it. This security of property rights in what farmers had planted made possible the huge amounts of investment that tens of thousands of Ghanaian farmers made in cocoa in the 1890s and 1900s and then again in the 1950s. The later 1950s and early 1960s saw the second great Ghanaian cocoa boom, and we have seen the third such boom recently. So I would say yes, the Land Tenure system was quite efficient before and during colonial rule.

The other thing is: was it changing? Before colonial rule, there were signs that the land market was emerging. As land was beginning to become scarce – just in a few areas – then you found the buying and selling of land, for example in Akyem Abuakwa. The colonial government rather tried to slow that down, but on the whole that became a trend it couldn't resist forever. So I would say that Land Tenure is quite a positive area.

I suppose the complexity would be the labour market in that, in 1874 when Britain colonised the Gold Coast colony in the South and then in 1896 when the same happened to Ashanti and the North, there was still internal slavery. And that was very important in the economy, along with pawning. The economic circumstances favoured it because if we all have access to land, there is no reason why I should work for you. If you want me to work for you, you have to give me a wage that you probably can't afford to pay me. I think it was really cocoa that changed that. More than anything else, it made it possible for a wage-labour market to take off and attract lots of voluntary migration from the North to the South and from neighbouring countries. It is true that without the colonial abolition of slavery, it would have taken longer, but it would eventually have happened.

As for capital, there was a longer-term problem: if you have a relatively modest saving and you want to put it into a large firm for Manufacturing or the Services Sector, or if you are an entrepreneur who wants to raise money for a large project, how could you actually get hold of the savings of lots of small farmers or other small producers? That really was a problem, I think. In a way, it wasn't yet a serious problem in 1900 – or it wasn't urgent – but by 1957 it was serious and not very much had been done about it.

IA-D: Why was it a big problem in 1957?

GA: In the sense that if you're thinking about at least beginning to diversify the economy – not full-scale Industrialisation, but a greater number of industrial enterprises, or even indigenous banking, for example, creating large-scale firms such as banks – and you want to raise money in the Private Sector, at that point having a capital market that will enable private entrepreneurs to raise money becomes important. Of course, in a sense, ideologically Kwame Nkrumah had no particular interest in that; he would far rather the State took the lead. But the result was partly the reliance on this combination of the State and foreign capital, in that there was a major foreign involvement in the economy – when it comes to aluminium of course – but there was not very much in the way of large-scale indigenous enterprise despite the many thousands of small-scale enterprises that existed.

IA-D: Tony Killick,[8] whose works concentrate on the early postcolonial independence, refers to the obvious characteristics of the colonial past, and says that by the 1960s the structures of the economy under Nkrumah were still maintaining colonial ones. Why was this so, since Nkrumah was known for his radicalism and anti-colonial posture?

GA: The most obvious answer would be that he hadn't had much time. Even though he had been in power internally to some extent since 1951, he couldn't do all that much while the British were still there. Then after that, in many ways he was constrained by the circumstances. The biggest example would be the Marketing Board on the one hand and the deal with Kaiser Aluminium on the other.

As far as the Marketing Board is concerned, the colonial government had created the Cocoa Marketing Board originally during the Second

---

8   Tony Killick, like Michael Roemer and Naomi Chazan, scholars and analysts of the postcolonial political and economic evolution of Ghana, are, as discussed in the Introduction, by their works, influential "outsiders" looking inside.

World War to hold up prices within the country when they thought that the world price would fall. But then the British discovered that it was also a very good way of taxing the farmers when the world price was high. The 1954 decision by the CPP government to keep the producer price low even though the world price was rising escalated the tendency. From then onwards all governments pretty much used the Marketing Board, on an even larger scale than the colonial government had already been doing, for raising taxation. This was understandable; governments do need taxation, so I wouldn't entirely criticise them for that.

That is an example of a colonial legacy that the government then turned to its advantage. An example of a colonial legacy that was more problematic would be the weak bargaining position that the government was in when it came to negotiate with a foreign multinational to exploit Ghana's hydroelectric potential and its bauxite. Here the basic problem was that it was an extremely expensive project so foreign capital had to be involved. That meant turning to either the Soviet Union or the USA; Britain had already withdrawn from the project. Crucially, the Ghana government wanted Ghana's bauxite to be used, to be combined with electricity from the Volta dam, to produce aluminium. This would be the basis of an integrated industry. But the aluminium company, partly for technical reasons, but also, as has subsequently been admitted, because they feared the possibility of nationalisation, wouldn't agree to that. So they imported bauxite from Guinea to combine with Ghanaian electricity, rather than put the whole facility in the country. You could say that is something that was rather easy to do with the politically fragmented nature of postcolonial Africa. Of course, Kwame Nkrumah would have said the answer to that would have been to integrate Guinea and Ghana. But there was a weakness in the sense of having to rely on foreign companies who, understandably, feared nationalisation. That resulted in a deal that was not particularly good from a Ghanaian point of view, and whose terms were really only corrected in the 1980s.

IA-D: Michael Roemer's works, which cover 1950–80, conclude that political leadership failed to utilise substantial potential. Does this mean that the structural inefficiency that Killick talked about had been dealt with and that the problem had become leadership?

GA: I think the key problem was policy. It certainly is in a sense a problem with the leadership, but there were, you might say, structural forces or interest groups that were also behind it. The crucial weakness of economic policy in the 1970s and early 80s was not so much the Marketing Board, which was already there of course, but the fact that the currency was to become hugely overvalued and effectively not convertible. The significance of that was that it acted as another source of implicit taxation on the producer. The producer of cocoa by 1981/2 was only getting something like 6 per cent of the purchasing power of his/her produce. The rest partly went to the Marketing Board, but partly went through the exchange rate mechanism. The Bank of Ghana would say, "OK here are 60 dollars' worth of cedis," but the actual dollars would buy you an awful lot more than the so-called cedi equivalent would buy you. And that was simply a penal rate of taxation on the major source of income in the economy. Although I have no doubt that Ghana needed to industrialise long-term, in the short run it was crucial not to cut off the branch upon which the population were sitting, and that was the cocoa industry. That was I think what was happening in the 70s and in the early 80s.

IA-D: Other scholars, including Naomi Chazan, have made similar analyses. What does your own research up to the 1990s tell us?

GA: I suppose compared to other scholars I put less blame on the Marketing Board System, because it was compatible with the growth of Ghana in cocoa output to a world record in 1964–65. That process was also very similar to what happened in Côte d'Ivoire when they overtook Ghana as the then highest producer in the late 1970s. So the real difference was this exchange rate point; it seems to be absolutely decisive.[9]

The significance of that is that, when it comes to reform, I don't think it was essential or necessary to abolish the cocoa marketing board, in principle. It's true that the marketing board had a lot of inefficiencies, employed far too many people – and after all the payroll apparently included some people who were actually dead in 1983 – and that definitely needed to be cut back. When you have a marketing

---

9   Gareth Austin, 'National Poverty and the "Vampire State" in Ghana', *Journal of International Development*, 8: 4 (1996), pp. 553-73.

board employing as many people as are actually producing cocoa beans then something is seriously wrong. But I think the government was right not to abolish it completely, as the Nigerian government did; that was going too far. Whereas the experience of the tumbling cedi in the 1980s and early 90s was very painful, it was actually less bad than the alternative of a completely fictional exchange rate, as had been the practice between especially 1975 and 1983. Going for Ghanaian monetary independence, as Kwame Nkrumah did, was essential for an independent country. It's a question of what you do with monetary independence, and in the Acheampong era and thereafter it went very badly wrong.

IA-D: Apart from teaching the economic history of Ghana, you also lived in Ghana for some time. Are there some common denominators that you think accounted for the decline of the economy in the period that you lived there?

GA: I first went for research in 1977 and continued to go for research, but I taught at the University of Ghana, Legon, between 1982 and 1985, so I remember vividly those conditions before and during Structural Adjustment. For instance, I travelled all over the country during that time. One thing economists and commentators have tended to overlook is the civil rights aspect of the licence regime that existed in the late 1970s and early 80s; notably the fact that, if you travelled, you were continually subjected to road blocks (barriers), and road blocks were inevitably open to abuse. Ordinary, peaceful market women were subject to verbal and occasionally physical harassment from the various people who in those days seemed to be entitled to set up road blocks. So it's not purely an economic thing. I would say, being there at the time, that was the thing that most struck me, and one couldn't experience that except by being there.

IA-D: For someone who has also taught African economic history, especially the political economy of Ghana, to international students and scholars, what would you say are their impressions when they measure this history against theories and models of economic development?

GA: Of course the fashionable theories, the dominant theories, have changed and will continue to change. By the time I was teaching the subject, it was becoming clear that State-led Import-Substitution Industrialisation had not been successful, so in that sense the dominant, orthodox development theory of the 1960s and 70s was no longer fashionable. One can see why, but at the same time, there is a danger of throwing out the baby with the bathwater. In particular, we mustn't lose sight of the fact that Industrialisation was a very worthy goal and something that, sooner or later, Ghana needs to work towards. Students vary in their response to that; every student has his or her own take on it. Today, clearly the most influential development theories, from a purely economic point of view, are the various forms of liberal market economics. On the other hand, from a political economy perspective, rational-choice institutional theory, represented by, for example, Robert Bates, who you mentioned, has been very influential for nearly thirty years now.

A danger in the rational choice analysis is that it can lead us to interpret government motives too narrowly. The theory tends to say that governments always seek as much money as possible for the ruling group. Now we all have experience of governments and we can all understand that view. But it turns out not to be the whole story, if we consider the history. There have been moments when, actually, governments decided that they had to promote economic growth, even if it meant that the rulers were not getting as much money for themselves in the short run. I think that actually is an important reason why many governments adopted Structural Adjustment, however reluctantly.

If African rulers were simply devoted to 'rent-seeking', far fewer states would have adopted Structural Adjustment. Market economists would say that, almost by definition, 'economic rents' are created when markets are interfered with.[10] Well, if Structural Adjustment, for all its strengths and weaknesses, was anything, it involved "getting the prices right", as Deepak Lal said. That is, it involved the restoration of market mechanisms in place of administrative mechanisms for allocating resources. And that meant fewer economic rents, i.e. fewer opportunities for getting money from selling import licences and the like. While I don't dispute that rents continue to be extracted in Ghana, and indeed in the economy that we are talking in, I don't have any doubt that there was a major reduction in government rents. I don't think the

---

10 An 'economic rent' is a surplus above opportunity cost; above what could be earned by using the asset concerned in its next most remunerative way.

orthodox theory has sufficiently taken account of that. And the reasons why many governments did that, in particular the Ghanaian government at the time; cannot be accounted for entirely by pursuit of individual economic self-interest, certainly not short-term self-interest.

IA-D: We've experienced state-led economics, during the Nkrumah government and for a very long time – 30 or 40 years – after. We now have a very liberal government, a government with traditions that challenged Nkrumah's rule in the 1950s. What do you think will be the future economic development of the country? We've now tried the two systems, and we just happen to have a liberal government at the time when liberal thinking is the dominant model for economic development.

GA: The most important change in Ghanaian economic policy since independence – even more important than the 1961 radicalisation of Kwame Nkrumah's policies – was the decision to adopt Structural Adjustment. Although Structural Adjustment was unpopular at the time, clearly by the time the democratic elections were held, none of the political parties was advocating its abolition; they were all competing to try to have Structural Adjustment with a human face, but not to go back on it. As you say, we now have a government that is committed to a liberal economic policy. I see that as lasting, in that I don't see a reversion to state-led policies in the foreseeable future. I think that to go back to the policies of the 1960s would be a major mistake. They failed before, and I think they would fail if they were adopted in the same form again.

However, it is very important that the State does lead in other ways. The State has an indispensable role in the economy, including facilitating the operation of the Private Sector. One asks now how Ghana can move towards a more industrial, certainly more diversified economy, with a more substantial Manufacturing sector. Of course what we have seen in recent decades has been the growth of small-scale industry, for example in Suame Magazine in Kumasi. But, also, I think the government needs to give attention to the possibility of a more labour-intensive style of Industrialisation. That was not possible in the 1950s, as W. A. Lewis rightly pointed out, because the price of labour was relatively high. But today, because of the increase in population and other things, the price of labour has come down quite a lot, which is painful if you're experiencing falling real wages, but it does mean that

Ghana may be getting closer to being able to do what the East Asian countries have done, which is actually industrialise, not by using the methods that Western countries did, but in their own way, taking advantage of relatively cheap labour. The fact that postcolonial governments have delivered a much more educated labour force, coupled with the relative fall in the cost of labour, may mean that it is not impossible to begin a process of intensive industrialisation at some point in the next generation, possibly much sooner than that. You could even say that that is a little bit like what happens in places like Suame.

IA-D: Now there is the possibility of Ghana becoming an oil economy. What does this mean for future growth? Is it good or bad?

GA: It's tricky, and economists have become, it is fair to say, more pessimistic about the developmental implications of oil. It can be very much a mixed blessing, particularly if, as in Nigeria, it attracts resources away from other sectors of the economy so that they decline prematurely. On the other hand, if it's used effectively, of course it can give the country extra options. In particular, it can allow the importation of machinery and other things that you need for industrial diversification. The crucial thing is to avoid the temptation to simply allow it to subsidise inefficient industries. In the Nigerian case, it wasn't all bad; despite the notorious waste, Nigeria also experienced some genuine industrial growth during the oil boom.

The trick for Ghana is to get the benefit of the income and the larger foreign exchange that oil offers without too much waste. The crucial part of that is simply how the money is spent. Because oil incomes are normally directed to the government, not to thousands of individuals, it creates opportunities for corruption and so on at the top. So it is absolutely crucial that that should be tackled. The political economy of oil will be a crucial area for Ghana's future if indeed the country does become the significant oil exporter that people expect.

IA-D: Thank you very much.

GA: Thank you.

June 2008

PART TWO

A Vampire Economy with a Silver Lining

Honourable Moses Asaga

Honourable Moses Asaga is the current Member of Parliament for Nabdam and the Minority Spokesman for Energy. He also serves on the Parliamentary Select Committees for Finance and Economic Planning, Mines and Energy, and Special Budgets. In these various posts, he has been vocal in his criticism of government Energy policy, particularly regarding the management of thermal power plants and the high taxation rates of fuel.

From 1997-2000, Honourable Asaga was the Deputy Minister for Finance, in which role he was in charge of managing Ghana's relations with the multilateral financial institutions. During this period, he was also a member of the Board of the Bank of Ghana and of the Central Bank's Monetary Policy Committee, as well as the sole Governor at the African Development Bank on behalf of Ghana. Honourable Asaga served as the Minority Spokesman for Finance and Economic Planning for six years up to 2006.

Before turning to politics in 1996, Honourable Asaga worked in both the Private and Public sectors, in the oil and banking industries, respectively. His career began in 1987 as a Staff Engineer on North Sea oil reservoirs at Occidental Petroleum in Aberdeen, Scotland. From 1988-1990, Honourable Asaga worked first as an Industrial Analyst, and then as an Economic Analyst, for Daishin Investment and Securities Company in South Korea. He returned to Ghana in 1991 and joined Ecobank as an Investment Analyst. For four years up to 1997, he worked for Ghana National Petroleum Corporation, initially in Corporate Finance, before ultimately assuming responsibility for all project finance activities.

Honourable Moses Asaga attended the Kwame Nkrumah University of Science and Technology in Kumasi, where he earned a BSc in Industrial Chemistry. He holds a Masters degree in Petroleum

Engineering from the University of Aberdeen, Scotland; an MBA in
Finance from the Yonsei Business School at Yonsei University, Seoul,
South Korea; and is a candidate for a PhD in Financial Economics at
Durham University in the UK.

**Ivor Agyeman-Duah: When the 31st December revolution of ex-
President Jerry John Rawlings was established in 1981, it didn't take a
very long time for the Economic Recovery Programme to also come
onboard. What was the purpose of the Economic Recovery Programme
under the Provisional National Defence Council (PNDC)?**

Hon. Moses Asaga: Well, first of all the Economic Recovery
Programme was a World Bank instrument, meant for economies that
had broken down, and in 1983 you'll notice that the Ghanaian
economy was really very weak. It was in a downturn, inflation was
almost about 140 per cent, infrastructure was almost destroyed, goods
and services were almost absent. So when the Ghanaian government
decided to have a programme with the World Bank, they thought that
the first instrument to use would be the Economic Recovery
Programme. And the word "recovery" speaks a lot for itself: that you
want to turn around. So when we subscribed to that programme,
initially what they were supposed to do was to make sure that the
International Monetary Fund (IMF) supported the Budget, and then it
also supported the Bank of Ghana with foreign exchange, so that we
would be able to import in the needed goods and services that were
critical in the economy. So that was the purpose of the Economic
Recovery Programme.

**IA-D: What were some of the strategies that were adopted to recover
what had been lost, and which sectors had been seriously damaged?**

MA: In the early-1980s and mid-1980s, the area that was seriously
damaged was the Cocoa Sector. If we can recall, most of the forests in
the Ashanti Region up to Eastern Region were burnt. Therefore cocoa
trees were burnt, and then the harvest of cocoa was very low. Also, if
you look at the Mining Sector: the Mining Sector was as old as 100
years, so a lot of the equipment was quite obsolete. And because at that
time most of the mining companies were state mining companies, and
controlled by the State, the State could not afford to re-tool the mining

sector. Because the Mining and Cocoa sectors were our major foreign exchange earners (also including timber) the government thought that the first area to tackle was to rehabilitate the Cocoa Sector and then the Mining Sector. When that was actually done, we saw that there was an improvement in the production of cocoa and gold. So that was the first strategy.

The second strategy was the fact that infrastructure was very much wrecked. For example, we didn't have roads. I mean, the roads were there, but they had been destroyed because they had not been repaired for several decades. Our ports didn't meet modern standards. Our airport, for example, was also very small and lacked a lot of facilities. So the ERP targeted itself at the infrastructure and the two commodities that I've mentioned.

IA-D: What were the results?

MA: The results were very good. Cocoa production went up significantly, and I can quote more from the Mining Sector: we were producing 230,000 ounces at that time, led by Ashanti Goldfields, but in this Recovery Programme Ashanti Goldfields started to pick up in their production, and by the year 1997 Ashanti Goldfields had already hit 800,000 ounces. Then, if you take the Cocoa Sector: by 1997 we were producing 350,000 to 400,000 tonnes of cocoa. In terms of infrastructure, I can use the Paga-Bolgatanga-Tamale-Kintampo-Kumasi road as an example. It used to take people seven days to travel that distance, and the whole road was riddled with potholes. By 1997-98, we had a very nice asphalt road, which is there today. And there are several such roads in other parts of the country – the Cape Coast-Elibu road to Côte d'Ivoire is one of them. The Akosombo-Tema road is another. There were a lot of feeder roads that were also constructed in the mining and cocoa-growing areas.

Another aspect of infrastructure that the Economic Recovery Programme targeted was the provision of electricity. If you recall, the hydroelectricity only ended up in Ashanti Region; the whole of the North did not benefit from the hydroelectricity. So, under the ERP we were able to construct all the pylons to take power to the North. In that same Programme, we had the rural electrification programme for most district capitals in Ghana.

IA-D: So how did all this infrastructural development translate into day-to-day economic progress, in terms of raising incomes of the people and improving the general living standards of ordinary Ghanaians?

MA: Because the Cocoa Sector improved, employment in the Cocoa Sector also went up. There were a lot of farming jobs for people to work on. The owners of the cocoa farms also earned an income. In the Mining Sector, Ashanti Goldfields recruited a lot of mining hands, including engineers. I can remember in 1984, we had not less than thirty engineers from the Kwame Nkrumah University of Science and Technology. Previously, it wasn't so. So I think that it created a lot of jobs. Then if you look at road construction, there were a lot of jobs for people at the construction sites.

Now, in terms of per capita income, I would not really say that it did improve because the Services industry was still very down and the economy was still small until recently. So, even though it created jobs for a lot of people, I did not think it created enough in terms of per capita.

IA-D: So the growth was not sustainable?

MA: No, the growth was not sustainable until we started what we call the Enhanced Structural Adjustment Programme (ESAP). When we say Enhanced Structural Adjustment Programme, it means that we have had a Structural Adjustment Programme before, because the World Bank was providing its support in a gradual manner, and you needed to graduate from one stage to the other. During the Structural Adjustment Programme, the government was forced to do some privatisation of state-owned enterprises, cut down public service recruitment, and because the state-owned enterprises were also privatising it meant that the bloated employment in those sectors had to be trimmed down. The Private Sector wanted to make profit, so the high cost of labour and wages was not attractive. When all that happened, it meant that some people lost their jobs. So the Structural Adjustment Programme – and the key word is "adjustment" – was to make sure that there were other programmes to cater for people who had lost their jobs.

I believe that the Structural Adjustment Programme also aimed at the macro-economy. We needed to look at our fiscal management of the Budget and at our monetary policies because, as I said, we were having very high inflation. By 1993-94, the inflation level was almost 70 per cent, our reserves were very low, and the cedi was not very stable as it is today. Therefore, the Structural Adjustment Programme looked at the macroeconomic front. I would say that there was improvement on this front from 1993-94 up to 1998. By 1997, inflation had dropped from 70 per cent to almost 20 per cent or thereabouts. And there was a miracle whereby in 1998 we got our first single-digit inflation of almost 9 per cent, an achievement which up to now we have not been able to get to again. Then, the cedi in those years depreciated at 4 per cent, and the money supply went down to almost about 40 per cent. So those were really dramatic years, which showed that the Enhanced Structural Adjustment Programme did work. Also, our reserves improved to two months' cover, when previously it had been something like one month or three weeks.

IA-D: But it was under the same government that these achievements relapsed. What happened?

MA: OK, the relapse came in 1999-2000. In 1999-2000, there was what I would call a little economic shock. First of all, gold prices went down to a record low of $230-250 per ounce. Cocoa went to a record low of almost $700 per tonne. And at that time, an increase in the oil price to $40 was considered an energy crisis. So these three external shocks destabilised the economy, because first of all we did not have enough reserves through the sale of cocoa and gold to support the currency. Then, we did not get enough for the fiscal budget, and the foreign exchange situation at the Bank of Ghana was also distorted. As a result of all that, we lost the macroeconomic stability that had been achieved throughout the preceding years. So I would say that the destabilisation was the result of these three external shocks.

IA-D: There was also the programme to mitigate the social costs of adjustment. Did this mean that structural adjustment faced challenges, or indeed couldn't work?

MA: Yes, that programme was called PAMSCAD, and the PAMSCAD came in the late-1980s to the early-1990s. It was more of a social event – that is, to see if it could reduce poverty, to see whether it could give social incentives to people who had been displaced as a result of privatisation. But I would say that that programme really did not achieve what it wanted to, because we still had problems with unemployment, we still had people who could not afford to go to hospital, and other social problems. PAMSCAD first of all was very short-term. It was not very well thought-out, because I did not think that was what we needed at that time, and I would not say that we got the full results. But after PAMSCAD, the ESAP brought us a lot of benefits that I have been describing so far.

IA-D: Let's get back to the role of ideology in economic management or reconstruction. The revolution was a socialist revolution. It was more or less anti-capitalist and anti-liberal in terms of markets. How was it able to adjust to especially the conditions of the World Bank and the IMF and to work with the European partners?

MA: What you said about the revolution is true. A lot of people who got involved in the revolution were left-wing in ideology – some of them extremist. But I do not think that the President at that time, the chairman of the PNDC, President Rawlings, really belonged to any ideology. If there was anything that he knew, he probably knew about Libya and Gaddafi, and probably the only book he read was *The Wretched of the Earth*, which just talked about ensuring that people were not cheated and that society bene-fited from the State. He was not a capitalist or a socialist; he just wanted to be a man of justice.

It was those who were his ministers or his advisors who were more left-wing. And as I said they were in various shades: we had the extreme ones who could be communist, some were socialist, some were left-wing, and some were moderates. Now it was the moderates who thought that you could not run an economy based on the socialist principle when you do not have the economic will-power. Therefore, they decided that we should do something which is more moderate, and lucky for us we had people like the former Minister of Finance Dr Kwesi Botchwey. They were intellectuals from the University, and they knew that, the way the economy was going, the best thing for Ghana was for us to sign up with the World Bank. And they were able to persuade some of the extremists...

IA-D: Like?

MA: I would say that people like Chris Atim were extremists, people like Alolga Akata Pore, people like Kama Sa, people like Zaya Yeebo in London were all extremists. Even Huudu Yahya at that time could be said to be an extremist. I would say the intellectuals and the moderates, though still left-wing, were people like Tsatsu Tsikata, people like Kwamena Ahwoi, Ato Ahwoi, Kwesi Ahwoi. If you then add someone like the then Finance Minister Kwesi Botchwey – he was a left-wing intellectual who I am sure could be compared to British Prime Minister Gordon Brown today. So among this mixed bag, the moderates decided to go to the World Bank.

Going to the World Bank, too, was almost a necessity; it was not choice, because we did not have any other choice. The Eastern bloc could not support us with the kind of resources we needed to support the Budget and to support our Balance of Payments, so the only avenue was to go to the World Bank, which was ready if you could come up with a good programme. And I think on that note, Kwesi Botchwey and people like Kwame Peprah (who was in charge of the Ministry of Energy) did a lot to come up with a programme which the World Bank agreed to support.

IA-D: So what was the reaction of Jerry Rawlings to this? You just mentioned that he was heavily influenced by Fanon's *The Wretched of the Earth*. How does someone with this limited knowledge engage in a revolution that was supposed to reconstruct an economy that was completely down?

MA: Yes, that is why he had all those ministers. And I do not think there is any President who really does his own work.

IA-D: But he was the inspiration.

MA: Yes, he was the inspiration, but behind the World Bank programme, I believe that the welfare of the masses was also key to him. So if you could convince him that in the midst of a World Bank programme you could also alleviate poverty, or you could give social justice, he would buy into it.

IA-D: What is your own ideological position in terms of managing an economy like ours?

MA: Well, I don't know how much you know Gordon Brown, but I think that I fit in the group of Gordon Brown. I am a centre-left, I believe in a free-market economy, but I also don't believe in property-owning democracy in its extreme. So once you know Gordon Brown, I think you know where I'm coming from.

IA-D: Do you think that the shift between the extremists of the revolution, those within the centre-left, the moderates in any way affected their ideological thinking beyond the revolution, because the revolution also transformed into a civilian administration that came to be known as the National Democratic Congress (NDC)?

MA: Globally it was not just the PNDC and Rawlings that adjusted to the free-market economy. Even the Eastern bloc, where we tried to learn left-wing economics in the extreme sense, adjusted too. Therefore, there was a wave that was blowing globally that even if you were left-wing, you must also embrace the free-market economy, you must free state assets into private hands because that could enhance productivity. Therefore, for a listening President like Rawlings, he also had to buy into it, and when the NDC came into government, it was a mix of people who came from the Busia-Danquah tradition, plus people from the Nkrumah tradition, and also people from the Rawlings revolution. So with that mix there was a good balance. And the important positions in the Ministry of Finance were still under Dr Kwesi Botchwey, and later on under Kwame Peprah, and Victor Selormey and myself who had been trained in the West. We knew that a free-market economy was good for Ghana so we continued to pursue those policies. And of course at the Bank of Ghana level, we had very good governors – Dr G. K. Agama and later Kwabena Duffuor – who had trained in the US and had worked a lot in the Private Sector in banking. So at that time, the free market economy was already operating.

IA-D: In terms of policy, had anything changed from PNDC to when Rawlings was elected democratically?

MA: The first four years saw a lot of privatisation, so that policy was different to when the PNDC was there and all the enterprises were state-owned. During the same period, too, we saw the Bank of Ghana getting a lot of independence so that they could manage the monetary policies very well. I was a member of the Board of the Bank of Ghana.

IA-D: When were you appointed Deputy Minister of Finance?

MA: I was appointed in 1997.

IA-D: And what were you supposed to do?

MA: I was in charge of the revenue agencies, which includes the Internal Revenue Service (IRS), the Customs and Preventive Department, and Value Added Tax (VAT). I was also in charge of the multilaterals, except the World Bank and the IMF. I was solely in charge of the African Development Bank and all the other multilaterals that we know about. I was also in charge of the financial sector, so policies governing the banking sector were all under me. That is why I was on the Board of the Bank of Ghana.

This was my schedule, but of course on a broader level we all attended the World Bank and IMF negotiations for the various programmes that we adopted, the most important being the Paris Conference, which used to take place in France – Paris, for that matter – for developing economies and most especially African countries. Ghana was so impressive because of the way we managed the economy by 1998 to the extent that the World Bank decided we could now have a home-grown economic programme, and therefore the Paris Conference, which is the consultative group meeting that brings together all the donors including the IMF and World Bank, should rather be taking place in Accra. That was one big achievement. That legacy is what we are still holding on to. So we've now made actually ineffective what used to be called Paris Conference, which everybody thought was a big thing.

IA-D: But by the time the PNDC became the NDC there was a constitution in place. The constitution exerted certain economic demands on the government. There was the National Development Commission but the party itself – that is, the government in power –

also had an Economic Advisory Committee. What were some of the new things that came in place in terms of strategy to move the economy forward?

MA: Well first of all, we had the Economic Management Team, which was headed by the Vice-President, Professor John Evans Atta Mills. It was made up of experts including people like Dr Joe Abbey, who is an independent economist; the Governor of the Bank of Ghana and his deputies; and some of the key Cabinet ministers. Therefore, this Economic Management Team was supposed to come out with the economic policies. I would say that the team did very well; it came out with policies that were based on consensus, and I think that is what led us to achieve a very impressive macroeconomic stability by 1998.

IA-D: All the economic policies were supposed to mitigate poverty and generate growth. To what extent would you say that the economic policies of the NDC performed in relation to rural development?

MA: First of all, let us take the social statistics, and especially the Ghana Living Standards Survey 4 (GLSS-4). We had the GLSS-3 and then we had the GLSS-4, which were supposed to give the poverty indicators. Things like infant mortality improved a lot. Maternal mortality also improved a lot. Certain diseases like guinea worm were wiped out completely. It was Zero Tolerance when we were in government. The guinea worm eradication is an indicator of the potable water situation, especially in the North, so that showed that the water and sanitation programme was working because there was more potable water than before.

Another area was the Rural Electrification. Once you start getting electricity in the rural areas, then their standard of living also improves. Ghana was chosen under a programme called Country Assessment Programme (CAS), instituted by the UN between 1997 and 1999. There were only two African countries that were being used as examples for other countries to follow, and those were Morocco and Ghana. I used to represent Ghana at the UN on this for other countries to come and study. What the UNDP didn't want to do was for each country to come and sign up for a CAS programme and then have to invent the wheel. But because Ghana was doing well by lowering some of the poverty indices, they decided that Ghana and Morocco should be the models for other countries. I believe that if the NDC government did not do well in poverty reduction, the UN would not have used Ghana. I was always there in those particular meetings with the UNDP representative in Ghana, Ahmed Abdul, who is now the UN Executive Secretary for Africa. He worked so much with us that the Ghana team, led by me, was always called the "dream team". So on the poverty level, the social level, this is what we did.

Getting to the year 2000, the World Bank then came with a new programme. The programme that we used was called Poverty Reduction Programme, but in Gabon in the year 1999, the donors and the World Bank decided that they were now going to come up with another, the Highly Indebted Poor Country (HIPC) scheme. By then, Uganda was already signed up to the HIPC, but nobody knew the results of HIPC to be able to say, "Yes, I want to sign up to it." So the first time it was to the NDC government in 1999 that the programme was introduced. But we did not want to go into a new venture that we did not understand at all. First, you were described as "highly indebted poor country" – what does that mean and why should I subscribe to it? What were the conditionalities attached? We needed to know all these details. By the year 2000, when we attended the African Development Bank annual session, a lot of the donors came to interview me to ask why we were not subscribing to HIPC and my answer was that we didn't understand it and we didn't know the conditionalities.

I believe that it was prudent enough for the NDC not to adopt that programme because it was a three-year rolling programme, so coming into an election year you would not be able to manage it. Secondly, even if you went in to negotiate, there would be so many conditionalities that you would not have time to negotiate properly in this period of elections when ministers were going to their constituencies and so forth. Our idea was to let the elections go through – we were hoping Professor Mills would win – then, since we were the people to whom they had dangled the carrot, we could sit in a more convenient manner and look at the programme.

Then the PRSP, the Poverty Reduction Strategy Paper, was also introduced, but we called it an interim PRSP – interim, because, again, the period in which it came was an election year so we did not have time to study how the PRSP was going to become a full-blown programme. It was from 2001, when the NPP came into government, that these two documents were looked at, and it was decided that they had benefits – or that their benefits outweighed the disadvantages – and therefore we decided to sign up.

IA-D: Do you think it was good for the NPP to have gone HIPC? They claim it has helped so much with the country – with growth, with infrastructure, and many other things. Do you think it was wise for the government to have signed up?

MA: Well before we come to the HIPC, one of the good things the NDC ever did for this country was introducing VAT, because it increased government revenue, even though the Opposition, which was the NPP at that time demonstrated against introducing VAT.

IA-D: Because it wasn't well thought-out perhaps?

MA: Well there was nothing to be thought out. It was a tax collection mechanism and we had the education all over the country. Even HIPC, which was not well thought-out, was promulgated without even education, without asking the Ghanaian people what they felt about HIPC. So our programme was even more well thought-out because we had a VAT Implementation Committee, which had worked for almost one year.

IA-D: But is it true that there were lapses in the system and that, if the system had been more disciplined, you could have gotten the same amount of revenue without introducing VAT at the time that you did?

MA: Well because everything has a beginning, you cannot say that things should be 100 per cent proven before you start a programme. It is when you are within the programme that you learn your lessons, and things that you need to do right, you do right. Otherwise, you will never start anything. So I said one good thing was this VAT. The second good thing that came to Ghana, especially in the area of education, was the Ghana Education Trust Fund, the GET Fund. That was another good thing that we did. Today, all the infrastructure and modernisation and everything in education is because there is a GET Fund. So if there is anything that the NDC left behind in education it is the GET Fund. Now, let's get back to your question about the HIPC.

IA-D: The good thing about a good government is the ability to foresee something that is good, something that will help your economy. Was the NPP able to do that; were they able to think ahead and realise that the HIPC was good?

MA: Actually, they never thought through HIPC, because they didn't even know HIPC. Maybe they took a risk and said, "Let's try it, it may work". But to say they thought it through – they didn't. President Kufuor came into government on the 7th of January 2000. The HIPC idea was introduced in the first Budget, which was in March. They could not have taken only two months to think through the HIPC programme of the World Bank. I think it was just guts. I think it was just, "Let's fill the gap with the programme. We've been told it will work." And the reason I'm telling you that they didn't think it through is, even at Kufuor's Ministry of Finance level and at the Presidency, there were dissenting views about HIPC. Why does the Deputy Minister of Finance go around on radio saying that Ghana will not go HIPC? The Presidency and the Senior Minister had a different opinion. At the same time as the Minister of Finance privately could tell you "We are not going HIPC", the President and the Senior Minister had a different idea to the extent that whenever HIPC was to be mentioned, whether in the Sessional Address or in the Budget, it was like an *addendum*.

IA-D: They say that we have an Executive Presidency, and that the President decided that he would go HIPC. But it is a credit to government, is it not?

MA: Yes, but you used words like "They thought through it" and I wanted to put the record very straight. They took a decision which has worked. I am anti-HIPC and I will give you my reasons. The first reason is the name: Highly Indebted Poor Country. They have not been calling us "poor countries"; they have been calling us "developing countries". Why is it that for the HIPC alone they used "poor country"? They could have called it Highly Indebted Developing Country, but they kept the "poor" so for me it is derogatory. This reason comes from thinking in a simplistic manner, but that was my first problem.

Secondly, I was privileged to see the whole HIPC document, and there were conditionalities attached to it. But the conditionalities were very technical, such that you cannot explain them to every Ghanaian to understand. Some of the conditionalities, and I insist that they were there, no matter how they have metamorphosed today, included things like full cost recovery for electricity, full cost recovery for fuel, and privatisation of water. Even in the UK, I believe there are safety nets to look at these social services. So that was another area I didn't like. Even in the same HIPC document there were other conditionalities about privatisation of certain key state enterprises which I think government should not free completely and be zero per cent holder. I think we should continue to have a share to make sure that we have some control because they are key areas. So for me, some of those conditionalities didn't make me feel comfortable with HIPC. The HIPC document was really an evolution of the Enhanced Structural Adjustment Programme, which could have still contained those conditions; some of these conditions were key. Tell me how many Ghanaians would want water to be privatised! So if I am speaking the voice of the masses about HIPC, I was right at that time.

Thirdly, the HIPC programme had a starting point, a completion point, and they gave you a number of things to do. And those things that we were going to do were those that the President was saying, "We must bite the bullet". When you are biting a bullet, it is not easy. It means you are really going through difficulties to satisfy those conditionalities. It is only when you have gone through all that and reached the completion point that you start benefiting from HIPC.

Now, for today, the only reason why I can say that HIPC has been beneficial is not because of its initial intent, but the windfall that came after former British Prime Minister, Tony Blair, and Chancellor Gordon Brown went talking to donors and the World Bank about debt forgiveness. And that is not the same as the initial HIPC. Because the initial HIPC did not anticipate that Prime Minister Tony Blair would come up with this initiative and force the G8 to give that kind of relief. The initial HIPC reliefs were to be coming in bits and pieces. That is, every year, we are forgiven a certain amount of our debt over 15-20 years. But the Gordon Brown initiative, which was hung on HIPC, said: you are forgiven the debt from today, so you have a clean sheet. So President Kufuor was only lucky in that sense, but if you are lucky, you are lucky! It has brought results. At the time I was talking, I did not consider an assumption that one day Prime Minister Tony Blair and Gordon Brown would say that if you run a HIPC programme you will be forgiven all your debt at one time. And it is that benefit that has been quite remarkable. So on that note, the HIPC achieved some good results for Ghana, but if it was based on the original HIPC, no.

IA-D: You have said some very good things that the NDC did. Looking at the way the economy has been run by the NPP, would you say that it has been run well, that there have been some very good things that they have done?

MA: The NPP government have done well as far as macroeconomic stability is concerned. Bringing inflation from very high – 30 or 40 per cent – to the current state – averaging 11 per cent – is a very good result. In the stabilisation of the currency they have done very well. The banking sector has improved a lot. Interest rates are down. There is a lot of competition in the banking sector. There is more lending to the Private Sector. Our international reserves have improved to three months' coverage. So if we look at the whole macroeconomic situation, it has improved a lot. Then, if you go to cocoa: production of cocoa has increased. Whether it came as a result of the Côte d'Ivoire situation or not, we know that production has increased and exports have also increased. So we see that the cocoa sector has also benefited.

When you come to roads: the NPP government has continued what the NDC were thinking of doing, because all the roads that are being constructed and modernised were things that the NDC was probably thinking about but didn't have the capacity to do. Again, I would say that a number of the road networks, especially the major ones that enter the regional capitals, especially in the South, have been brought to a very good level. For example, the Accra-Kumasi road is excellent, the Accra-Cape Coast road is also excellent and they are doing the Tema-Aflao, which will also become excellent. I can pick out some of these roads because they are quite major. Then, the Tetteh Quarshie roundabout is good. What they are doing from Accra North Post Office at Circle up to Nsawam is also very good – maybe four lanes or six lanes of good infrastructure. Regarding the modernisation of our international airport, they came and continued with the Phase 3 and Phase 4. We did the Phase 1 and the Phase 2. Regarding the Tema Harbour, we had already started with the expansion of the container terminals. They have come to also improve it more. So I would say that all in all they have also contributed their part.

The only problem I have with the NPP government is: if corruption was five times in the NDC, they have increased corruption levels to twenty times. It is one of the governments that have allowed corruption to become an incentive. And if we don't change it, the oil that we are getting as a blessing will become a curse. I am being honest. Corruption has gone up so high in this government. Drugs and cocaine are a menace in Ghana, and they need to be addressed. The donors cannot tell them, but the donors are not happy with the level of corruption and the drugs menace in this country.

Also, one area they have not gotten a handle on is employment, but that one I cannot just blame the NPP government. I don't know what the NDC would have done but unemployment is still a problem; it is a problem because the NPP magnified how quickly they could fix unemployment. If they had been modest with their promises, maybe they could have justified the present situation. But they created an expectation that was too high, and that expectation has not even been met half way. I tell people that if you want to know the situation of unemployment in a country, just look on the streets and you will see it. It has nothing to do with statistical data, labour data – just go on to the streets. If the youth had employment and were well catered for, they would be working in factories or if they wanted to be small-scale entrepreneurs they would be owning shops. You have been there and have seen how it is in South Korea. I think that is an area we need to look at.

IA-D: Final question: Now we have oil. What does it mean for our economic prospects? What does it mean for economic growth?

MA: The discovery of oil is very good for Ghana. We are all happy that we have discovered the oil. Even though oil is considered to be a curse in some situations, we in Ghana believe it can be a blessing. Already I've highlighted that the number one enemy of oil is corruption. It means that one of the issues we must tackle immediately is corruption and transparency. You know very well that we are producing small quantities of oil at Saltpond and we've been doing this production for almost three years. But not a single Budget of the NPP government mentioned the small production at Saltpond. Nobody tells us the revenue that is coming from Saltpond, no matter how little it is. Nobody is telling us the royalties that we are accruing. So as early as their second Budget, I challenged them on these sales, production, and revenue figures. As a result of that, these days there is a bit of transparency. The Ghana National Petroleum Corporation came out with an advertisement notice in *The Daily Graphic* and *The Ghanaian Times* to respond to me, and they gave all the necessary information that we needed to know. But did they have to wait until I talked about it? So there is an improvement.

The biggest improvement in the transparency issue that I am seeing on the ground is the fact that the government decided to get the Norwegians and the donors to come up with what we called an Oil and Gas Forum. Ghana is probably the first country among developing economies that have discovered oil to come up with a national forum to discuss the way forward into the future. Other countries start producing the oil and mismanage the oil funds before they say, "Oh! Now let's hold a stakeholders meeting". But we were able to do that. They brought all the stakeholders, they brought international experts, and in particular I was there at centre stage. We have gone through the Oil and Gas Forum for National Development and we are now to come out with a final document. Government will have to come out with what we call an Oil Policy and Plan, which will be a blueprint. A number of suggestions have been made and, limiting myself to what I know, I am limiting myself to Oil Revenue Management.

For best practice, we need first and foremost to make sure that when we are granting concessions and oil licences for both exploration and production, it should be done in a transparent manner. Now that the risk of discovery has reduced, we could even attempt a bidding round for people to come and bid, and therefore the best company should get the licence. And the best company will be the one that has technical competence, and the financial muscle to do it. We do not want a situation where because someone knows the Presidency, they just form what we call a Shell company: come in front, take a licence, and not be capable of doing the work. So that is where we must start from.

Having started from there, the next step is to make sure that the Ministry of Finance understands Oil Tax Administration. The IRS must understand Oil Tax Administration. The GNPC engineers should understand how the reservoir of oil economics is managed. They must understand what we call Oil Costing. They must understand Oil Auditing. From there, we must establish what is called an Oil Account, and this Oil Account must be co-Chaired by the Minister for Finance and the Governor of the Bank of Ghana. There should be other members on it – that is the prerogative of government as to who they will bring onboard. There should be one person from Parliament, ideally from the Opposition, but since in Parliament we work on both sides, two people should be represented in Oil Account Management. The Minister for Finance, the Governor, and the other nominees are all appointed by the President, so if you don't get someone from Parliament it means that the other side will not be involved. Therefore there will be a question of transparency.

Having done that, we are now talking of Oil Revenue. We must decide how much of this revenue will go into the State Budget. It is only when it has gone into the Budget that the Minister for Finance would control it. How much of this Oil Revenue that we keep aside for bad times? How much of this Oil Revenue should we invest, and in what instruments and assets are we investing in? These questions will be key. When it comes to the amount of Oil Revenue that has gone into the State Budget, we must decide what we want to use it for. Is it just for current consumption? Is it for infrastructure? Last but not least, is it for poverty reduction – that is, providing schools, good health, etc.? Then beyond that, for us to be more transparent, without any ambiguity we must put our Oil Account and Oil Revenue on a website so that if you click it can tell you how much came in, how much has been spent, how much is in our investment account. That is a tedious thing, but I believe we will get there.

IA-D: Otherwise you believe in the future of Ghana?

MA: Yes I do.

IA-D: Thank you very much.

MA: It's been nice.

March 2008

Ambassador D. K. Osei

Ambassador Daniel Kofour Osei is a Career Diplomat who since 2001 has served as Secretary to the President of Ghana. In his role as Private Secretary to the President, Ambassador Osei provides economic, diplomatic and administrative support for the smooth functioning of the Office of the President. He is also a member of Cabinet, the Economic Management Team, the Diplomatic Advisory Council, and the Government Strategic Analysis Committee.

Ambassador Osei, who speaks French and English, as well as a few local Ghanaian languages, has worked with three former Heads of State and travelled with them extensively around five continents in different capacities, including as bilingual translator. He has attended all ECOWAS Summits and African Union (AU) Heads of Government Meetings between 2001 and 2007, as well as other specialised conferences hosted by, among others, the G8, the World Health Organisation (WHO), the World Food Programme (WFP), and the United Nations Development Programme (UNDP) over the same period. He has been involved in Conflict Resolution Missions in a number of African countries, including the Democratic Republic of Congo, Angola, Liberia, Côte d'Ivoire, and Sudan, and was part of the team led by Ghana to support the election of Kofi Annan as United Nations Secretary General. He was recently awarded Togo's highest national decoration, The Commander of the Order of Mono, by President Fauré Ezzozimna Gnassingbe in Lomé in recognition of his efforts to improve Ghana-Togo relations. In Ghana, he has received the national honour, the Order of the Volta (Companion Division).

Ambassador Osei joined the Ghana Foreign Service in September 1976 and has subsequently served in Paris, Guinea, Kinshasa (Charge d'Affaires), and Denmark as Head of Mission. He has been promoted through the diplomatic ranks of First Secretary, Councillor, Minister

Councillor, and finally Minister Plenipotentiary in 2000. In 2001, he was appointed Ambassador at Large.

Ambassador Osei attended Achimota School, before proceeding to the University of Ghana, Legon, where he received a BA (Hons). He attended a Cours de Langue et de Civilisation Françaises at the University of Dakar, and then returned to the University of Ghana, Legon, for a Post Graduate Diploma in International Relations. Ambassador Osei also holds a Post Graduate Degree in International Relations from the Institut International d'Administration Publique, and a Diplôme d'Etudes Supérieures Specialisées from the Sorbonne, both in Paris. He is married with three children.

Ivor Agyeman-Duah: Ambassador D. K. Osei, it is said that you are one of the most powerful Secretaries to the President that we have ever had in the history of this country, and not only that, that it is because of your efficiency in running this office. How true is this?

Ambassador D. K. Osei: I think that around the corridors of power there is always an exaggeration of how powerful X is and how powerful Y is. I have always taken the view that if you are not directly interested in running for political power, your concerns in government should not be about the power play. That is where I am coming from; I have never run for political power and I have no such intention. I am really functioning outside the ambit of the power play. I think it is hugely exaggerated.

Secondly, you talked about efficiency. I think that cannot really be determined by me. I must say, though, that governance in a developing country has not benefited from some of the capacity that has been built in the developed world by years of consciously training people to take over political power. In France, they have the Ecole Nationale d'Administration, which trains the best from all the areas and eventually many of them become Prime Minister of France. I can cite several. It is not by accident that many people from Lincoln's Inn have been Prime Minister of Britain. We have not consciously developed that kind of system and that is the reason why I find that those with a lot of career Civil Service experience can make a very useful contribution to running the country *if* they themselves do not get involved in the politics. That is what I tried to do: not get too actively involved in the politics and be interested in dealing with the institutions and the systems, and outlining the structures which will assist politicians to make decisions.

IA-D: You are the gate-keeper to the President's office. You see people trooping in and out: Finance Ministers, Governors of the Central Bank – mostly from Ghana, but outside of Ghana as well. How do you personally relate to these people?

DKO: Coming from a background in Diplomacy, where you have to deal with people from all sectors, from all countries, has made it pretty easy for me to deal with a lot of them. And do not forget that in order to gate-keep properly, you have to understand the issues that you are gate-keeping about. I mean, you have to be able to determine what is extremely urgent and what is not. For instance, if the Governor wants to see the President, if you have an idea about what has happened in the Central Bank, you will probably ensure that nobody sees him before he does because you understand what the Monetary Policy is going through, how it is going to affect the Budget in the next six months or so. This has made it easy for me.

IA-D: How is the time space allotted to special people, players in the economic/financial sector? How does the President spend his time with them?

DKO: Basically, in the past when we began, because he set off with a clear reform programme, we had to also accompany that with institutional reforms. One of the institutions we introduced was the Economic Management Team (EMT), which had a very experienced Chairman, J. H. Mensah, and the Finance Minister and a lot of others in the financial sector. A lot of the economic and financial matters dealt with by the President were first discussed at that level, so in between the EMT, the Minister of Finance, and the Governor of the Central Bank, we usually discussed how much time they would require a week. With the Central Bank, it was once a week; with the Minister, as and when it was urgent. The Minister and I would usually go through the issues and I would say, "Look, on this matter – maybe because it is going to Cabinet or because X, Y, Z is happening now – can you delay your discussion until Thursday?" That also tended to be twice a week. Then of course there was the sub-Cabinet Finance Committee which also did a bit of the rough work. But the President also determined, as and when he determined his priorities, which player he wanted to see. So a lot of it was determined by him, and also by what was happening to the economy. On the average, it was once a week with the Governor, twice or thrice with the Finance Minister, and since the EMT does not exist anymore, depending on which sector of the economy we are dealing with, the President will talk to the Chief Advisor, the Chief-of-Staff, and me.

IA-D: What is the structure here in terms of economics and finance? There is a policy unit – the Chief Advisor, the Chief-of- Staff, etc. How do you personally fit in?

DKO: There is an official strategic team which is supposed to meet once a week. There is also supposed to be a diary team which is supposed to meet once a week, including the Chief Advisor, the Chief-of-Staff, and myself. This team looks at all requests for an audience with the President, including the economic- and financial-sector requests. We then make recommendations to the President, but a lot of those recommendations would have been determined quite often by the President himself. Usually, by the time we get to first thing on Monday, the President has an idea which sectors he wants to give a lot of attention to, so by the time I have done my Monday briefing or my Friday briefing, I know exactly what weight to attach to which sector in the economy before I present the diary to him. A lot of that is driven by he himself.

IA-D: What is the nature of your briefing normally?

DKO: We start off normally in the morning by discussing the President's programme and reviewing what has happened the previous day or the previous week. Then the President guides me as to what he wants to do during the day. I then take him through what he has earlier agreed on, like: "You have four meetings. There is a meeting with the Executive Director of the International Monetary Fund. These are the issues he wants to raise." By this time, the President will have received written notes relevant to the meeting he is going to have, and if there is some portion of the notes he wants to review, he talks to me, takes me through what he wants the positions to be. From his briefing, then, there is usually some data to pick up before he meets so you quickly come and source the data and make sure it is added to the notes. Then the meetings roll.

IA-D: I am sure there are many important economic and finance meetings that you have sat through, especially in the early years of the regime. Can you enlighten us on some of these? You told me in a previous interview about the loss of institutional memory and the difficulty the government encountered when President Kufuor took over. There were no files and things like that.

DKO: Along with the reform programme that the President wanted to institute as soon as he took over power, there were major decisions to be made about Monetary Policy, Currency Reform, relations with the International Monetary Fund and the World Bank, and mostly about HIPC, which then implied a lot of other decisions, about the energy sector deregulation, budget deficits and so on. That process of taking a decision about HIPC was a very tortuous route, because first of all you had to demonstrate that you had put in place sound policies to stabilise the macro situation. We were having these discussions not only with the Fund and with the Bank, but with all the interested donor parties who would be involved in the multi-donor budgetary fund.

When I hear people talking about how Ghana took the decision to go HIPC, I just laugh. I can tell you today that most members of the Economic Management Team were against going HIPC, so you can imagine the debates that we had! The President took a firm decision that it was in the interests of this country to ensure that the overhang of debt would be removed. In fact, I can tell you when the decision was finally made. The decision was made the morning the Budget was going to be read and that decision was taken by the President to me over a telephone conversation, after all the discussions that we had had.

IA-D: He called you at home?

DKO: Yes, I was at home and he said "Can you wake up?"
   And I said, "Yes, what is it about?"
   "Have you got a copy of the draft Budget?"
   I said, "Yes sir."

He said, "Look, I want you to go through the following paragraphs" and he actually started dictating the portions about Ghana deciding to go HIPC. So after he had given me his rendition I spoke to the Chairman of the Economic Management Team, the Finance Minister, and in the end it turned up in the Budget.

IA-D: Why do people talk about the HIPC and personalise its implementation?

DKO: How can such a major decision be taken by any one person, particularly under an Executive Presidency? More importantly, a lot of the discussions about HIPC were done in confidence with a lot of foreign governments. We had discussions with the British government, the French government and even some of the Fund officials; no one else but the President had these direct discussions. In fact, two days before the budget, the President was in touch with two donors – major development assistance countries – and making the arguments with them himself. I really do not understand it when people say, "I am the father of HIPC"; I don't know where the story is coming from. I know people that were dead against the HIPC who are now claiming that they took Ghana to HIPC.

IA-D: To what extent can ministers, or people working in government, claim credit for things that happened, policies that were successful? And to what extent can we say that this is a collective decision of government?

DKO: When you have the kind of Constitution that we have and you have an Executive President – let me remind you that even Cabinet is only Advisory to the President in the strictest sense – the one person who can take credit for what has happened is the President! He appoints the Cabinet and the Cabinet advises him, but *he* takes all the decisions. Now, when any minister, along with his colleagues, decides collectively in Cabinet that we are going to pursue this policy and that policy pursued becomes successful, how can any one individual lay claim to it? I find it very strange! Quite often you might bring forward a proposal to Cabinet, but the quality of contribution from your colleagues will enrich the document so much that the original document might not mean very much to you yourself. Of course, I am not a politician and I am not in a position to understand the motivation of such claims, but it is very difficult to justify particularly when you have an Executive President who can take a lot of those decisions on his own – in fact, who is allowed constitutionally to take a lot of those decisions on his own.

IA-D: One of the interesting things about the early days was the creation of an independent Central Bank. People talk about it preceding the President. What was the state of the Bank when the President came in?

DKO: There is a very good history of the Central Bank, *Bank of Ghana: Commemoration of the Golden Jubilee*, which has just been produced in this fiftieth year of Ghana. When you have time, just take a quick look at it; it tells you exactly what happened. I will say that the mere fact that the Bank of Ghana Act was passed during this period should tell you something. Don't forget that the current Governor was picked out of the IMF, and this was a decision the President took. He did not know Paul Acquah very well, but he saw his background and said, "I am looking for somebody who understands central banking, who has the independence of mind to assist government to ensure continued stability." See what has happened! The Act was driven by a desire to ensure that an independent Central Bank would be a major player in ensuring monetary stability. And it has happened!

IA-D: So the President did not know Paul Acquah?

DKO: He did not know him individually. In the financial sector, a lot of the decisions the President has made were made on very objective grounds. I'll give you a typical example: You know the Social Security and National Insurance Trust (SSNIT) and the State Insurance Corporation (SIC), two of the biggest institutions in this country. When the President said to me, "Look, I want the best in the area of Actuarial Science in this country to run SSNIT and State Insurance Corporation" we did a search on paper and gave him what the industry itself considered their best lot. He looked at it and picked number one and number two and said, "I want you in SSNIT, I want you in SIC". He didn't know them from Adam, so he was acting purely on merit.

That was how it happened with Paul. The President didn't know Paul before. He asked around and said he was looking for a good Ghanaian with a lot of experience in international finance, well-educated, and Paul's name popped up. We did a search, due diligence, we talked to lecturers, we talked to his colleagues at the Fund, the Bank and so on. I am not the President so I cannot say, but I am very pleased with the way the Central Bank has played a major role in reforming this economy.

IA-D: We do not only get revenue from our commodities and our international trade, but also the bulk of our revenue is from multilateral institutions, especially now on the bilateral front – Aid from the UK, the US and elsewhere. You have been on many of these trips, soliciting for Aid – assistance in whatever form. What has been the terrain? This is the most-travelled President we've ever had.

DKO: It started with the first meeting we had with the World Bank and the IMF in Bamako in the very early days of the President's first term in Office. I remember that speech very well. That was the first time the President was meeting both the boss of the World Bank and the boss of the Fund. After his speech, they both came to the President and said to him, "John, we know you believe what you are saying. If that is what you are going to do with the economy of Ghana, we know that you are going to transform the economy of Ghana." So he built a very close relationship with the then-President of the World Bank, James Wolfenson, and the Managing Director of the Fund. On the road to HIPC, they used to speak to him directly when there were hiccups here or there, when maybe the targets for containing salary levels were getting a bit out of hand, or there were Budgetary deficits. He was communicating directly with them – that is what set the tone.

You know, there is something that must be said for the President. A lot of people do not trust politicians; they come across as not believing what they are saying. But the impression you get when you sit through some of these meetings with his colleagues who lead countries which usually contribute to our economy is that they trust him. I am talking of Chirac, Bush, the Chinese President, the former Prime Minister of Japan – Kuozumi. Just to give you an example: we recently went to see the Prime Minister of Japan officially. In the evening, Kuozumi sent a message saying that he would not let the President leave Japan without having a private dinner with him, so we went and had dinner with Kuozumi. This is the kind of relationship he developed with them.

Before the second discussion with the Bush administration about the Millennium Challenge Account (MCA), we were in the US to premiere other things; we were not scheduled to meet President Bush. President Bush heard that President Kufuor was in the hotel. He called us and said, "John, I am waiting for you in the Oval Office. Come now." So we sat in there and he said, "Look, I hear you're having problems signing a compact with the MCA. Tell me, what can I do for you?" So the President told him this and that and it led to all kinds of things subsequently. Lo and behold, we signed the compact! He built a very good relationship with all of them.

In a period when Japan could not continue providing assistance to Ghana, we had a loan of $80 million for the Cape Coast road from them. Parliament had passed certain rules that we were going HIPC, we could not access Japan funds. The President said, "Let's go to Tokyo". He had meetings upon meetings with his colleagues, and you know what happened: the loan was converted into a grant! The Accra-Cape Coast road you see was built for zero out of direct negotiation with them.

One of the summits we went to, the President went to the Chinese President's hotel. He said to him, "Mr. President, you are an engineer and we know what your background is, so you know how crucial Bui Dam is to the country's energy requirements. If that is all you can do for Ghana, please do it for me." So we kept at it, because you know this had been on the drawing board for a very long time, and we have signed the Bui Dam agreement.

IA-D: You have argued that for a developing economy like ours, foreign policy is very critical.

DKO: Absolutely.

IA-D: How has our foreign policy been in relation to our economic growth in the last seven years or so? Have we crafted a sort of policy or do you think it is the President's own personality that is driving this growth?

DKO: I think it is beyond his personality; it is policy direction in foreign policy. The first time he appointed non-career ambassadors and he spoke to them, he said to them in his speech, "My number one priority in diplomacy will be economic diplomacy". This was the President's message to his first batch of non-career ambassadors. After training for a month, they come and say farewell to the President. Invariably he tells them, "You know where we are, you know where our economy is. I am asking you to do whatever you can while you are there to improve our economy." I think we have fashioned what I will call a more direct and aggressive policy-implementation foreign policy, which has brought numerous benefits to our economy.

IA-D: You have been in the Diplomatic Service for a long time. Do you think this is a unique period in our Diplomatic history?

DKO: I think that posterity will have to admit that our foreign policy has been extremely successful, and I will be brief in giving you examples. After President Kufuor took over, I believe that our relations with our neighbours have been so good, we have never had it like that. That is the first one. During President Kufuor's tenure as Chairman of ECOWAS – don't forget he became Chairman of ECOWAS very quickly after he took over, against his protestations – Liberia was resolved, and Accra Accords (One, Two, Three) for Côte d'Ivoire was excellent. Don't forget that President Kufuor is currently Chairman of the African Union (AU), and usually in citations from foreign leaders they say, "We want to thank you for your leadership, for bringing peace and stability to your sub-region". It has been so consistent that you have to believe that foreign policy direction and implementation since 2001 have been very positive.

IA-D: What kind of construction can we make in terms of his legacy, as he is about to leave office in a year's time, in terms of economic policy and foreign relations?

DKO: In foreign policy I could mention a lot of examples, but one example that the Ghanaian public for instance is unaware of is that during his turn as AU chairman, this is the first time that the organisation has been audited. The regional economic groupings have been involved, the Economic Commission for Africa (ECA) has been involved, and he set up a panel of experts which has combed through all of what the Organisation of African Unity (OAU) and currently the

AU had done. He is just about to instruct his panel of experts to explain all this to the summit. He will be having a meeting with a number of Heads of State in January, and the resulting documents, the outcomes, will transform implementation programmes of the AU forever. This has about 195 new recommendations to improve policy implementation in the organisation. I think this will be one of the greatest hallmarks of President Kufuor's tenure as AU chairman.

IA-D: And in economic terms?

DKO: You know I am amazed that anyone can doubt that President Kufuor has transformed this economy. Anyone who brings inflation down by about 30 or 40 per cent in five years is extraordinary. Any economy which is able to reduce interest rates by 30 per cent in five years is extraordinary. Look at the currency. This currency has never been this stable. Look at the comparison between the Ghana cedi and the dollar, and the consequential effect on business in Ghana. This currency has been so stable that business is flowing! The economic indicators *are* impressive, and I think that over a longer period when President Kufuor is no longer President and economic historians are actually writing the history and they are dealing with cold, objective data, they will have to admit that this government under President Kufuor has really transformed the economy of Ghana. From this point onwards, achieving the Millennium Development Goals (MDGs) will be relatively easy and we will become a middle-income country. I believe we are on the path already, and the evidence is there. The data speak for themselves.

IA-D: Thank you.

December 2007

Dr Anthony Akoto-Osei

Dr Anthony Akoto-Osei is a Minister of State at the Ministry of Finance and Economic Planning, responsible primarily for resolving budgetary issues and managing Ghana's economic relations with the multilateral financial institutions. He is also the Member of Parliament for the Old Tafo/Pankrono Constituency in the Ashanti Region. He has previously served as Deputy Minister of Finance and Economic Planning, from 2003–2007, and as Special Advisor to the Minister of Finance, from 2001–2003. His professional career in Ghana began in 1995 as a research fellow for the Centre for Policy Analysis (CEPA), an independent economic think-tank in Accra.

An economist by trade, Dr Akoto-Osei's expertise lies in Monetary Economics, International Economics, and Quantitative Economics. He has taught as Assistant and then Associate Professor of Economics at Dillard University, New Orleans; as Lecturer in the Department of Economics at Howard University, Washington, DC; and as Assistant Professor in the Department of Economics and Business at Morgan State University, Maryland, all in the United States. He has also consulted for the Institute of Urban Affairs at Howard University and the World Bank in Washington DC.

He has a number of publications to his credit, including "The Demand for Heating Fuels: A Disaggregated Modelling Approach", with Rodney Green, et al. *Atlantic Economic Journal* (1986); "The Effects of Different Types of Income on Age-Sex-Race Specific Mortality Rates in the United States", with Jack Hadley, *Journal of Medical Care* (1982); and "Income, Education, and Mortality Rates", with Jack Hadley, in *More Education, Better Health*, Jack Hadley, ed. (Urban Institute Press, 1982).

Dr Akoto-Osei holds a PhD in Economics from Howard University; an MA in Applied Economics from American University; and a BA

(Hons) in Economics from Oberlin College, all in the United States. He is married with three children.

Ivor Agyeman-Duah: Dr Anthony Akoto-Osei, you studied in the United States before coming to Ghana. When did you come to Ghana and what did you come to do?

Dr Anthony Akoto-Osei: Yes, I stayed in the States for about 21 years, did all my college – First Degree, Masters, PhD – and got back to Ghana in 1995 on Thanksgiving Day to work as a research fellow at the Centre for Policy Analysis (CEPA).

IA-D: What were you doing there?

AA-O: I was designated as a Research Fellow, but with the responsibility for doing most of the real sector economic work for the Centre. We did – and they still do it – an annual review of the economy, commenting on the Budget; gave public speeches; and various other things that a think-tank would normally do.

IA-D: What were your impressions about the economic history of Ghana during the period before you got in – I mean, during the post-independence period, if your research went as far back as that?

AA-O: The general conclusion of the information we got was that we have not had an opportunity to really have a steady economy with growth that was always moving upwards – we had too many disruptive changes in the economy for a variety of reasons. All the work we did indicated that, even in the times of the Economic Recovery Programme (ERP), when we were supposed to be doing well, there were some weak points. We had never really had a period of continuous, sustained growth – maybe two or three years at best – but on the average it was not the best history we have had, up until about 2001.

IA-D: From there you became Special Assistant to the Minister of Finance and Economic Planning?

AA-O: Yes, in 2001 when the New Patriotic Party won the election, first we were appointed as a team to run the Ministry until the ministers were appointed – myself and a few other people. Then I was asked to be the Special Advisor to the Minister of Finance and Economic Planning, officially in 2001.

IA-D: What was the state of the economy when you became part of the team?

AA-O: You will know that as soon as the President was inaugurated in 2001, our first task was to prepare the Budget, in February. Because my work had been similar to what was being done here, we quickly set out to find out how to prepare the first Budget. You will recall that that was when the President decided to take advantage of the Highly Indebted Poor Country (HIPC) initiative of the World Bank. But we found an economy – at least by the information I had – which said that if we did not take some serious measures, then we were going to be in serious trouble. Reserves were low, inflation had been high, the exchange rate depreciated badly, so the first Budget was really tough. In my view, even in hindsight, without taking advantage of the HIPC initiative it would have been almost impossible to survive the first year.

IA-D: What were the elements that made the economy look bad at the time?

AA-O: All the typical indicators were in the wrong direction. The cedi had depreciated almost about 50 per cent, inflation had hit well above 41 per cent, economic growth was not the best, reserves were up to I think about one to two weeks' level of imports. There is no way you can run an economy with such indicators. Interest rates in those days were high; the Treasury Bill rate was about 45. Things were really not in the best framework. We had been paying our bills – external debt – consistently, but after that there was nothing left to do any serious development programme.

IA-D: For how long did it get to that point? We also heard the outgoing government singing the praises of its policies.

AA-O: I think around 1998, CEPA had started giving indications that where we were headed was not the best. It got worse by 1999 and of course 2000, but by the end of 1997 going into 1998, it was clear to us at CEPA that things needed to change radically. Allegedly, the former Minister of Finance at that time, Mr Kwame Peprah, was saying that any government in the world would have difficulty managing that economy, and we found out he was right.

IA-D: Was it a result of policy failure or…?

AA-O: It was a combination of factors. One of the discoveries I made when I got to the Ministry formally, in terms of working with the people there, was that you always had a small team of people working on the economy and I was not sure they were necessarily the best. The majority of people didn't really have an idea of what was going on. We tried to change that by forming what we called an Economic Policy Coordinating Committee, where all the key actors from the Ministry and from The Bank of Ghana met monthly. The situation was so bad that almost every day we needed to know where every indicator was going. Immediately after the Budget we needed to monitor seriously almost on a daily basis, so you needed to get a team of people, which was chaired by myself and somebody from The Bank of Ghana, almost on a daily basis checking on ourselves and where things were headed. Without that, I think it would have been difficult. That brought a sort of new professionalism, where people now began to really make serious contributions. All the revenue agencies were there, every key member at the Ministry of Finance was part, every key member of The Bank of Ghana met around the corner, and we had to monitor the economy with more seriousness than we had noticed before.

IA-D: Before then, what was the profile of the Ministry of Finance and Economic Planning in terms of professionalism?

AA-O: One thing I must say about this administration is it has always had enough serious, hard-working people; the issue is how you work with them, how you manage them. I think that if you go around most ministries after a certain time you will find most people there, but at this ministry, usually, even at 9:00 pm or 10:00 pm there are staff working because the issues are many. We have the Policy Analysis Division, and the Aid and Debt Management Division, and so on. On the average there are very serious, hard-working people, but they need to be directed, let me put it that way.

IA-D: What was your position as Special Assistant to the Minister? What were you supposed to do?

AA-O: One good thing about being a Special Advisor with a technical background was that I had no position. I was allowed to go to every place where there was a crisis. Essentially, I needed to advise the Minister on everything about the economy, so I was allowed to have interaction with every person around. I was acting as his mouthpiece, and because it was a technical position, there was some respect. People knew that I was not coming to talk politics *per se*, but I was worried about how we were going to bring the economy together.

After we took the HIPC initiative, it was obvious that, given our relationships with the international institutions, we needed to craft a programme that was respectable to be able to manage the economy. We worked very closely with The Bank of Ghana. My counterpart there was Dr Mahamudu Bawumia, who is now the Deputy Governor. We had a very good team, which was led by himself and our focus was straightening up the economy to arrest the rot. We had the focus that, unless we took certain decisions and monitored them and ensured that they were successful, things were going to be serious. I think people accepted it that I had the authority to speak for the Minister and so I could put my nose every place, and that helped a lot.

IA-D: In terms of the HIPC, I understand that there wasn't a consensus. It was a new initiative that the Bank had come up with and initially there wasn't a consensus.

AA-O: That is not entirely correct. There was a consensus that we needed a way; the question was did we have to do it on our first Budget. There was discussion that it doesn't look good to come out and say that you are poor, that you are crying for help, but that issue was resolved very quickly by the President. We had Honourable J. H. Mensah working with us on the last day of writing the Budget and we knew that the statement had to come in there, but where we were not sure. Of course we were in touch with the President, and when he gave the order that it must be inserted in the last paragraph, the decision was made. But I think there was general agreement that there was no way out. First of all, there was nothing to lose, but everything else to gain, because immediately after we opted for that decision, some relief was given. We didn't have to pay some debt service – that gave us room to fill the gaps. Then we knew the follow-up was to craft a programme that could be monitored for two or three years to get us back to where we were going to get the bigger relief, so the focus was right.

IA-D: In terms of the relief component of it, how did it cushion economic activity?

AA-O: At that time we were paying over $400 million in debt service – cash that we had to pay every year. Even if you got 50 per cent immediately, then you were able to have more reserves for example; the President doesn't have to go to Nigeria to negotiate for crude oil, because we didn't have to pay all that amount. We were able not to spend all our money on debt servicing, but to spend it on real economic growth areas. We needed to pay salaries; we needed to pay arrears that had been built up in the system, particularly in the road sector. That allowed you some room to really function. In the first year, that was not a huge amount, but we followed the programme with the Fund and then two years later we formally got into the HIPC thing. We came out very quickly because we got bigger relief, and that gave us more room to arrest the trends that we had seen. You could see everything was going in the right direction, and it was as a result of the relief that we got.

IA-D: What is the structure of the Ministry of Finance and Economic Planning? What does it do?

AA-O: The Ministry has the responsibility, a duty, to ensure that the economy is managed well, particularly on the fiscal side – government expenditure and taxes. It has the responsibility to liaise with The Bank of Ghana to make sure that the economy is doing well. We do a lot of things. Of course, the revenue agencies come under us, so we have a responsibility to make sure our revenue targets are met. Then, on the expenditure side, we have a constitutional obligation to make sure that whatever Parliament approves, people respect that. We have to present the Budget. Most of the time, one of the key products for this Ministry is preparing the Budget. The last two or three years, we have had to prepare two budgets a year – the normal one and a supplementary one – and then we have to monitor implementation during the year, so it is a whole lot of things. We have several divisions that come together to help us achieve these objectives.

IA-D: Apart from the divisions, there was also at the early stages of the NPP government the Economic Management Team.

AA-O: I don't know if there was a formal economic management team *per se* because the Minister of Finance is constitutionally responsible for that obligation. Certainly you need consultation. This ministry is at the heart of government business for a variety of reasons, so you are forced to coordinate with all ministries. I think in that sense the EMT, so to speak, was an Advisory group. I would call it a Cabinet sub-Committee on the economy, because we have that mixture of a system. There was what I would call a Cabinet sub-Committee, but the crux of the work happens here.

IA-D: There is also the constitutional body, the National Development Planning Commission.

AA-O: Yes, but the two are not mutually exclusive. The NDPC has a constitutional obligation to look at the long-term issues in the economy and to advise the President, but in the short-term the Ministry's role is very clear. But the two must work together. We have the Ghana Poverty Reduction Strategy (GPRS) II now, we had the GPRS I; the NDPC has the responsibility of getting the GPRS II together. One, the budget flows out of the GPRS I, and two, it is a yearly thing, even though we used to do a three-yearly roll-ever. I think the two institutions are different.

IA-D: What would you say has been some of the critical stimulation that this government has brought to the economic management of this country, in terms of the three principal sectors?

AA-O: I think first, in my view, we have not yet begun to see the successes that have come in these sectors. They are yet to come really, because the first order of business was to stabilise the economy and that meant that the macro environment had to be right. Interest rates are down; inflation is moderate – still a bit high, we think we need to go down; growth has been steadily up, from about 3.7 to 6.5 per cent.

Now, in that environment, it is easier for us to expect industry to begin to move, the financial sector the same way.

I am now expecting the Private Sector to play its proper role because they cannot be complaining about a destabilised economy. Now we have moved from stabilisation to accelerated growth. That requires that they look at the environment and go to areas where they are most powerful. Of course, we have had to deal with the energy crisis so the government still has played a role to arrest the energy deficits that have come about, but we are yet to see the Private Sector exerting itself. You have some mines coming in, but manufacturing is yet to show itself properly. There are areas like tourism which can really be at the heart of our growth potential but are not yet there. ICT – they have barely scratched the surface. We are now getting involved in the infrastructure there – rural telephony, fibreoptics – so the ICT industry is yet to grow. You have seen some growth – teledensity has gone up – but I think we can move much faster, and this is the challenge. How do we keep the economy on an even keel but accelerate growth? That is the challenge we need to focus on in Ghana's next phase of economic development.

IA-D: There is also talk of the independence of the Central Bank and policy formulation at that level. There has always been this argument that others started the process and then this government cashed in and made sure it went very well. Has that independence reflected economic outcomes?

AA-O: We helped the Central Bank craft The Bank of Ghana Act which gave them what I call operational independence. We have always worked very closely. In fact, I suspect that this economic management team in Finance and The Bank of Ghana is probably the best team that I have seen around. The cooperation has been stellar, we work very closely together. The Act gives The Bank of Ghana operational independence and we respect that, and that has allowed Paul Acquah, the Governor and a former employee of the IMF, and his team to also work religiously. I think on that level we have done very well.

IA-D: Do you think the infusion of the Ghanaian Diaspora coming in – the Governor was at the IMF, you were also outside, there are many others too – has stimulated thinking in a particular direction?

AA-O: Well, the thinking had been around for awhile, but the difference has come in implementation. Some of the things that we are doing we had always said at CEPA, but the issue was who was implementing it. Now, the difference is that some of us are involved in the implementation, and it makes a difference. When you are in the kitchen it is different, but our experiences have helped. One cannot say that that is what has made a difference, but certainly our understanding and our experiences have really helped bring things together.

IA-D: What is your own interpretation of the country's economic development in the coming years? You've worked in the field of research, you've been part of an implementation team and you are still working towards a particular direction.

AA-O: First, I am convinced that we have not reached our potential yet. There are several avenues that are in the pipeline that if we can just continue on the trend for two or three years we will be on the way to reaching our vision of becoming a middle income country very soon. I don't need to mention the discovery of oil – it could have both positive and negative implications. There are things like bauxite development. We still have a lot of infrastructural development to do. I believe that 8, 9, 10 per cent growth is possible. We cannot afford to reverse where we are, and I think that this is what people must focus on. Any relaxation of the discipline we've put in place will set us back. We don't need that. I'm sure if we keep it up for two or three years, in three years' time you will be looking at a Ghana that you have never seen before.

IA-D: What will be our relationship with our development partners and the multilateral institutions in the coming years, even as we withdraw?

AA-O: Right now we have the Article 4 relationship with the IMF. We have been talking about negotiating a policy support instrument programme. We have the same relationship with the World Bank, the PRSC is still ongoing. I do not believe that it will change that much. However, I think the need for Ghana to have other sources of funding, as we have done by going out to borrow $750 million from the market, is going to become important. I have no doubt in my mind that the ability-to-pay issue will disappear very soon, but we still have to manage our debt very well. We will continue to have a very good relationship with them, but more and more the ownership issue in terms of how the economy is run should be dominated by Ghanaian thinking.

IA-D: I guess the dependency is still strong because we are looking at 30 per cent...

AA-O: 30 per cent is not bad and we should aim to reduce it; we can do it because we have not reached the potential of the domestic revenue mobilisation target that we can reach. There is a lot of room for improvement in all the three revenue agencies. Barely, we are 22 million people. Assuming even half of the population is working, less than one million are in the formal sector paying income tax and so forth and so on. Just imagine if we got even three million people paying it. It is almost double the tax collection effort. So there is a lot of potential, even relying on our own self, but there is nothing wrong with using other people's resources to develop, as long as you put it into growth-enhancing areas and you are able to pay it back. That is what it is all about.

IA-D: When we listen to such good indicators of an economy, yet at the same time people working on the streets complain about difficulties in obtaining basic necessities of life, what does it mean?

AA-O: The perception is wrong. It is an issue of perception and high expectations. Ghanaians ought to have high expectations, but nobody in his right mind can compare where we have been and where we are going, and say that things are not moving forward. The real income of workers has gone up. If you look at the Public Sector Wage Bill, it is bigger than the Private Sector. Private doctors are now moving to become Public-Sector doctors. Why? The salaries are high. It did not used to be this way not so long ago. They have other amenities. Even teachers' salaries have increased. If prices generally go up, on a relative basis things are better.

The issue of distribution is always going to be there, and that is why we must grow bigger in order to have more to distribute. You cannot distribute what you do not have, but expectations are very high, and that is on the basis of where we've been. You talk about the Capitation Grant, the National Health Insurance Scheme (NHIS) – you name it – these programmes are expensive! You need money to fund them. If I am a parent and my child is going to public school and I have school feeding and a Capitation Grant, what I do not use for these expenses becomes extra money in my pocket. My salary is higher – that is also extra money. Ghanaians have high expectations, and they should, but the high expectations mean we must grow the economy bigger to be able to distribute more.

IA-D: People say that if the economy is growing at 6 per cent, and Capitation Grants and other programmes are making things a bit easier for parents to accommodate their children in school, we should also look at the quality of what is coming out. They think that the quality of education *vis-à-vis* the Capitation Grant is not the same.

AA-O: Yes, there are legitimate issues of quality, but because of that it does not mean that we should not increase the quantum. If the child does not go to school then the issue of quality will not even arise! We have to address both problems at the same time, and I agree that there is a problem. The new Educational Sector Reform is meant to address some of these issues. Certainly with National Health Insurance the quality of Health must get better. We know people are going to hospital more often; it's going to be expensive, but these things are necessarily expensive. Quality issues are real, but if you don't have the quantum, you can't worry about the quality. If I were living in a village where none of my siblings had gone to school, the issue of quality doesn't matter. First, I have to be part in order to deal with the issue of quality. That is being addressed, but it takes some time.

IA-D: Have we diversified the economy enough or are we still dependent on the traditional commodities like cocoa?

AA-O: Yes, the structure of the economy has not changed much since independence and we need to be moving away from that. The issue about non-traditional exports must be taken seriously. If you think of the potential for products like sheanut butter, and you look at what is happening in the tuna industry and the few Ghanaian firms that are involved in that, we have a long way to go and we need to get there. We have to trade our way out of poverty. That is the issue and we need to continue to expand our range of products. In the cocoa sector, we need to process more cocoa here. Even food production – the Millennium Challenge Account (MCA) and other such instruments are going to help in that sense.

IA-D: Why has it taken us so long to diversify? We talk about it all the time.

AA-O: I think it is because we have not had a successful, continuous, sustained trade. We are always trying to fight fires. When you stop fighting fires you are able to focus and concentrate. We are still fighting the fire in the energy area, but it is better than before. If the macro environment is so bad and the micro areas like energy are bad then you are lost! You have to be able to arrest this deterioration and focus. I think now that we believe we are doing that, we should be able to focus properly. I mentioned the ICT area – we have barely scratched the surface. There is room for improvement. I mean the Youth Employment Programme is good, but it is not the best type of employment we want. We want people in ICT and the few examples that we've seen where Ghana is becoming like India and processing medical records over here is a very good area where we can get revenue from.

Now is when we expect the Ministry of Trade and Industry to begin to give Policy Advice in the area of Industrial Policy. For the first time, Industrial Policy is going to be approved by government so that it can be cohesive. The same will apply in the Transport Sector. We have a Transport Sector that is not coordinated: railway, harbours, we need to put it all together. We are about to have a new Transport Policy. I think things are beginning to come together and then the implementation is what we need to watch.

IA-D: A few years ago, Ghana achieved a B+ rating from Standard & Poors' and others. What has this done for the image of Ghana?

AA-O: Well first of all, this is the first time that the Ghanaian government had looked for a rating. I think that is for a reason. We wanted the discipline that the international market imposes to come on us. What it then allowed us to do was to issue a bond on the back of that rating, which was well-received; in fact, it was over-subscribed. We think that the review should have been better than the last time, but we need to work harder. The B+ is positive but we think it could be a bit better. We are working on that. The market puts some extra discipline, and that's what we're looking for.

IA-D: Since then, what has happened in terms of our standing in the financial market, in terms of our image among international economies?

AA-O: On the 14th of January 2008, we went to London to receive an award. Ghana has been identified as being the 2007 Emerging Market Bond of the Year, and the Eastern Europe, Middle East, and Africa (EEMEA) Bond of the Year. That is good, that is positive news. When the international market believes that you are disciplined enough, they will respond to you. We are going to need that type of huge monies from there. It is good that sometimes in Africa you say, "We are doing well", but you need to compete globally, and this is the type of thing that helps us.

IA-D: You're looking at East Asia?

AA-O: That is why for us it is good that among emerging markets, all those nice countries, we have been considered one of the best. We need to strive to be like the East Asians, like the Malaysians, like the Singaporeans.

IA-D: There are people who do comparative economic analyses and pitch Ghana against South Korea and against Malaysia. They look at the economic starting points of these countries and they think that we didn't do well over the years.

AA-O: For a variety of reasons. If you look at the starting point without going beyond that you will think that because the starting points were the same we have done badly. The starting point is important, but the dynamics of moving forward are important too. I am sure that in Korea, if you didn't have the US presence there for a long time, the type of injection that was going on there may not have happened.

We have also had political instability. They have had continuous political stability; even if it was not quote-unquote "democratic", it served the purpose. Mahathir Mohamad, Lee Kuan Yew – that type of political leadership helped them focus, and we have not had that. We have had disruptions. Think about it: this is the second time we have had a civilian government that has gone on for eight years, the first time being the Rawlings era, in our fifty-year history. Nkrumah came, gone in 1966; Busia came in 1969, gone in 1972; Acheampong came; Limann came. That type of instability cannot help you! They have not had that and that makes a difference.

I think there are other things. Foreign capital goes where it feels safe in a politically stable environment, no matter how autocratic people might perceive the leader. If the investments seem to be doing well, people will take their money there. We have not had that kind of infusion of investment in Ghana; we have had to rely on our own resources. I think we are getting there. At least in the West African region we seem to be gaining the advantage. We have allowed ourselves not to have gone as far as we could. It doesn't mean that it's too late; we can reverse it. We are, and we should continue.

IA-D: What is being done to reverse some of these structures that you are talking about? I was at the Ghana Investment and Promotion Centre and there were more drivers and office clerks than there were official investment officers.

AA-O: Yes, these are the areas we need to reform and reform better. The type of skills we need in Ghana are not the type you just mentioned. We need to be globally competitive, so our educational system must begin to focus on getting the right type of skills. We have some young Ghanaians, who are very good in ICT, but we don't manufacture, we assemble, and we are competing with Malaysia and Korea. It will not happen, so we need to move beyond that.

We need to reform the Public Service but also the Private Sector. Our Private Sector has had to depend on government a lot. You go to any private person: "Government give us this, government give us that". Government can create the environment, and then the Private Sector can move in. We need to change attitudes – I think that is important. All these things require continuous education. People like to see success stories and then their attitudes will change. If we continue to be successful, I am sure Ghanaians' attitudes will change.

Now there are a lot of quote-unquote "returnees" who have come and gone into areas where they wouldn't have dared go six or seven years ago. Ashesi University is one of them, and they are making progress. You go to the financial sector where there are young Ghanaians coming back and willing to take risks; if you look at the quantum of remittances coming from Ghanaians to Ghana, it is an indication of the confidence that people are beginning to have in our economy. We need that. Ghanaians must build Ghana, not everybody else. This is what I expect to see in the next five to ten years, and once it is sustained, if in ten years I have not retired, I shall retire to enjoy the fruits of my labour.

IA-D: In the next ten years what will make this achievable? Has it got to do with political change, continuity of policy, or other things?

AA-O: I am convinced that, in terms of political stability, we are heading in the right direction. Now we need to think 'outside the box' in the economic area. We need to build initiatives in certain areas, and those are coming. How we use our own potential revenues is going to be important. We need to do other things too. The President has done very well by pointing out the fact that our infrastructure gaps are huge. We should build a railroad from Accra all the way to the North, and that should happen in ten years, not twenty years, because of the volume of traffic. We have spent money on our roads, but they are being destroyed because of the traffic. That I can see happening. If we can get VALCO to do what it was expected to do, that would be a huge boost. The bauxite mining – I think that is what I am looking at. All our internal airports should be improved, and that should happen earlier. I see a lot of potential.

IA-D: How much of our Budget goes into infrastructural development?

AA-O: I cannot give you a precise figure off the top of my head, but it is not small. Now, it has gotten bigger because we have had to do a lot for the Electricity Company of Ghana (ECG) and the Volta River Authority (VRA) and roads. But we need more, not less. For our farm products to survive and the marketing must be there, we must build storage facilities and airlift them. If you go and produce in my village, and you think that you can get it to the port without a problem, you are lying! We ought to be able to build storage facilities at these production centres to guarantee that they are safe to come to the airports. We should have a Kumasi International Airport and Tamale should deal with the northern borders. That is feasible and I think we can do it in about three years. That is not difficult.

IA-D: Do you have faith in the future of Ghana?

AA-O: I have absolute faith in Ghanaians in particular. Ghanaians are beginning to believe in themselves and for that reason I am confident that we will get there.

IA-D: Thank you very much.

AA-O: Thank you.

October 2007

Professor John Evans Atta Mills

Professor John Evans Atta Mills is the former Vice-President of Ghana and current flagbearer and Presidential candidate for the National Democratic Congress (NDC) in the December 2008 general elections. He has previously served on the Council of the Ghana Stock Exchange, the Board of Trustees of the Mines Trust, the Management Committee of the Commonwealth Administration of Tax Experts, the United Nations Ad Hoc Group of Experts in International Cooperation in Tax Matters, and the United Nations Law and Population Project.

Professor Mills' illustrious career began in academia, when he joined the Faculty of Law of the University of Ghana. In more than 20 years there, he was promoted through the ranks of Lecturer, Senior Lecturer, and Associate Professor, and served on several university Boards and Committees. He also spent time as Visiting Lecturer or Professor at a number of educational institutions, including Temple Law School in Philadelphia, USA (from 1978-79 and 1986-1987), and Leiden University in Holland (1986-87). He was a Visiting Scholar at the Liu Centre for the Study of Global Affairs, University of British Columbia, Canada (2002), and has presented research papers at conferences and symposiums throughout the world. Professor Mills has more than a dozen publications to his credit, among them: *Taxation of Periodical or Deferred Payments Arising from the Sale of Fixed Capital* (1974); *Exemption of Dividends from Income Taxation: A Critical Appraisal* (1977); and *Report of the Tax Review Commission, Ghana, Parts 1, 2, and 3* (1977).

In 1988, Professor Mills became the Acting Commissioner of the Internal Revenue Service, and was subsequently named Commissioner in September 1996. As the running mate of President Jerry John Rawlings, Professor Mills was sworn in as Ghana's Vice- President on 7 January 1997. He held this position until 2001, during which period he also chaired the government's Economic Management Team. In 2002, he was elected NDC flagbearer to lead the party into the 2004 elections, and by a majority of 81.4 per cent, he was re-elected flagbearer in December 2006.

Professor Mills attended Achimota School, and then proceeded to the University of Ghana, where he earned a Bachelor of Law and a Professional Certificate in Law in 1967. He continued his studies at the London School of Economics and Political Science, where he earned a Masters degree. He pursued a PhD in Law at the School of Oriental and African Studies (SOAS) in London, UK, receiving his degree following a Doctoral thesis on Taxation and Economic Development. While at SOAS, he was selected as a Fulbright Scholar at Stanford Law School in the United States.

Ivor Agyeman-Duah: Professor, taxation is one of the three major sources of government revenue in Ghana. Would you say that the tax base had been sufficiently built during postcolonial rule to generate the necessary revenue for governments over the years?

Professor J. E. Atta Mills: Let me say that until the mid-1980s, when the PNDC government decided to tackle our tax system seriously in order to ensure that enough resources were generated by potential taxpayers, the tax base was very narrow. Apart from employees, who paid taxes regularly, many self-employed people did not pay tax. The result therefore was an onerous burden on employees. But since 1986, when the PNDC government embarked on a reform of the tax system, the tax base was broadened. But it is something that should be a continuous affair because more and more people keep making money, generating income, and therefore you need to broaden the tax base. My suspicion now, having been Commissioner of Internal Revenue for eight-and-a-half years, is that the base is not as broad as it should be. There are quite a lot of self-employed people, and they are the ones who are hard to task, who I believe are not really paying their fair share of taxes. If the revenue collecting agencies were given enough resources and given the right motivation, they should be able to collect much more than they are doing.

IA-D: Why did it take so long – from 1957 to 1986 – to do what you are saying?

JEAM: You know, normally when governments face the crunch, when they are in dire straits then, they begin to look frantically for sources of income. This was the time when we had the Economic Recovery Programme and we had to look at all the sources of revenue, expenditure, etc., so there was a complete overhaul of the economy, as you would say. I believe that in the years before then, either the governments did not find the need to look for additional sources of revenue or they just did not care. So I believe a good start was made in 1986 when we had to take a holistic look at our economy, and indeed at our own development path.

IA-D: Obviously, you played a part in this as a seasoned Tax Professor and someone who had also worked as Commissioner of Taxes. What were the strategies that were adopted in 1986?

JEAM: The most important thing I believe that we did was to get the right calibre of people. You know, before then, I do not think that professional Accountants – I mean Chartered Accountants – had found it attractive enough to work in the then-Central Revenue Department because the Conditions of Service were not attractive. So one of the first things we did was bring in a group of young professionals, who were committed to proving themselves. So we did that; we looked at the personnel. Then we looked also at the laws. And then we decided to give them the adequate resources, the resources that they needed. You know, if you go through the history books, you will find that in the Central Revenue base – that is when they were part of the Civil Service – it was even difficult for them to get paper to write on because if there was no allocation, there was no allocation! So what we did was that they were hived off from the Civil Service and made into an autonomous institution with their own Budget, their own Governing Board and all that. That raised morale and improved efficiency. We also gave them the resources so that they could update the Tax Register.

When it comes to Taxation, nobody likes paying taxes except Sir Oliver Holmes! What we did then was to bring the Tax Office nearer to the people, so we embarked on an expansion exercise where we built a number of offices in the districts and in some other important towns, so that the collectors could be near the people. Apart from the taxpayers finding it easier to walk into the Tax Offices, if Tax Officers were resident in the community they could get vital information so that they would be able to find out who was making what and therefore bring them easily into the tax net.

IA-D: So what is the state of the Internal Revenue Service now, in the year 2008?

JEAM: Well let me say that I haven't been there for quite some time, but if some of the stories that I hear are true, it looks as if morale has gone down; it looks as if they are not being given sufficient attention; they have complained also about lack of resources to enable them to do their work, carry on the expansion exercise, operate more efficiently. It's a human institution and it's important therefore that you look at what can lift morale, and they will need the resources also to do the work. And then the most important thing is that a Tax Officer must be honest, transparent, but *independent*. When there is political interference, you are not going to get Tax Officers doing their best, and from some of the hints I got, there is the impression that the Executive is leaning on some of the Tax Officers to bend the rules or turn the other way when taxpayers are not paying their taxes. While this creates difficulties for Tax Officers, others get encouraged to evade taxes.

IA-D: We are talking of a period when the government has said it has been able to give more technological advancement to the Internal Revenue Service (IRS) – computerise the systems and things like that. Is this still the case?

JEAM: I don't think that the computerisation has been fully done in the IRS. You will have to talk to the IRS officers. There are a lot of things that they feel the government could do in order to enhance their performance which the government (NPP) is not really doing. All kinds of claims have been made.

IA-D: Including, of course, talking of meeting targets. Is that also an issue?

JEAM: Well I really don't know. Here you are, you have a government who's Domestic Primary Balance – that is its revenues against expenditure – in 2007 was 6.7 negative of GDP, which meant that it spent more than it collected. In 2006, it was 4.6 negative of GDP – Domestic Primary Balance negative, which meant that it spent more than it collected. And yet this is a government which is talking about meeting targets! Now, in 2007, the government had a Budget deficit of close to 10 per cent, and if you look at the record of 2007 and 2006, the government did not meet a lot of its performance targets. So when they say they have been able to meet their targets, why is the Domestic Primary Balance the way it is?

IA-D: All governments agree on the need for government to generate revenue, but the strategies have been different. For instance, when the NDC came out with the Value Added Tax (VAT), there was massive resistance to that by the then-Opposition and now Government-in-Power, and when the NPP government started talking of the Talk Tax, which is now a law, there was also disagreement from the NDC side. Is it normally a politicisation of the tax policy, or is it reflective of real policy differences?

JEAM: Well, you know in any democracy people should feel free to express their views, and you cannot ram anything down the throat of anybody. Sometimes it's the mode of introduction; sometimes people find it convenient to make noises where there is really no need. But I think you have to look at the substance of the argument. Especially when it comes to Taxation, you will not get everybody welcoming the imposition of tax without looking at it very critically. Nobody wants to pay tax, I will tell you! Therefore, the introduction of some of these taxes will generate some very lively discussion. Sometimes it turns a bit sour, but I think it is to be expected. We don't regret that we introduced the VAT, and I believe that we have been proved right, and I would claim that that is what matters. As to whether the noises which were made were justified or not, we'll leave posterity to be the guide.

IA-D: You became Vice- President with a lot or experience in revenue generation. What was supposed to be your role in government as Vice-President?

JEAM: One, just to assist the President in the performance of his duties. My constitutional responsibility was to perform whatever assignments were given to me by the President, pure and simple.

IA-D: The NDC had the Economic Management Team, of which you were the Chairman. What was the team supposed to do?

JEAM: What we did was that we met regularly, and brought together the various actors in the economy. We had The Bank of Ghana, we had the Ministry of Finance, we had the Private Sector – we had all of them. We would discuss policies, we would get reports, and then we would decide on the way forward. But of course, you could not go into detail; you had a general idea as to what had happened and you had a general report. As to what had to be done specifically, you left that to the various agents, but you had an overview of what the economy looked like and in what direction it was going to go.

IA-D: How different was this from the Cabinet decisions for instance or the role of the National Development Commission?

JEAM: Well, you know what I chaired was really Advisory. You couldn't take decisions; if we took decisions they had to go to Cabinet for approval. Cabinet would then discuss it and decide that, "Well, this is the way forward. We're going to pass this law; we are going to issue this directive." So whilst the first one was Advisory, the Cabinet meetings were really decisive. That is where the Executive made its intentions known, and where you required an Act of Parliament to implement your policies, we went ahead and did that. Where you needed to signal to the people of Ghana what else you wanted, Cabinet went ahead and did that.

IA-D: So why do your opponents associate you so much with being Chairman of the Economic Management Team and then blame you for failures and sometimes praise you for successes?

JEAM: Well I think many of them are just being mischievous. I think that is the political game. That experience is something that people talk about, but I don't regret that I was Chairman; I believe that we did something which was quite commendable. These days, with all the so-called "geniuses" who are members of the Kufuor Economic Management Team, the Domestic Primary Balance is in the negative! You are not achieving your targets! You are recording fiscal deficits! Let me tell you, you can look at the records: even in the four years when I was Chairman of the Economic Management Team, we were recording surpluses in the Domestic Primary Balance, which is something. Let us also be mindful of this fact, which people run away from: at the time that we were in power, cocoa was selling at $700, gold was $235. Now, cocoa is selling at about $3000 and gold is close to $1000 because of what we did – we handed over peacefully, we opened the doors for debt cancellation running into billions. The Kufuor government has had more resources to deal with than any other government and yet there is little to show for it as far as the ordinary Ghanaian is concerned. They pride themselves on being the economic gurus – well, we'll live to see.

IA-D: Every economy has its good and bad days – as was the case with the NDC. What led to the good and what led to the bad?

JEAM: Well, you know, when your economy depends a lot on exports, primary products, gold, timber, cocoa, and you import oil, then when cocoa prices are up, gold prices are up, timber prices are up, and oil prices are manageable, you enjoy a windfall. But the moment there is a drop in these prices then you begin to feel the crunch, and that was exactly what happened to us. And of course there were other factors too. Mind you, the NDC had taken over from a government, PNDC, which had also taken over from a government which was recording negative growth. When people say, "Let's compare", they forget that we built the foundation. When we had inflation running at 122 per cent, when for years the economy was recording negative growth, we were able to stabilise the economy. We were recording an average of 4.5–5 per cent growth a year, and this is what they came to build on, but it can never be the same.

IA-D: I know the ideological position of the NDC has been Social Democracy. What are the economic dimensions in the world today when we are talking in general terms of liberal markets?

JEAM: Well, you can talk about liberalism – each man for himself and God for us all – where the forces operating are equal, but not when you have things skewed. For example, in African terms, you'll find that the majority of our people cannot, unless the State takes care of them, fend for themselves. This is why we are Social Democrats, because we think that our development imposes on us the obligation to ensure that we make it possible for the vulnerable, the marginalised, for the *average* person, to have a good education, to have access to medical care – these are things that they normally would not have because they do not have the means. So when people talk about, "Oh yes, liberalise", we are liberalising for what? I think that, yes, some amount of liberalisation can go on, but if you want fair and equitable development, you must pay attention to those sectors which need governmental support. I, for example, might have found it extremely difficult to attend tertiary education if at the time they had insisted that we pay fees, and there are so many people like that. They have to be helped! This country has benefited from government intervention and I think that where it is possible, we should be able to pursue it.

IA-D: Thank you very much.

JEAM: Thank you.

July 2008

Ambassador Isaac Osei

Ambassador Isaac Osei is the Chief Executive of Ghana Cocoa Board (COCOBOD), a position he has held since April 2006. He is also the current Vice-Chairman of the Executive Committee of the International Cocoa Organization and a member of the Consultative Board on the World Cocoa Economy. Under his leadership at COCOBOD, the Board has attained a production level of over 740,000 tonnes, the largest ever output, and has managed to secure a trade facility of $900 million and a medium-term facility of $190 million for its operational and investment activities. In business, Ambassador Osei serves as Chairman of Intravenous Infusions Ltd; Director of Aluworks (Ghana) Ltd.; Chairman of Ghana Cocoa Marketing Co. Ltd.; and Director of Cocoa Processing Co. Ltd.

Ambassador Osei's career began at the Ministry of Finance and Economic Planning, where, in the early 1970s, he worked in the Industry, Mining, and Forestry section and later in the Macroeconomic Division. He subsequently became Chief of the Commercial Operations Department at the Ghana Tourist Development Company Limited, from 1978-1982. He was the founder and Managing Consultant of Ghanexim Economic Consultants Limited, a leading economic consulting firm involved in the planning of infrastructural projects and socio-economic and environmental impact analyses, as well as the preparation of financial, marketing, and business plans for Private Sector companies. He has also worked in various capacities as a consultant to government, USAID, the World Bank, JICA, and DfID. He was an international trade consultant for UNCTAD and is an expert on the multilateral trading system.

He was the Managing Director of Intravenous Infusions Limited, the largest manufacturer of intravenous infusions and small volume injectables in West Africa, until his appointment as High

Commissioner of Ghana to the United Kingdom and Ambassador to Ireland in 2001. While in London, Ambassador Osei served as the Chairperson of the Board of Governors of the Commonwealth Secretariat from 2003–2005. He also travelled extensively as a member of Ghana government delegations to Commonwealth Heads of Government meetings, the UN General Assembly, Commonwealth Foreign and Finance Ministers conferences, and to the G8 meeting in Gleneagles, Scotland.

Ambassador Osei is the recipient of the national award, Order of the Volta (Officer Division) conferred by President John Agyekum Kufuor, as well as the International Non-Governmental Organisation (NGO) Award, the Daasebre Award for Excellence, the Ghana Professional Achievers Award in 2003 and 2006, the Eagle Wing by the Research Department of the Ministry of Foreign Affairs, the Economics Department (University of Ghana) Distinguished Service Award, and the Old Achimotan Association (OAA) Merit Award.

He began his education at the State Primary School in Kumasi and then attended Achimota School and the University of Ghana, where he obtained a BSc (Hons) degree in Economics in 1973 and was elected National President of the Ghana United Nations Students' Association, then the largest students' organisation in Ghana. He pursued further studies at the American Economic Association's Economic Institute at the University of Colorado, Boulder, and, in 1977, received a Masters degree in Development Economics from Williams College in Massachusetts, both in the USA.

Ivor Agyeman-Duah: Ambassador Isaac Osei, how important was cocoa as a commodity in the immediate post-independence era in Ghana?

Ambassador Isaac Osei: Cocoa was very important, not just in the immediate post-independence period but even before independence. You will realise that the Ghana Cocoa Board or the Gold Coast Cocoa Marketing Board as it then was, had been established by the British colonial administration in 1947. Clearly they saw a need to have a Marketing Board in place as a way of raising revenue for development purposes. In fact, in the immediate post-independence period, Kwame Nkrumah relied heavily on revenues from cocoa to finance a large part of the Development Budget of our country, so cocoa definitely has been important.

Even today, cocoa is just as important as it was then, and perhaps even more so, because, not only is cocoa the principal foreign exchange earner, which has been so since independence, it has also been the sector which employs most of our people. From time to time a commodity like gold comes up but you know that all cocoa revenues are retained in Ghana and therefore if you were to take one single commodity in this country, it has got to be cocoa. This is why the adage is: "Ghana is cocoa and cocoa is Ghana."

IA-D: So what is the structure of the cocoa industry in Ghana?

IO: Well, the structure of the cocoa industry has at its base the farmer. The farmer is actually the bedrock of the industry, because it is the farmer who grows cocoa, tends cocoa and harvests cocoa. But the farmer cannot do it alone. The farmer has to interface with a number of operators within the industry. First of all, the Ghana Cocoa Board, through its Seed Production Unit, provides the planting materials, which enables the farmer to plant the cocoa. Secondly, we have a responsibility of educating the farmers in good agronomic practices, to ensure that the spacing is correctly done, that the planting material that we have recommended is what they are using, that the cocoa farmer is looking after the farm in the manner which will enable him to have the high yields. So, at that stage, the Ghana Cocoa Board interfaces with the farmer.

When the cocoa farm is properly established, and the farmer harvests the cocoa, Ghana Cocoa Board, through the activities of the Cocoa Research Institute of Ghana, also moves in to educate the farmer as to maintenance and proper fermentation and drying. You see, in some countries they allow all the pods to ripen, but in Ghana we don't, because to assure quality you will notice that we are able to harvest *some* of the crop, which is just at the right stage for harvesting. And then also, the farmer has the responsibility of fermenting the cocoa. Our duty is to interface with the farmer to ensure that the fermentation process is done rightly. Fermentation is for six or seven days, with at least two turnings. You can see all these cone-shaped beans piled up in many of our villages in the cocoa-growing areas. That is the period of fermentation. We cover it with a local material – leaves from the plantain tree – to ensure that the heat is maintained in there, to ensure proper fermentation of the beans. Once you have fermented the cocoa, then you have to go through the drying process. These are things very well known to our farmers.

Ghana Cocoa Board uses private licensed-buying companies to interface when we come to the purchasing of cocoa. So we have private licensed-buying companies – about eighteen or nineteen of them – all Private-Sector Limited Liability companies, with their own independent management structures. They practice their trade, buying cocoa all over the country, and operate according to the rules and regulations that Ghana Cocoa Board has set. These rules and regulations are known to all. For example, you shouldn't buy cocoa which has been mixed with inferior-quality stuff, or which has not been properly dried. You shouldn't buy cocoa which has been mixed with foreign materials.

These licensed-buying companies have a responsibility for buying the cocoa. They also have responsibility for primary evacuation, moving the cocoa from the farms to the individual warehouses at the society level. Most of our farmers are organised in cooperatives or in societies. So at the society level, there will be a warehouse where these bags of cocoa are received. Licensed-buying companies also have a responsibility of ensuring that they deliver cocoa to us at 64 kilograms – not 65, not 63.5, but at 64. That is the weight at which we buy cocoa.

But having purchased the cocoa on our behalf we have a responsibility to ensure that the cocoa is of a quality which we can export, not just as cocoa beans, but as *Ghana* cocoa beans. There is a reputation attached to our bean, and that reputation says that our cocoa bean is very well fermented, is thoroughly dried, and is free of foreign materials. You're allowed 5 per cent on the market, or thereabouts, but ideally Ghana cocoa should be free of any foreign materials. And so our Quality Control Division moves in, examines the cocoa, by horning bits and pieces from every single bag to make sure that the cocoa is of the quality that we require. And then when that has been done, we will grade the cocoa, and we will seal it with a specific seal so that we can identify the area and the grader who did that job. There is an element of traceability in Ghana cocoa, because that seal that we put on the cocoa bag shows you exactly where the cocoa is coming from. Once it is sealed, then it has to be transported to the three takeover centres. At the takeover centre we also conduct another quality check to ensure that the cocoa that we graded and sealed up-country is the same cocoa that we have received in our warehouses for export or for delivery to the local processing factories.

So, if you look at the structure; we have private hauliers moving the cocoa, we have private licensed-buying companies and we have private individuals who are farmers. And then we have Ghana Cocoa Board, through the Seed Production Unit; Cocoa Research Institute of Ghana; as well as the Cocoa Swollen Shoots Virus Disease Control Unit, which looks after a particular disease of the cocoa tree. So there is a real example of public-private partnership in the cocoa trade.

But when it comes to marketing, that responsibility is left to the Cocoa Marketing Company of Ghana, which is a fully-owned subsidiary of Ghana Cocoa Board. The Cocoa Marketing Company is probably the only company from a producing country which has exhibited the capacity to move in and out of the market as and when it requires, or as and when we see that the price is good or bad. Our duty is to maximise the earnings for our country, and that duty falls on the Cocoa Marketing Company. We watch the various Reuters screens that we have, and watch what the price is at every particular time of the day, to ensure that when the prices are rising we can then move in and sell Ghana's cocoa. We can sell spot and we can sell in the futures market as well.

IA-D: In terms of industrial growth – that is the industries within the country – how is cocoa related to it? How do you feed the industries? And how many industries operate at this moment?

IO: I believe you're talking about the processing industries that we have in Ghana. We do have quite a number of processing industries, and it is the policy of the Kufuor government to ensure that processing capacity increases to at least 40 per cent. The way we're going, we're going to get there. Prior to 2000, before this government came into office, we had the Cocoa Processing Company (CPC), which was at that time publicly-owned but is now a limited liability company with some government ownership, but other institutions also have shares, the general public have shares. And then we had the West African Mills Company (WAMCO) in Takoradi, which was a public-private partnership. These were the two companies there. CPC had a theoretical capacity of about 50,000 tonnes but was actually doing 20,000 tonnes. WAMCO has a theoretical capacity of 80,000 tonnes but is operating way below that capacity and certainly was at that time.

Since 2000, we have had Barry Callebaut, the world's biggest chocolate manufacturer, operating in our country. They set up a 30,000-tonne capacity factory which was opened by President Kufuor, and about a year or so ago they have expanded that capacity to 60,000 tonnes. CPC has had a complete re-fit, it has been fully rehabilitated, and by the end of the year it will be a 65,000-tonne capacity enterprise. We have Cargill, the biggest food processor in the world, a US company, and H. E. the President cut the sod earlier in the year and the factory should be ready, up and running at 60,000 tonnes per annum from October 2008 in Tema. A few months ago we signed a bean supply agreement with Archer Daniels Midland (ADM), so we have the three "big boys" in Ghana. ADM will set up their factory in Kumasi. Apart from that, we have had two other smaller factories – Afrotropic and Commodities Processing Industries Limited – so we are looking at a capacity of about 350,000 tonnes by the end of next year, 2008. Clearly you can see that, given the current level of production, we will exceed the 40 per cent which the government has targeted.

But apart from these industries, we have spawned a number of other industries. People are doing cocoa powder all over the place. They also take from these secondary manufacturers to produce their tertiary products. As we look into the future, we are looking at artisanal chocolate manufacturing in Ghana. This is something that we are well-positioned to undertake because of the levels of cocoa butter and cocoa liquor which we are producing domestically. We have the capacity to do all these things, and I think these are exciting times for COCOBOD and for the cocoa industry. It's also a time when Ghana Cocoa Board has set itself a target of attaining one million tonnes in terms of production. This will represent about a 40 per cent increase over a three-year period. I believe that, with the measures that we have put in place and also with the active collaboration and support of government, we should be able to attain our target.

IA-D: There was this syndicated loan that you were raising in London – I think it started some years ago. What were these monies being used for? What is it being used for now?

IO: Well, Ghana Cocoa Board does not rely on the government Budget to finance its operation. Ghana Cocoa Board has to finance itself, so we have to look for the cheapest money wherever we may find it, and this is precisely what we've been trying to do over the years. This syndication has been going on for the past thirteen years. In its last year, for this current season, we were raising $900 million, and we raised it at a price which is probably the best price we have ever done: just a little above 5 per cent. We think we are poised for growth. We raised this money to finance the operations of the Ghana Cocoa Board – i.e. the purchasing operations especially. So what we do is we borrow the money, we bring it to Ghana, and then we advance monies to licensed-buying companies to purchase cocoa on our behalf, to ensure that as soon as the farmer delivers his cocoa he gets paid. This has been going on successfully for a number of years, as I said earlier about thirteen years now.

But this year, 2007, another element was introduced by COCOBOD, in February. For projects which have a long gestation period – for example, the target we have set ourselves to increase cocoa production from 700,000 tonnes to one million tonnes, which is something we will do over a three-year period – borrowing money over one year is not the way we should look at it. We went into the market and for the first time we were able to raise a medium-term facility, initially $150 million but now totalling $190 million, so this year Ghana Cocoa Board has borrowed more than $1 billion, but we have the capacity to pay. Last year we borrowed $810 million. By August, we had paid the money. This year we will pay, because we have the systems, structures and capacity to do so.

IA-D: As an economist, how would you explain the fact that we have been dependent on cocoa for a long period of time and that we are still depending on it? Have there been other ways that the economy has been stimulated in terms of adding more revenue to what we have already, in GDP terms?

IO: Cocoa certainly is a major contributor to GDP and certainly over the last five or six years, the Kufuor government has shown an interest in diversifying the sources of revenue for the country. This has been exemplified in the Presidential Special Initiatives. Whenever an initiative is taken, it takes time to bear fruit, and this is what I think the people of Ghana have to understand: you don't put in place policies which have long-term effects and expect to achieve results in a single year. So the Presidential Special Initiatives on palm oil, on textiles, will bear fruit, but we have to have the policy and stick to it. If we stick to the policy, then we will be able to attain the results that we expect.

There have been also a number of other activities, especially in the area of construction. All these have not just supported the cocoa industry, but also have boosted the economy in general. COCOBOD for example has a partnership with the Ministry of Finance and the Department of Feeder Roads to tar certain cocoa roads. This is just the first phase of it, but the important thing is that we are putting in place the infrastructure that will support the development process of our country. It is not just for cocoa; it is for the economy as a whole. Once you have tarred that feeder road, it is not just cocoa that you move along that road; you are moving food crops along that road to feed the urban populations who do not grow these food crops. In order to establish a cocoa farm you have to provide a canopy of plantain to provide the shade for the cocoa seedlings. That also provides food for our people. We are adding value by establishing processing industries within our economy and increasing the quantity of cocoa which is processed locally.

As an economist, I can say that this government has moved forward to diversify the economy in the manner which will sustain growth in this country way into the future. The important thing for us is to stick to the policies that we have put in place. These are not policies just for this government, these are policies for Ghana. Whichever government is in place should realise that these are policies for growing our country and for the future of our country, and we should pursue them. There might be different modes of pursuing these policies, but the policies have to be firm. I think when you have a firm policy framework; that in itself provides the basis for the development of our country.

IA-D: Obviously Ghana has no monopoly over cocoa. There are other countries which produce cocoa in West Africa. How has the country been able to withstand this global competition to still be on top, with cocoa as one of our major export earners?

IO: The key to Ghana's cocoa is quality, the way we take care of our cocoa pre-harvest and post-harvest. Every chocolate manufacturer wants a bit of Ghana cocoa to blend. Even those who buy from our neighbours want Ghana cocoa to blend because of our flavour. Our

flavour is different. Our flavour is the best for the making of choco-
lates, which is the main thing that cocoa beans are used for. So it is
the quality. And it is not because I work for COCOBOD that I am
saying that ours is of the top quality. The fact is that the market is
saying that cocoa from Ghana is of top quality. That is why they are
paying us a higher premium. Quality is market-determined; what
you do will be reflected in the market-place. That is why whenever
we see any difficulties with quality we move in very quickly. For
example, when there is talk of purple beans, which is a problem with
fermentation, we move in quickly to re-educate the farmers. Now,
the incidence of purple beans has reduced tremendously in our country.

In terms of competition, we used to be the number one supplier of
cocoa beans to the world market. That was a long time ago. I think
about twenty years ago Côte d'Ivoire took over as number one. Côte
d'Ivoire produces about twice the quantity that we produce, but their
revenue from cocoa certainly is not twice. First, the quality aspect is
very clear. Secondly, our marketing strategies are very effective. We
sometimes sell in the futures, we play the market. In other countries,
they may not have the capacity to do so, because they do not have an
institution which has the strength that Cocoa Marketing Company or
Ghana Cocoa Board has. So we are able to compete and stand on our
own. And I have no doubt that we will produce one million tonnes,
because we are marketing our cocoa not just as cocoa beans, but as
Ghana cocoa beans. We will have a place in the market mainly because
of our quality.

**IA-D: The World Bank and the other multilateral institutions certainly
must be interested in the commodity for what it does to the country.
What is the relationship between COCOBOD and the World Bank for
instance?**

IO: Well our relationship with these multilateral institutions has to be
a relationship through our sector ministry – that is, the Ministry of
Finance. Many multilateral institutions – the EU and the Japanese
government, for example – have been assisting COCOBOD in its
work. The EU, for example, under its STABEX, assisted us by ensuring
that when swollen shoot struck in many parts of the country,
replanting grants were available. But that programme has been phased

out and Ghana Cocoa Board has taken on the responsibility of ensuring that we continue with the programme. We have a programme with the Japanese government whereby the Japanese government has kindly provided resources, and we are in the process of establishing a centre within the Quality Control Division which will enable us to test for chemical residues and issue certificates of analysis before export. Ghana will be the first country to do this, and we are in the process of achieving this with support from our Japanese friends.

The World Bank has also been supportive in various ways, but you will understand that it was the World Bank which supported the then-government to rationalise the cocoa industry as it were. The only part which was retained of course was the marketing. And I think it makes sense to retain the marketing as we have it today, because we are playing a market where there are very few operators. You have three or four big processors, and you have four or five major traders. You cannot open it up and allow the Ghana cocoa farmer to compete: the traders will buy the cocoa at any price, and we cannot afford that in our country. What we want to do is to enhance the value of the bean to the farmer. This is precisely what we are trying to do.

IA-D: There were complaints, not specifically against Ghana, from consumers in European countries about child labour on cocoa farms and other plantations. Did this in any way affect our production or how people look at our industry?

IO: No, it has not really affected us because in Ghana child labour on cocoa farms is not prevalent. We look at cocoa as an investment, and if cocoa is an investment we have a responsibility to pass it on to succeeding generations. So when a farmer takes his child to the cocoa farm, it does not mean that that child is going to do all the work which older people would do. Child labour does not mean that child work is not permitted; child labour means you do not involve children in hazardous work and deny them the opportunity for normal development. But the government of Ghana itself has provided the policy framework which makes it difficult for children to work. One, it is illegal not to send a child under sixteen to school. Through the implementation of the policy and as a result of the Capitation Grant which has been offered by the present New Patriotic Party (NPP) government, children can go to school tuition-free.

Let me say that COCOBOD does not accept that a single child in our country should be working on farms and not going to school. We do not accept that a child should be trafficked from another area of Ghana to work on somebody's farm, whether the person is paid or not paid. We do not accept that. And this is why we are sensitising the farmers about the dangers of engaging children in this sort of difficult activity. I think also that because we in Ghana have small farms and not the huge plantations that you may find elsewhere, the requirements for labour are rather limited. Therefore the need to employ people to assist on farms is very limited. We will be welcoming very soon Senator Harkin from the United States. The Harkin-Engel protocol, which industry has ascribed to, is what laid out this issue about child labour on some cocoa farms. We are confident that the system that we have put in place will, even where it exists, eliminate it.

IA-D: You have worked in the Private Sector – initially you started with the Public Sector, then you went to the Private Sector, became High Commissioner to London, and you are now serving in a very sensitive position as CEO of Ghana Cocoa Board. This government, I mean the NPP government, has been talking of Private Sector-Public Sector partnership for economic growth. Do you see this happening? Are there any indicators that this has worked at a level that is commensurate with what the government talked about when it came to power?

IO: The government has done very well, first in providing the environment in which the Private Sector can actually operate and grow. The whole regime for doing work in this country has been tremendously enhanced under the NPP government. There is absolutely no doubt about it. And I am not just talking simply about the macroeconomic framework, although that is important. When I was running Intravenous Infusions Limited in Koforidua (in the Eastern Region of Ghana) before I was appointed High Commissioner, I borrowed at 52 per cent. And not only that, inflation was 42 per cent at that time, which meant that we could not plan. It was all on an *ad hoc* basis. Today, inflation has been lowered tremendously and interest rates are in the lower twenties, and for some firms even they can get a little lower than that.

What is important is that, if the policy framework is moving in the right direction, then business operators can plan. Take the question of exchange rates. Exchange rate stability is fundamental for any business, whether it is a public sector business or it is a private business. And all of us are witnesses to the stabilisation of our Cedi over the last few years. So the policy framework has enabled us to have a more efficient environment in which Private Sector operators can do their work. But this is also true for the Public Sector. When you have stability of economic conditions, coupled with stability of political conditions, then the various economic operators within the economy can plan, work and make money. That is what it is all about: making money, either for the Public Sector or as a private individual.

I also believe that, for people who go into Public Service, if they really want to get to the top they have to deal with the Private Sector, because the Private Sector has to assume the commanding heights of our economy in order for our economy to grow. That is the only way. The government or the Public Sector itself can't do it. The duty of government is not to do business; government's duty is to provide the environment for the people who understand and know business to do business.

IA-D: Would you say that for the first time in Ghana's history we have seen a liberal democratic government at work, in terms of policy, in terms of implementation, in terms of allowing people to own property? Property-owning democracy – is it at work in Ghana?

IO: Well one thing is very clear. Every Ghanaian wants to own something. If you are a fisherman, or you are with a fishing cooperative, what you want to do is to be able to own your own canoe. When the NPP government talks about property owning, it does not mean just houses, but owning your own property, owning anything which you can use to do your work. If I am a farmer, I do not have to go and borrow or have socially-provided cutlasses. I have my own cutlasses and I have my own tools of trade to work. I own my farm; it is not owned by all of us. Ghanaians like to say, "This, I have worked for it, and this is mine." And that is what property-owning democracy is about. I agree with Abraham Lincoln when he says, "Property is the fruit of Labour".

It is also about ensuring that everybody has a chance. And, for me, when you talk about Liberal Democracy, I see Liberal Democracy as being exemplified not only in Private Sector development, but also in the multi-party democracy that we have today, where people have a choice. Even within parties, I know some have lately noticed the importance of also conducting elections in order to choose their leaders. But this has been the tradition of the NPP government. Since the days of Dr J. B. Danquah and others, the NPP's tradition has always been to elect leaders through the process of elections. We do not confer leadership on people; people must present themselves and be elected. I think that is good for the country. And you not only do it at the party level, but you do it at the national level, so that President Kufuor, whom everybody knows has been in this game of politics for a long time, even within the NPP had to go for elections and to win those elections; we did not just confer leadership on him. And in the country he had to fight national elections, he lost and then won. That is the essence of democracy.

Not only that: this is the first President who has also said that if he falls foul of the law, he will subject himself to it. I don't know in the history of our country where a President has appeared before or has written in response to questions laid before him, as President Kufuor has done with the recent case involving his son's hotel business and so on, responding to the Commission on Human Rights and Administrative Justice (CHRAJ). I think he sets an example for us to follow. So the rule of law is critical. Development of the Private Sector is also important, as is multi-party democracy. Everybody must have a chance to advance himself, to acquire property, and not fear that somebody is going to take it from him. I think this *magye-magye* (envy) politics is all over. We are now ushering ourselves in a new era. And I certainly would not have joined government if I didn't know that this NPP party was founded on the best political traditions of liberal democracy.

IA-D: How do you see the future of Ghana in the coming years, that is, twenty years from now?

IO: Twenty years from now, I would hope that a party like the NPP would retain power. The longer you retain power, the better opportunity you have for advancing these values that I am espousing. So I am looking forward to us having Liberal Democracy deepened in Ghana. I am looking forward to Ghanaian enterprises expanding:

growing new businesses, expanding existing businesses, making this country and its people rich. We need wealthy individuals in this country who can grow the country, and bring up others who may not have the capacity. What we need to do is to all grow together, not have a small section of the community wealthy and then the broad masses of the people poor. But to everybody his due: your hard work will determine where you will be in the future. The future is bright. It's looking good for Ghana.

IA-D: Thank you.

October 2007

Dr Charles Wereko-Brobby

Dr Charles Wereko-Brobby is an Energy Specialist whose principal research interests include Climate Change and Sustainable Development. Now retired from active work, Dr Wereko-Brobby intends to use his expertise to ensure that Ghana manages its energy prudently, particularly after the recent discovery of oil, and to encourage African governments more generally to be more assertive in their demands for development and self-dependence.

After a long and prolific career, Dr Wereko-Brobby most recently served as the Chief Executive of the Ghana at 50 Secretariat, responsible for commemorating independent Ghana's Golden Jubilee in 2007. Ghana at 50 projects included the construction of the African Union Village, where Heads of State stayed during the Anniversary celebrations and at the subsequent African Union summit in Accra, and the Greening Ghana initiative, as part of which 6.7 million new seedlings were distributed to provide new natural resources and to combat global warming.

Prior to his appointment as head of Ghana at 50, Dr Wereko-Brobby held a variety of important positions within the Energy Sector. His career began in the UK, where he worked first as a consultant, then as a Research Fellow at the Imperial College School of Management Science, and as the Energy and Environmental Planning Programme Chief at the Commonwealth Science Council in London. He returned to Ghana in 1988, where he served the dual role of Energy Policy Advisor to the PNDC government and Executive Director of the National Energy Board, until 1993. Concurrently, and since 1987, Dr Wereko-Brobby worked as a Private Consultant for such institutions as the United Nations and the World Bank. Before Ghana at 50, Dr Wereko-Brobby was Chief Executive of the Volta River Authority (VRA), a position he assumed in 2001 after a brief stint as Chairman.

Turning to politics officially in 1992, Dr Wereko-Brobby formed his own political party, the United Ghana Movement (UGM), in 1996. He mounted a Presidential campaign for the 2000 elections, but was unsuccessful in his bid to succeed the ultimate victor, the incumbent President J. A. Kufuor. In 1994, he founded the first private radio station in Ghana, Radio Eye, to break the state monopoly of the airwaves.

Dr Wereko-Brobby attended primary and secondary school in Ghana, before completing his education in the United Kingdom. He received a BSc in Fuel and Combustion Engineering and a PhD in Solar Engineering from the University of Leeds, where he was elected President of the Students' Union in 1978. He also has an MBA from the University of Middlesex, UK.

Ivor Agyeman-Duah: Dr Wereko-Brobby, energy has been very important in the economic development of Ghana. What have we had in terms of structures in the postcolonial economy; that is from 1957?

Dr Charles Wereko-Brobby: I think the most important development, which really started just before independence, was the construction of the Akosombo Hydroelectric Dam. The basis for that was that it should provide the energy to industrialise Ghana. Our first leader recognised, and it had been recognised all over, that the basis of any development in any society was the use of very important, efficient energy sources such as electricity and petroleum products. In that sense, Akosombo was to provide a platform, and even though it was recognised from the word "go" that the dam was far too large for the pace of industrialisation, it was always going to be there to ensure that over the first 30 or 40 years we would have enough energy.

IA-D: What did it do in terms of the early industrialisation that characterised the Nkrumah regime?

CW-B: There were several attempts to produce value-added goods through manufacture of various products, primarily from agro-based products, but of course one of the key things which was lacking was not energy but the fact that we were not operating at the sort of economies of scale that would make our industrial processes competitive internationally. Unfortunately, much of the early industrialisation was focused on what was called Import Substitution, which was just producing locally what we would have normally imported. We should have looked beyond the local production and used it as a platform to produce for the wider market. So energy wasn't the problem, but rather industrial strategy was the problem.

IA-D: So without the Akosombo Dam, do you think the early industrialisation plan that Nkrumah set out to do would have taken place at all?

CW-B: It would have if it was based on a real assessment of what industry required rather than simply trying to do for ourselves what we normally import. It would have worked. As I said, energy was not a very major constraint in the early years of our independence. Unfortunately, later on as we tried to get the strategy right, it became a major constraint.

IA-D: Fifty years after our independence, what is the significance of the Akosombo Dam in terms of our industrialisation? I am sure things have changed.

CW-B: Unfortunately, it has made very little impact on our industrialisation. You will remember that Akosombo came in the early years, and much of it was used for the aluminium refining plants at Tema, VALCO. As time has gone on, the electricity from Akosombo has not gone to feed Industry; it has actually now gone to feed very basic needs of the people, to the extent that now I believe that the amount of electricity used for industrial production in Ghana is a very small and insignificant proportion of what we produce here. Don't forget also that Akosombo now does not even produce enough electricity to meet the country's needs; we are now supplementing with thermal power. Regrettably, very little of this major increase in the use of energy is contributing to our industrialisation in Ghana.

IA-D: When you returned from abroad, what was the situation, and what were you supposed to do?

CW-B: Well, we met a situation where the country had just been through a major crisis in 1983 and it was realised at the time that we needed in a sense to supplement the power from Akosombo with thermal generation, so we began the development of a number of power plants which would add new power generation to our requirements. Unfortunately, the problem I met then, which has continued for many years, and which has been the cause of subsequent power crises, was that the gap between planning and actual delivery and implementation has been so large that far more often than not we get caught up in situations where we delay so long in implementation that the demands increase and we run into a crisis again.

IA-D: What is the role of the VRA – that is, the Volta River Authority?

CW-B: The Volta River Authority was set up at the time of Akosombo's construction to be the main generator and transmitter of power in this country through the hydroelectric dam. Subsequently it assumed the first part of thermal generation, so for the moment, with the exception of very small projects involving a joint venture with a foreign partner, the VRA remains the sole generator and transmitter of power in this country. That is set to change with the introduction of independent power producers.

IA-D: What is the relationship between the VRA and the Energy Commission?

CW-B: Well the Energy Commission is the successor to what used to be called the National Energy Board, which has two functions. When it was decided we needed a more structured planning of our Energy sector to ensure that we did not enter into any more crises, the National Energy Board was set up around 1984-5. It was firstly to advise government on what should be the appropriate policies. It was also to then assist the Ministry and government to monitor the policies as they were being implemented by the various energy-producing and delivery services. The Board was subsequently dissolved and replaced by the Energy Commission, which has fairly similar functions and also regulates Industry, so the Commission is supposed to be the body that essentially collates policies which are appropriate to the sustainable development of energy sources, and then assist government in a sense to shape the policies according to the government's own industrialisation or other socio-economic goals. It also then ensures that government is assisted in monitoring those things, and regulates the operators in the industry.

IA-D: Is there duplication between the Energy Commission and the Ministry of Energy?

CW-B: Absolutely not. The Ministry, as in any government, is the beholder of government policy and is the one that ensures that government policy is implemented by the agencies. The Commission is supposed to provide technical support to the Ministry, and to regulate the operators in the industry, so it is really meant in a sense to be the repository of technical knowledge that the Ministry relies on to ensure that government policy is implemented.

IA-D: When you were Energy Advisor to the government, what were some of the processes that led to policy formulation?

CW-B: You know my role as Policy Advisor was pretty much in what you might call a non-multi-party democratic sense. We were in a military regime, therefore the structure of government was quite different, but I had the dual role as Policy Advisor and also at the time Head of the National Energy Board. It was very much integrated into the work of the Ministry. Our work was first of all to coordinate the first coherent Energy Policy framework for Ghana, which we called Energy and Ghana's Socio-Economic Development. It looked at how we were going to move from a situation of energy deficiency to one of surplus and relate that to what the key socio-economic objectives of government were.

In terms of power generation, we looked at what we were going to do to add thermal complementation to the Akosombo Dam, we looked at how we were going to increase the use of petroleum products in the country, and we also looked to ensure that sources like electricity and petroleum were widely available, because if you go back to what I was saying about part of the problem associated with the Industrialisation strategy of the first President, you will realise that many of the areas of our country which have the raw materials needed to produce value-added industrial products were not served with energy or electricity or reliable petroleum resources. Therefore, if you were going to set up factories that would turn basic agricultural produce into value-added end products and there was no electricity or reliable supply of petroleum products, or reliable roads to ensure transportation, or even reliable electricity to give good telecommunications, etc., then it wasn't going to work.

One of the things we focused on essentially at the time was to establish what we called the National Electrification Programme, which aimed over a thirty-year period to extend electricity to every community in the country which had a population of 500 or more, but we tied this to the decentralisation policy. Everybody realised that there was an over-concentration of administrative power in the centre, but then we realised that if we were going to decentralise and the heart of the decentralised government structure was not served by adequate infrastructure, then you were not going to make much progress. So we established the National Electrification Programme, the first focus of which was to ensure that every district capital in the country was given electricity within a period of about four or five years. With electricity you could have proper water, you could establish proper communications, you could establish proper Health Care facilities, etc. I am pleased to say that by and large that was achieved. The second part of the electrification programme was then to extend it through the Self-Help Electrification Programme to ensure that all communities got served. We were all very worried about the drift to Accra, the population intensity, but at the end of the day we could only really encourage a decentralised governance structure if within every community there were basic infrastructure utility services. That really was the core of that Energy Policy.

We coupled that with building of strategic and storage depots for all petroleum products around the country so that now we have depots in every region of the country, we have pipelines that carry petroleum products from Accra to Akosombo, we use the lake to carry products to the North, pipelines are just being built to go from the North to the border – again, so that every region of the country would be well served with the provision of products. We were a little bit ahead of ourselves in looking at, for example, global warming, etc. We used to extract a lot of LP gas from the refinery and we thought that one way in which we could improve energy use and energy efficiency and be sensitive to the environment was to switch much of the cooking here from firewood and charcoal to LP gas. It has been extremely successful and I believe that it continues to be quite successful.

The elements of Ghana's formalised energy policy and plan were laid out in around 1989-92 and I think not much has changed. The challenges have been how to implement and sustain the implementation.

IA-D: So what is being done now? Do you think that there is continuity of policy?

CW-B: I believe that, by and large, not a lot has changed. Not even the changes in government and the return to democratic rule have changed the essential building blocks. The major problem has been implementation. You see, you are dealing with basic utilities, and there are certain things that go together. If you say that you want to give people basic utilities – electricity and fuel – and yet there is a problem of affording the service, that is a major problem and it has been one of the biggest of our time. Fortunately we have managed, by and large, that of petroleum so that now it is totally accepted in this country that when oil prices go up, our petroleum products go up, and when oil prices come down the same would happen with petroleum products. By and large, after some time, I believe we have effectively achieved liberalisation, and it is having a major impact – apart from the negative impact of too many vehicles on the road. Clearly, we don't have a problem with constraints in the supply of petroleum. If you remember in the late 1980s when people used to queue for petrol, we haven't had that for the last eight to ten years. By and large we've got that right.

Electricity continues to be a major challenge but we also need to get that right. I think that is possible if people use electricity efficiently and avoid waste. I have been on record and I want to remain on record as saying: electricity, even though it appears very expensive, for the basic person who wants basic use of electricity, it is far cheaper than buying oneself a candle, or even using the lamps. It is cheaper, it is cleaner, it is better. People need to get used to waste management and to pay a proper price. At the moment the country really hasn't got the kind of money to invest in new generation. We need to encourage independent, private power producers to come in and deliver the power, and they will only come in if they know that they will make a profit from what they are going to invest in. But they will only make a profit if we charge the right price for the electricity they produce. Significantly, bringing in independent producers to compete would in my view even reduce the cost of producing that power. Now that is the challenge: coming to terms with producing electricity in an environment in which we accept that the cost of production must be fully recovered to ensure sustained production.

IA-D: Independent producers like...?

CW-B: "Independent producer" means anybody who wants to do it. There is a lot going on right now. There are about four or five major international producers who are building power plants that are going to run on gas and light crude oil. Two of them have already signed power purchase agreements with the Electricity Company of Ghana. That means that the Electricity Company of Ghana does not have to rely on VRA for power; it can buy power from these people directly, and they are offering very competitive prices. These prices are, in my view, probably better than what VRA can offer them for the same type of energy. I don't want to mention names here, but it is happening already and the thing is to sustain it.

Unfortunately for us, the amount of power use in Ghana is very tiny. If we want to achieve middle income status in ten or even twenty years, we have to increase energy use by at least twenty-fold. Much of that is going to come from the Private Sector, so that government can utilise natural resources to provide the basic needs of the people – Health, Education, etc. So as the demand for Energy grows in this country, the structure of production will see a reducing role for government and a move towards what we might call a market production system, which of course will make the work of PURC, the Public Utilities Regulatory Commission, more important because they have to regulate those producers to ensure that they get a good deal, but more importantly, that consumers in Ghana also get a good deal out of it. So government's role, through bodies like PURC, will increasingly be one of regulation. VRA will become less important. There's the Bui Authority, which is quite separate, and in my view, as events unroll, we should inject more efficient management into even the publicly-owned utilities by floating shares on the Ghanaian stock market and employing world-class management to take over those things.

IA-D: There is the Bui Dam that is being constructed. What are your views?

CW-B: Well I think that any addition to our power supply systems is welcome. My speciality is in solar energy and I hardly promote solar energy because what every consumer is looking for is the most reliable power at the cheapest possible cost. Already we are getting a lot of complaints from consumers about the cost of energy, so we must be very careful that we do not introduce into our power mix any source that is very expensive, but we need to look at the numbers.

The main advantage of Bui as it comes into our energy mix is that the whole world, as you know, is consumed by global warming, climate change and its effects, and the more we continue to inject thermal power, clearly we are not going to help global warming because we are going to inject more carbon dioxide into the environment. From the perspective of having fewer carbon sources of energy, Bui and sources such as solar and wind are very much welcome, but they need to be looked at in the context of better sources for generating power as an aid to reducing carbon emissions globally. Therefore it may well be that, even if the nominal cost of power generation from non-carbon sources is quite high, it may be important for support to be given to these sources as an alternative to having to clean up the environment or reduce carbon emissions. So from the point of view of looking for an acceptable carbon-friendly energy source, it is a major development for us and we should continue to explore what I call "the mix" – the mix of various energy sources.

Having said that, even with climate change and all the problems, carbon-based energy technologies such as coal, oil-fired, and gas are going to play a very important role in the world in the future. We need to address some of the basic environmental problems that will come, because you're going to flood up whole habitats, you're going to lose huge reservoirs of fairly important ecosystems, flora and fauna. We need to look at all those things and make sure we address them well, but in terms of adding a much-needed, carbon-friendly addition to our power generation, it is a major thing. But what people need to understand is that we should always look at these things in a time-frame. Right now, we are energy-constrained, so in the next three to four years, Bui is not a solution. Bui will come in maybe five or six or seven years' time, so for the moment we need to inject a lot of thermal-powered, hopefully gas-fired power generation plants because those can be built in a year to two years to meet the immediate to short-term needs of the country and look at Bui as adding to the needs let's say five or seven years from now.

IA-D: We have found oil. Some are talking of Dutch disease, others are very hopeful for the future. What will oil do for the economy of Ghana in the coming years?

CW-B: Look, our largest neighbour in the West Africa region is Nigeria. In terms of per capita income, we are richer than Nigeria. The way I see the oil is that it is essentially a source of additional foreign exchange revenue and additional revenue to the country. Don't forget it's like mining gold: much of the actual receipts are going to go to the companies that are coming to dig for the oil. We will get royalties and taxes and a few things, so it is a very useful source of additional revenue for the country. It is also going to be a very useful source of foreign exchange, but the most important thing is not having the oil, but what we do with the additional revenue that accrues to us. Are we going to use it to improve the pace of our socio-economic development, to offer better facilities to our people? The example of many of our neighbouring countries who are oil-rich has been that a very few in the country have gained an enormous benefit, but a substantial, overwhelming majority have remained poor, so let's not see oil as some panacea to all our problems. It preserves many opportunities, but whether we will realise those opportunities will depend on the kind of policies that will be pushed by government to utilise the resources and the revenues.

IA-D: What will be the outcome of this in relation to the West African gas pipeline?

CW-B: The West African gas pipeline is producing and giving us gas from the Nigerian oil fields. Every oilfield comes with some gas, so if the gas that is associated with what we have found in Ghana is in commercially-producible quantities, it will enable us to have our own source of gas to fire power stations that we will increasingly need to put up in the next few years. For a direct benefit to us, if the gas that comes from those oilfields is in commercially viable quantities, then I suggest we should take hold of that gas and use it here to add to the power generation. With the West African gas pipeline, we should be very careful. My recent assessment suggests that, even with the pipeline, the amount of gas coming from Nigeria is not going to be enough to meet even our short- to medium-term needs for the power generation systems that are being put up in the country at the moment. Unless Nigeria is willing to provide more gas, or we are prepared to build another pipeline from there to send more gas, a fairly major constraint is going to come from that project fairly soon. The opportunity there for us is that if we get gas in commercial quantities from our own fields, then we can use that to facilitate the generation of new power systems.

IA-D: What will happen to our economy over the next two decades from the perspective of the energy sector?

CW-B: I think we have tremendous opportunities. If we really want our economy to take off, we will need to produce and sustain energy production ten- to twenty-fold in the next ten to twenty years. Now, a lot of people will want to come and establish value-added industries in this country. Ghana has got some advantages within the sub-region as a major place for very stable economic development, peace, stability, stable government – an environment that is welcoming to investors. But I can tell you, if all of that is here and an investor walks in here and sees an economy which every two or three years is faced by an energy supply constraint, they are not going to bring their money here.

We need to be bold to encourage people to invest in energy development, to assure them that their investment will yield good returns, to assure users here that they can come and get energy at a competitive international cost, and, more importantly, that it is going to be there for the duration of their investment. For example, Newmont came in here. Their start-up was delayed by about six to nine months because of power supply problems. I am aware of people who are interested in establishing major industrial production facilities here for steel mills, etc., but they have not been able to consummate their investment because of their uncertainty of the power system. It is therefore absolutely crucial to the socio-economic development of this country that we make power available on a sustainable, ample, and reliable basis. I would encourage this by encouraging investors, especially in the power sector, to bring their investment here.

IA-D: Thank you very much.

CW-B: Thank you.

December 2007

Dr Ellen Bortei-Doku Aryeetey

Dr Ellen Bortei-Doku Aryeetey is a Senior Research Fellow at the Institute for Statistical, Social, and Economic Research (ISSER) and the acting Head of the Centre for Social Policy Studies at the University of Ghana, Legon. In these roles, she undertakes Social Policy Research and also teaches courses in Social Development for the ISSER Masters Degree in Development Studies.

With the exception of two years in Malawi working on an agricultural project, Dr Aryeetey has spent her entire professional career at the University of Ghana. It is a campus she knows well, her father having been a Professor there. Her research focuses primarily on the changing interests and practices in Rural Production Systems; the relationship between Gender and Development, particularly the empowerment of women at work and in the community and the institutionalisation of Women's Rights; and the broad Social Development Agenda, encompassing Education, Health, and the family. In this vein, Dr Aryeetey has just concluded a study on the effects of Capitation Grants on basic schools in Ghana.

Dr Aryeetey has a number of publications to her credit, including: "Legal and Institutional Issues in Land Policy Reform in Ghana" (with N. A. Kotey, N. Amponsah, and K. Bentsi-Enchill), ISSER Technical Publication No. 74 (2007); "Coming to Terms with Sexual Harassment in Ghana", ISSER Technical Publication No. 64 (2004); and "Behind the Norms: Women's Access to Land in Ghana", in Toumlin, C. P. Lavigne Delville, S. Troare, eds. *The Dynamics of Resource Tenure in West Africa* (2002). She has also undertaken a variety of consultancy assignments for such institutions as the Government of Ghana, the Department for International Development (DfID) in the UK, the International Labour Organisation (ILO), and the United Nations Development Programme (UNDP), and The World

Bank. Most recently, she was a member of the team that produced the 2007 UNDP Ghana Human Development Report, and served as Team Leader of the Livelihood Empowerment Against Poverty (LEAP) Implementation Design commissioned by the Ministry of Manpower, Youth, and Employment.

Dr Aryeetey's study of Sociology began at the Kwame Nkrumah University of Science and Technology, where she earned her BA in 1975. She subsequently received a Masters degree in Social Development from the University of Reading in the UK, and a PhD in Sociology from Michigan State University in the United States. She is married with two children.

Ivor Agyeman-Duah: Economic policies have the objective of improving the social conditions of people. Would you say that the formulation and implementation of these policies in the postcolonial era has been helpful?

Dr Ellen Bortei-Doku Aryeetey: I think that since independence we have had a mixed bag in terms of provision of basic Social Services for the ordinary Ghanaian, very much linked to the fortunes of the economy of the country. In the early part of the post-independence era, there was a lot of enthusiasm and attention given to providing universal basic services for Ghanaians, but by the 1970s, as the economy took a downturn, obviously investments in these areas also declined. Gradually, Ghanaians lost that basic access to core services in Education, Health, and even subsidised Transportation. It has been a bit of a mixed bag.

IA-D: What is the state of Social Policy formulation in Ghana today, in terms of the people involved?

EB-DA: Obviously, the lead player is still the government, particularly for providing infrastructure in the Social Services, and also, based on its constitutional mandate; it remains the lead player in driving the Social Development agenda. We as a country have never quite formulated a Social Policy. We have had a series of policies that have implications for the Social Sector, but we cannot say that we have a Ghanaian Social Policy as such. We have had activities that provide Social Services for the people.

IA-D: Should we have a formal Social Policy? Is it necessary?

EB-DA: Many people, myself included, are of the opinion that we need to have a more direct Social Policy statement. Considering that the social arena is a very wide stage for development activity, it is not very easy to talk about *a* Social Policy, but there have to be Social Policy indications which, taken together, will then give a more concrete direction to policy-makers, development practitioners, and also to ordinary citizens on what our Social Policy is. We need something like that.

IA-D: When we talk about strategies or even Social Policy in a broader framework, what are we talking about?

EB-DA: Talking about strategies in Ghana, we have adopted a strategy now that is more pro-poor than perhaps we had in the 1990s for example. I say "pro-poor" because the intention is to provide services that are accessible to the poor. At the same time, this is underlain by a philosophy of, to some extent, cost recovery in some of the Social Services that we provide. Again, it is a bit of a mixed agenda, but I think increasingly if you look at what development partners and NGOs – who are also major players – are urging us to achieve, it is becoming a rights-based, pro-poor agenda that we are pursuing in the social arena.

IA-D: Have non-governmental organisations been effective in this area?

EB-DA: Very much so. They have contributed immensely in shaping what today we are calling a rights-based, pro-poor agenda in Ghana by the way they have approached Social Development, and the kind of advocacy work that they have done to encourage government and others to adopt a rights-based approach. In my view, yes, NGOs have played a critical role.

IA-D: How has this affected women and development in agriculture and associated areas?

EB-DA: Women have been major beneficiaries of the shift from what we had originally in the 1990s with the Structural Adjustment Programme.

It was originally a fairly strong, neo-liberal trend in our economic policy direction. Our approach now is still liberal, but interfaced with strong Social Democratic principles, and I think women have been major beneficiaries here. NGOs, for example, have championed the Women's Cause, drawing attention to women's lack of productive assets, such as credit especially, and their lack of control over labour. They have made inputs in these areas which have helped increase women's access to key productive assets, but there are still strong social and cultural beliefs and practices which tend to constrain the access of women, particularly rural poor women. Here you have to look at women not in a homogeneous manner, because women come in all shapes and sizes; women belong to all different categories of economic well-being. We are looking particularly at the rural poor women whose access and ability to improve their livelihoods still leaves a lot of room for improvement.

IA-D: Compare the status of women in the immediate post-independence era to this period. Would you say that there has been any improvement, if so, in which areas?

EB-DA: It is difficult to answer that question because we have a sort of schizophrenic situation where in formal legislation, and based on our Constitution, really there are very few restrictions on what women can do, what they can achieve, where they can go. On the other hand, culturally we still have a very strong male-biased decision-making process and leadership structure, which therefore tend to put a lid on how far women can go: the glass ceiling effect. Yes, women can stand for any political office, but putting a woman up to campaign, to run for office, is subject to the sentiments of the people. The people are still largely influenced by social-cultural constraints on women's involvement in public life.

IA-D: But at least for the first time we have a chief justice who is a woman, we have people like you in sensitive positions...

EB-DA: We do not want token representation as women, and I think you know that. We are looking for a more open environment in which women can run for office as MPs and expect that, if they are good candidates, they should be elected. The electorate should not be influenced by their gender, which is the situation we have at present.

IA-D: So what kind of social engineering is required to change the minds of a critical mass?

EB-DA: We have to go back to basics. A lot of it starts from the home, from the way we socialise our daughters and sons into believing in themselves. It depends on community socialisation also, as well as at the workplace, with acceptance of women in leadership positions. A lot of that has happened. As you said, we can look across Ghana and find women in all manner of positions, but there is still that cultural handicap that we have to overcome.

IA-D: According to your research, what has been the trend regarding the access of women and children to Health and Education services?

EB-DA: There have been constraints in terms of access to Health and Education for women and children, but I do not think this should be looked at in isolation. We are talking about ordinary poor Ghanaians and their access to Health and Education. Yes I acknowledge that women have faced more constraints; young girls have faced more constraints accessing school and completing school compared to boys, but I prefer to look at it across the sexes. We have a situation that ought to be looked at in terms of boys and girls in education, because our numbers are not quite where they ought to be with respect to access and completion for both boys and girls. I would prefer to say that we still have a long way to go to achieve universal access and completion for both sexes. Girls' situation has improved compared to the past, but there is still a long way to go.

IA-D: What has been the role of the Department of Social Welfare in all of this, especially in matters relating to women and children?

EB-DA: The Department of Social Welfare has a huge mandate and a very small purse to go with it. This has been the case over the years, and in fact it has finally caught the attention of government and of donors. We talked about the strategy for improving social development in Ghana, and I think I should have indicated that a major step has been taken in the last year or so with the formulation of the National Social Protection Strategy. This is being championed by the Ministry for Manpower, Youth, and Employment. It is intended to directly target extremely poor households in Ghana. It is anticipated that the major beneficiaries will be women and children, so steps are being taken. In fact, in a couple of months you will hear about the launch of an initiative known as Livelihood Empowerment Against Poverty, or LEAP for short. It is intended to provide some kind of support to these very poor households, identifying in particular women as caregivers of households. The conditions would be that, for beneficiaries, children have to go to school and the family has to be registered with a National Health Insurance policy. Women and children therefore stand to gain from these new initiatives. You will find similar references in the Ghana Poverty Reduction Strategy (GPRS), which is now the Ghana Growth and Poverty Reduction Strategy. Again, there is a focus on improving the conditions of women and children, as well as vulnerable and excluded groups.

IA-D: What is the role of the Ministry of Women and Children? Are there too many bureaucracies? Do you think there should be some sort of coordination?

EB-DA: It is known as MOWAC – Ministry of Women and Children's Affairs. MOWAC has a coordinating role to play, and therefore has to liaise with all the ministries, departments, and agencies to ensure that appropriate consideration is given to providing resources that will enhance the well-being of women and children. It has a big mandate also, like the Department of Social Welfare.

IA-D: To get back to the Department of Social Welfare, would you say that monetary considerations alone have been responsible for its inefficiency?

EB-DA: Well you are assuming that the Department is inefficient! If you were to see what the Department does, compared to its resources, you would be humbled by their commitment and their perseverance. The Department lacks basic inputs and human capacity. The Department in many parts of this country is manned by one officer. One officer, who is expected to roll out its Community Care programmes, Child Rights and Child Protection programmes, Justice Administration programmes – you can imagine! It is only recently that you will find in some of these places that the Ministry of Manpower has posted young people from the Youth Employment Programme to assist these Social Development Officers in their work at the district level.

The Department often lacks adequate office space. I have been to places where the Department is housed in one room with the most archaic facilities you can imagine. Invariably they have no means of transport, but 90 per cent of their work is field-based. They have to depend on taxis and *tro-tros* to do field visits – it is not easy at all. They could be more efficient, but I hesitate to put their inefficiency, as you put it, down to lack of commitment. I think there is a lot of capacity deficiency that has to be addressed. I am happy to say that the National Social Protection Strategy regards this institutional development of the Department of Social Welfare as one of its major activities.

IA-D: Have these problems always existed?

EB-DA: It has gotten worse as the population has grown. It has gotten worse as the Department has failed to attract the necessary resources from the Budget. These are some of the reasons.

IA-D: What have been some of your research findings that could help the government develop better social policies?

EB-DA: Well, basically it is clear from available research that to have successful social development and to have a successful policy-making capacity, you have got to invest. You have got to invest in training people with the necessary competencies to lead the social policy and social development process. Indeed, at the Institute of Statistical, Social and Economic Research (ISSER) and at the Centre for Social Policy Studies and at other departments on campus, we are increasing our attention to the training of people with this kind of capacity. ISSER has a Masters in Development Studies programme; the Centre for Social Policy Studies is about to launch a Masters programme in Social Policy Studies, so we are taking those kinds of steps to increase capacity.

Our research also indicates quite clearly that there are a lot of practices out there which hinder particularly children from attaining their full potential because of widespread child labour. If you look at the statistics from the Ghana Statistical Service, you will see that quite a sizeable proportion of Ghanaian children between the ages of 10 and

15, and also up to 18, are engaged in forms of labour that retard their progress in education and also impede their health. There is a lot of research material around that shows clearly that we are underachieving in terms of social development because of poverty – it is poverty that drives households to release children into early child labour – and it calls for a more concerted effort, more direct measures, such as the National Social Protection Strategy and the LEAP, to put children in school and ensure their completion. You know that government has also introduced capitation and school feeding programmes, trying to arrest some of the backlash from poverty. The Centre for Social Policy Studies has recently conducted research into the extent to which the Capitation and School Feeding Programmes have encouraged poor households to send their children to school. We are about to disseminate the findings from that study.

IA-D: And what are those findings?

EB-DA: It is clear that, as all the reports have indicated, this has improved enrolment. However, there is still a large issue related to quality, which does not appear to have been touched by the Capitation and School Feeding Programmes. These measures have brought children to the classroom in anticipation of one good meal, which is very good and is something we have to find the resources to continue, but the issue of quality still remains. Access to quality Education, quality Healthcare – these are areas that Capitation and School Feeding alone will not resolve. It calls for other measures, which I think we now have to sit down and seriously discuss.

IA-D: When you put all this together, people are expressing mixed feelings on the social and economic front. What is the future for Ghana?

EB-DA: I think you have said it: we have mixed feelings about the outcomes of all the initiatives that have been taken. Part of the problem comes from the fact that the interventions have been piecemeal. The investments in all the Social Sector areas we have talked about have been sort of fragmented; they have not been coordinated to give you that critical value that you are looking for. I think that with the GPRS II and also with the National Social Protection Strategy, we are gradually moving to a stage where there is a convergence of ideas and intentions. We need to go the next step of establishing a broad Social Policy framework which brings all these initiatives together from the different players we talked about earlier – the government; the development partners, that is the donors; the NGOs; and also ordinary Ghanaians. We have got to get all the intentions, ideals, and values that we place on Social Development together to formulate a strong, clear, coherent Social Policy Framework from which all of these different players will take their cue. Of course, that should leave room for innovation, and this is where support for research is critical and must be considered one of the pillars of the Social Policy environment.

IA-D: So if we do all this we will be happy as a nation?

EB-DA: We will be on the right track. If we talk, but we do not walk the walk, nothing will happen. Let's put our framework in shape, and then let's start implementing activities under the framework. Then we will be making progress.

IA-D: Finally, what is the Health situation in Ghana today?

EB-DA: The Health status of the average Ghanaian has more or less fluctuated over the years, in some areas quite seriously. I would like to make particular mention of Child Health, based on the Ghana Demographic and Health Surveys over the years. One gets the sense that Child Health has fluctuated quite seriously. In fact, there have been reversals between 1998 and 2003 in areas like stunting, wasting, infant mortality – these are quite serious. On the whole, the Health status of the under-five-year-old in Ghana is not good, and this is something that we really ought to pay very special attention to because the status of any nation should be seen through the status of its children. The economy may do well, but if the Health status of children is not good, and there have been reversals, then we have a problem that ought to be addressed.

Then of course Ghana is also like many other African countries battling HIV/AIDS. We have been going up and down in this area. Then we have the malaria "curse" if I may put it that way. There are things we can be doing to control malaria better, besides bed-nets and medication. Environmental Hygiene, Sanitation – somehow we have not been able to get a handle on this. The District Assemblies are struggling with it. I think that for all of these areas, the public campaign that has been launched is good, but obviously does not go far enough because of the HIV/AIDS spread. We thought we were on a decline, but it looks like we are not on a decline after all. These are areas in Health that I think we need to take a very serious look at.

IA-D: Thank you very much.

EB-DA: You are welcome.

January 2008

Professor Jeffrey D. Sachs

Jeffrey D. Sachs is the Director of The Earth Institute, Quetelet Professor of Sustainable Development, and Professor of Health Policy and Management at Columbia University in New York. He is also Special Advisor to the United Nations Secretary-General Ban Ki-Moon, and President and Co-Founder of Millennium Promise Alliance, a non-profit organisation aimed at ending extreme global poverty. Prior to his arrival at Columbia University in June 2002, he spent over 20 years at Harvard University, most recently as Director of the Centre for International Development and Galen L. Stone Professor of International Trade. From 2002-2006, Professor Sachs served as Director of the UN Millennium Project and Special Advisor to UN Secretary-General Kofi Annan on the Millennium Development Goals, the internationally agreed goals to reduce extreme poverty, disease, and hunger by the year 2015.

A celebrated economist, and one of the world's most influential people according to *Time Magazine* (2004, 2005), Professor Sach's current research interests include the links of health and development, economic geography, poverty alleviation, globalisation, international financial markets, international macroeconomic policy coordination, emerging markets, and economic development and growth. He has written more than 200 scholarly articles and a number of books, among them New York Times best sellers *Common Wealth: Economies for a Crowded Planet* (Penguin, 2008) and *The End of Poverty* (Penguin, 2005).

Professor Sachs has worked as an Economic Advisor to governments in Latin America, Eastern Europe, the former Soviet Union, Asia, and Africa, as well as to several international institutions, including numerous UN agencies. From 2002-2005, for example, he directed a comprehensive worldwide study of poverty reduction as Director of the UN Millennium Project. During 2001 and 2002 he was Chairman of the Commission on Macroeconomics and Health at the World Health Organization, and from September 1999 – March 2000, he served as a member of the International Financial Institutional Advisory Commission established by the United States Congress.

Professor Sachs is the recipient of many awards and honours, including membership in the Institute of Medicine, the American Academy of Arts and Sciences, Harvard Society of Fellows, and the Fellows of the World Econometric Society. He was the 2005 recipient of the Sargent Shriver Award for Equal Justice and was awarded the Padma Bhushan, a high civilian honour bestowed by the Indian government, in 2007. He also received the 2007 Cardozo Journal of Conflict Resolution International Advocate for Peace Award. Distinguished lecture series include the London School of Economics, University of Oxford, Tel Aviv, Jakarta, Yale, and the BBC Reith Lectures 2007.

Professor Sachs graduated from Harvard College with a BA in 1976. He also holds an MA (1978) and a PhD (1980), both from Harvard University in the United States.

Ivor Agyeman-Duah: Professor Jeffrey Sachs, Africa's growth rate in the last decade has been consistent and hopeful. What kind of growth are we talking about?

Professor Jeffrey Sachs: The economic growth has risen to 5 or 6 per cent per year, which of course is a major step forward for Africa, but we also have to make sure that the growth means higher living standards for all the population. When growth is based on the mine sector, or hydrocarbons, or a narrow sector of the economy, it doesn't necessarily help everybody. We have to turn this into very high-quality and even faster growth so that it reaches the villagers and the small-grower farmers; makes clinics, schools, roads, and power; and provides the basis for long-term development.

IA-D: How has this affected or helped reduce poverty since we last became interested in Ghana's economy?

JS: Well in Ghana, of course, we've had very strong political leadership, we've had political stability, we've had faster economic growth, and we've had development-oriented investment in health, in education, in infrastructure. There is still a long way to go, of course, but I've seen real improvement, and I think that the broad-based investments that Ghana has been making will serve it for a long time to come.

IA-D: In the last two decades or so a lot of things happened to the Ghanaian economy. What would you say has been fundamentally positive in this economy in the last twenty years, if we should go back that far?

JS: Well for a long time there was a lot of crisis, and a lot of instability in the 1970s and into the 1980s. Then growth started, but slowly then, some stability came back. There were ups and downs of commodity prices. I think the return to democracy and to political stability and to the era of the Millennium Development Goals has been very positive, because that has put a focus on the farm sector, it has put a focus on infrastructure and it has put a focus on schools and on clinics. Under President John Kufuor's leadership, there has been a very broad-based strategy of economic development. Now, if the basics of energy can be resolved, through Ghana's new oil finds, as well as through the West Africa gas pipeline, as well as other investments; if the road system can be consolidated; if agriculture can be strengthened, we should have a lot of confidence.

IA-D: What have been some of the new strategies, if you have been observing, that have stimulated the economy? We've been talking of the School Feeding Programme in Ghana for instance.[11] How far has it helped with economic growth?

---

11 The School Feeding Programme under Ghana's Ministry of Local Government started in 2004. It was a policy which initially evolved out of the Maputo Declaration of African Heads of State in 2003 on how to improve the quality of and access to education in food-insecure regions. By 2007, the Local Government Ministry figures said a total of 987 schools with a pupil population of 447,714 were benefiting from the programme in 138 districts. The Greater Accra region, with 239 schools, has 112,272 beneficiaries; the Ashanti region has 251 schools; Brong-Ahafo, 167; and the two poorest regions, Upper East and Upper West, 18 and 17 schools respectively. The Catholic Relief Services and the World Food Programme run similar programmes in the latter two regions.

JS: The School Feeding Programme is a commitment that every child in school will have a midday meal. It hasn't yet reached everybody, but it is reaching hundreds of thousands of children, and this is a big step forward. The world is looking because Ghana was the first to say, "We will do it for everybody". Everybody is rooting for Ghana's success to achieve the full objectives of this project. I think it is extremely important for a number of reasons: one, it brings the children to school; two, it helps them to learn, because when they are fed they can be more attentive. It helps with long-term physical development of the children, of course, with better nutrition. It also can help the local farm community if the School Feeding Programme is based on purchasing foodstuffs from local villages. It builds a commercial economy locally, and this is how I would like the School Feeding Programme to work – that it is building by buying from small-grower farmers, providing a market for them. Then those farmers can become commercial farmers. They can buy fertiliser and better seeds so that they can have a higher yield, and then the benefit of the School Feeding Programme itself can take place inside the schools.

IA-D: You are also an activist and you have this Millennium Village Project in Ghana. In what ways does it contribute to the growth of the village that it operates from?

JS: We have a village project with Bonsaaso village, near Kumasi. It's a very exciting project for us. Bonsaaso was initially a very poor area. It's a cocoa-growing area near Kumasi. It had no infrastructure – basically no roads, especially during the rains, when it was almost impossible to get there; it had no communications; the healthcare was almost non-existent – many people under-nourished, many people sick from malaria, buruli ulcer, and other conditions; agriculture was at a very low level. So the concept of the Millennium Village Project is to empower the community to take its lead by helping with better food production – by fertiliser, better seeds, and water management; helping with infrastructure – paving the roads, bringing the power in, bringing telephone connectivity with mobile telephony, bringing electricity and computers to the schools and to the clinics; helping with the midday School Feeding Programme; and building more health facilities so that a sick person can reach the clinic and doesn't have to walk ten kilometres.

All of these things are happening in Bonsaaso. We're only two years into the five-year project but we see a lot of progress: higher food production; the road getting completed to link the village with Kumasi; the electricity being brought in as the grid is expanded to the village; School Feeding Programmes in place; clinics being built; malaria being brought under control by helping the villagers to get the anti-malaria bed-nets on a comprehensive basis, and the Artemesinin Combination Therapy, so-called ACT, which is the best medicine to fight malaria. A lot of wonderful things are happening in Bonsaaso and we think that that model can be a base for development in nodes all over the country.

IA-D: Do you think it's an effective way, as you advocate, for non-governmental or governmental – I mean European, American – aid to be channelled to the non-governmental sector in Ghana?

JS: Well the village project is Aid to the village itself, but it works very closely with government so it's not a non-governmental project exactly. It's help at the lowest level of the village, working with the district officials. In general, I would like to see effective government, and I would like to see help so the government can carry out public investments in critical areas: agriculture, health sector, education sector, roads, power, water and sanitation, and cellphone and internet connectivity. If those things can be done, Ghana can just take off. That is the base of the Millennium Village Project, but we would like to see those investments country-wide.

IA-D: You've also worked in Malawi. What models – particularly in agricultural development – do you think are suited to the situation in Ghana, as they have been able to create an indigenous formula?

JS: Malawi did something very interesting. Three years ago they were in the middle of a drought. People were very hungry, and the President was extremely concerned, so President Mutharika said, "Look, we can't go on like this with such hunger. I want a guarantee that every small-grower farmer – every farmer with two hectares or less – should have the fertiliser and improved seed varieties that they need to grow a proper crop." So in 2005, they created voucher tickets. Every household got a voucher ticket and then if you presented the voucher ticket, you got a bag of fertiliser and you got seed. With that simple step, the production doubled the next year in the 2006 harvest. Then they improved the project even further, and the grain was again twice the yield that it had been in earlier years. Now we are into the third harvest season. Again, it's twice the level that it was before this programme started.

So what Malawi has shown is how to double food production, and it didn't take ten years to do! It was from one year to the next, and the key was to get improved inputs – fertiliser; seed; small-scale irrigation, where you can do it – to the small-grower farmers to help them organise in a more commercial way as a farmer cooperative. Get the inputs, store safely the outputs, and be able to market them: that's the model that I would like to see spread everywhere. Of course, we call it the "African Green Revolution", and the time has come for Africa to raise its productivity in food dramatically.

IA-D: In your recent 2007 Reith Lectures, you accused the advanced economies of doing very little in terms of percentage GDP allocation for Africa. In the economy of Ghana, for instance, can't internal strategies be devised to help trigger its own growth?

JS: You know I would love nothing more than to be able to stop asking for Aid because it's no fun. Nobody likes it, neither the giver nor the receiver, and I spend so much of my time complaining. The problem is that when we are dealing with the poorest people, they really need help. My feeling is that we give the Aid, not as a handout, but as an investment, so that it can actually raise production enough so that we can stop giving the Aid. That's the key. I am amazed at the stubbornness of the rich countries because we're not talking about a lot of Aid; we're talking about less than 1 per cent of their income. Believe me, there is enough income in the rich countries to help the poor countries for 0.7 of one per cent – that's all that it is! So I'm going to continue the fight, not because I love Aid – and of course there are many things that need to be done even aside from Aid, and we need private investment and we need self-help – but still the rich countries should be more generous. It is in their own interest and it is not a lot of money we are asking for.

IA-D: Why is it in their own interest?

JS: It is in their own interest to help poor countries because when poor countries are unstable, nobody benefits. Of course the poor suffer the most, but then if it is violence, if it is unrest, if it is radicalism, if it is spreading disease, if it is displaced populations – all of these things become a problem for the whole world. It is terrible to let people suffer anyway, but it is absurd, when at low cost people could be helped; instead of waiting for a massive crisis to explode and then to try and send in the troops. That is what I try to tell my fellow citizens in the United States. We keep going with the military approach, thinking that if you send the Army you can solve a problem in Afghanistan or in Somalia. There's no way that an Army can solve a problem when people are hungry and there's not enough water, so we need to be sending engineers and agronomists and seed and fertiliser and bed-nets. Those are the things that can really stop the conflicts.

IA-D: Final question: you've worked with President Kufuor in other capacities. How differently has he managed the economy since he inherited it, compared to previous administrations, and compared to Africa in general?

JS: President Kufuor is one of Africa's great leaders. He is a great democrat, he is a man of great dignity and consistency and he is somebody that everyone looks up to. When Kenya is in crisis, we turn to President Kufuor to help resolve the crisis, because President Kufuor is someone that people count on to be open, democratic, and very far-sighted. For me, it has been an enormous pleasure to work with President Kufuor. It is not that he has not had his hands full with crises from the day he came in – Energy, Water, Food, Healthcare, Aid promised but not delivered – so it has not been easy. It isn't easy for an African leader and an African democratic leader, but think of how respected he is and how people admire him and can count on his consistent follow-through, and that is a great accomplishment. He has made a great mark and set a very high standard for leadership.

IA-D: So, from what you say, this political situation has had benefits for the economy?

JS: When you operate with this kind of leadership, the economy is bound to develop and you can develop the resources, bring in the foreign investment needed to build the projects. That is how to achieve the long-term development.

IA-D: Thank you very much.

JS: Great, thanks.

May 2008

Ms Joyce Aryee

Ms Joyce Aryee is the current Chief Executive Officer of the Ghana Chamber of Mines, and the first woman to hold such a post in Africa. In this role, she has travelled widely and participated in several mining-related workshops, both locally and internationally, including as Guest Speaker at the International Women and Mining Conference in Australia in November 2001. She was awarded the Order of the Volta of Ghana (OVG) (Companion) by His Excellency the President of the Republic of Ghana in 2006.

Ms Aryee has had an illustrious career, spanning more than thirty-six years of public service. In the political arena, during the 1980s Ms Aryee served as a non-Cabinet minister at the National Commission for Democracy, as well as at various times the Secretary for Information and for Education with Cabinet status. She has also led several government delegations to international conferences, including the Conference of Non-Aligned Ministers of Education, and UNESCO. A Fellow of the Institute of Public Relations, Ms Aryee has worked in this capacity with Ghana's two main Environmental and Standard Regulatory Bodies in the late 1980s and participated in international conferences on behalf of these bodies. She was also the Editor of an educational magazine and Contributing Editor of a leading Ghanaian business publication.

Ms Aryee has a passion for developing African leadership, and focuses particularly on the empowerment of women. To this end, she mentors the Women's Initiative for Self Empowerment and Leadership Development (WEILD) Foundation and serves as Senior Mentor for the African Leadership Initiative. She has also spoken at a number of leadership conferences and seminars, including the third Annual African Business Leaders Forum in South Africa, November 2005.

Ms Aryee holds a BA (Hons) from the University of Ghana, and a Post-Graduate Certificate in Public Administration.

I

Ivor Agyeman-Duah: In what ways would you say that women have most effectively contributed to the economic development of Ghana over the years?

Ms Joyce Aryee: I think over the years, politically and in the area of Commerce, women have done a tremendous job. I still believe that today, if it were not for the women, the areas of Commerce and even political activities would not be as good as they are now. We still haven't *made it* politically, but we do a lot of background work.

IA-D: In which sectors of the economy would you say this is very much felt?

JA: Again, I will go for Commerce, but I need to add Agriculture also because more than 60 per cent of the food we eat is really produced by women, and definitely, even though I am not a statistician, I can say that perhaps 90 per cent of what comes from the rural areas to the cities for consumption – that is, food-wise – is done by women. They travel to the hinterland to buy the food and come and sell it to those of us in the cities. Then they are also the ones engaged in a lot of commercial activity. From little things to big things, it is still dominated by women. You know commerce plays a big role in the economic development of this country.

IA-D: Who are some of the prominent ones that come to mind when we talk of women in economic development?

JA: Well I must admit that some may not even want their names mentioned. Without asking them I wouldn't want to do that, but you know I don't know the market queens, I don't know most of the bakers, and those who move goods around, clothing, textiles, household wares, and so on. I don't know all of them by name, but I think those who do know them by name would be able to tell you that if you enter any of the markets, there will be some very significant people who have made a big difference.

IA-D: Are women being empowered enough in terms of credit facilities in the informal and formal sectors to contribute to development?

JA: No. I would say no. Part of it I don't think is a deliberate decision to discriminate. Part of it is also the way women have been put into groups to be able to access these facilities. Some work is going on but much more can be done. You know, especially outside the cities, a lot of the women are involved in very micro activities, and sometimes they could be overlooked. And yet most of the time, perhaps even 25 or 50 or 250 Ghana cedis (about $200) would go a long way and make a big difference in their lives. Putting them into groups is something that is going on gradually. The Ministry of Women and Children's Affairs and a lot of NGOs are working on that. The Ministry of Fisheries is also pushing that a lot in the Fisheries Sector.

IA-D: You have served in government in a very senior position and you have been all over. How do policies affecting women come up for discussion? What are the mechanisms that help to develop relevant social policies?

JA: Well what was happening really for a long time, and perhaps until recently when President Kufuor's government created a dedicated Ministry for Women, was that decisions were taken in general and then a lot of times maybe the Department of Social Welfare or one of the NGOs would take up the matters critical to women's empowerment and deal with them. Now, the Minister for Women and Children's Affairs is a Cabinet Minister, so she really has been pushing some of these issues. I must admit that, for the past ten years, some of the NGOs have done very well, such as The Ark Foundation, Abantu, and Netright, to mention a few. They have done a lot to really bring women's issues to the fore, and perhaps also the Parliamentary Caucus for women have been quite sensitive to some of these things and have helped.

II

IA-D: What has been the role of the Ghana Chamber of Mines in the economic development of Ghana over the years? You have been around for more than seventy years.

JA: In fact we are going to be eighty years this year, 2008. You know, a lot of the work being done in the sector has not been fully recognised and so a lot of people think that Mining has not contributed much. If you measure Mining purely from the GDP perspective, you may not get much because it is still a fairly small sector even though it generates a lot of money. But if you think of the level of infrastructure that has gone into the mining communities, then you can see that a lot has happened.

You will notice, for example, that a railway link even into the country was largely because of mining, timber and cocoa, and over the past several years, if you take the Western line, it has really been propped up by the bulk minerals of manganese and bauxite. Cocoa these days hardly goes by rail, and as for timber, you can forget it. It is not going by rail anymore, so it is largely these two mining companies that have done that.

When you talk of roads also – I am not even talking about trunk roads, but I am talking about roads into the mining communities – these have been built largely by the mining companies themselves and maintained by them, and it has served to open up some of the communities. A lot of schools are either built or are supported by the mining companies; hospitals are built or supported by the mining companies. You go to Obuasi, really it is the mine hospital that offers more of the facilities. The Bibiani Government Hospital started as a Mining Hospital; the Tarkwa Government Hospital started as a Mining Hospital, and in addition to that you still have other hospitals.

If you go to Amansie West District in the Ashanti Region, when the Resolute Amansie Mining Company was there, it really did a lot of things to help the community to develop. Two major things I would say: one was the introduction of citronella farming into the communities, and then extraction of citronella oil. The company built a pressing facility, which pressed the oil from the dry citronella leaves and created a market for soap-making. Then they also introduced fish farming into the communities. I mean, in largely agricultural areas you will now find major fishermen and fisherwomen in the Amansie area. The mine wanted to use some of their old pits for a fishing lake, but in order to do so they felt they needed to introduce the people to fish farming. They helped them, with the assistance of cooperatives as well as the fisheries department then – it wasn't a ministry – of the Ministry of Agriculture to generate interest, to teach them how to fish, to show them how to smoke fish and so on, and then helped them dig ponds, even as they were preparing some people to work on their larger lake, teaching them how to swim, teaching them how to row boats, teaching them safety methods on the large lake and so on. Now it is a major fishing area, which has added to the economic development of the area.

We are also doing a lot of what we call Sustainable Alternative Livelihood Projects. Even though people feel that there must be some very major things happening in the mining communities, when it comes to Industry, we need policies to get other companies. You know, a mining company is a mining company; what they know is how to mine. They do not know how to make machines; they don't know how to create other things like limestone or cement, so we do need some integrated activities that will actually expand much more what has happened so far.

When you talk of revenue also, quite a lot of revenue has come into government coffers, even though government has never indicated that this is mining money. They don't need to. They don't need to say, "This is cocoa money, this is timber money, this is mining money", but mining has expanded the revenue base of government. Even in terms of PAYE (pay-as-you-earn), it contributes about 11 to 12 per cent into the Ghanaian economy. 30-something per cent of foreign exchange earnings is coming from Mining. Two years ago, the mining companies returned about 48 per cent of what they earned in foreign exchange back into the country, which is not bad.

IA-D: How many people are in this sector?

JA: In terms of real production – that is, the companies that are producing – we have, in the Chamber at least, AngloGold Ashanti with two mines, one in Obuasi and one in Tarkwa; we have Golden Star Resources, with one mine in Wasa in Western Region and another mine in Bogoso, also in the Western Region; we have Goldfields with two mines, both of them in the Western Region; we have Central African Gold, which is also in Western Region, in Bibiani; and then we have Ghana Manganese, also in the Western Region; and then Ghana Bauxite, also in the Western Region; and finally Chirano Gold, also in the Western Region. There are the beginnings of another mine in the Amansie West – they bought the old mine but they are not producing yet; about eleven mines, mostly gold because Ghana is preponderantly a gold country.

IA-D: So what do we mine, in what form, and what are the export trends and growth patterns?

JA: We mine mainly gold. In fact, of the mining revenue, about 95 per cent is from gold, which sometimes frightens me because it is almost like a mono-economy. We have bauxite and we have manganese. We have bauxite in three major areas: one is Awaso, which is the only one being mined now; another large deposit is in Nyanahin, which might be mined pretty soon, maybe in the next two years or so; and the other one is in Kibi, which I hope will also get mined. In terms of export, both manganese and bauxite are exported in their raw form, although prepared ready for Industry. In terms of bauxite, government is making plans to have alumina produced in Ghana. It would really improve even the revenue we get from bauxite. Bauxite in its raw form only gets about $21 per tonne, and manganese also about that, but when you produce alumina it increases three-fold, and when you produce the ingots of aluminium, even better still. So I hope that the country does that. Gold is also exported in a purity of about 89 to maybe 91 per cent, but in terms of selling gold you want 99.9, so it has to go to a refinery.

Because most of the mining is being done by Foreign Direct Investment, what we gain really is the revenue we get from royalties and other taxes. There are small-scale mining companies, and the thing is to expand the small-scale mining companies in Ghana that are locally done and then move them into medium-scale mines, and then maybe one day large-scale mines. We really look forward to that.

IA-D: What is the role of the multilateral institutions – the World Bank group – in the Mining Sector in Ghana?

JA: I remember I may have mentioned to the predecessor of the current World Bank representative that the World Bank hasn't done that much in Mining, although through the International Finance Corporation (IFC), Newmont and AngloGold Ashanti Iduapriem have benefited from some of the resources of the World Bank. As a result, some of the environmental best practice, as well as community best practices, have been adopted that go along with the loans the IFC gives.

In terms of policy, I do not think that the World Bank has done enough, because the World Bank should be promoting a policy that ensures that the backwards integration into the Ghanaian economy from Mining is very good. By "backwards integration" I mean creating the facilities where companies can come and establish here – local companies as well as foreign companies – and produce the things that the mining companies will need rather than always importing them. As a country, if we really want to benefit from Mining, that is what we should be doing; we should be making sure that it is an integrated industry. The equipment, the other services – whether in terms of chemicals, in terms of tyres, or other things that are needed – should be produced in this country to feed the mining industry. That way, you broaden the base of industries that are servicing the mines. And looking forwards, we should also introduce some form of processing that would enable the economy to expand.

As far as gold is concerned, you don't actually make that much money when you refine gold, because you refine it and later on marketing is a major problem. Besides, it is so capital-intensive, if you want to do major refining you need a lot of power, you need a lot of equipment, and so on. But we could promote small-scale refineries which would then refine gold for jewellery-making. I think we should really begin to zoom in on jewellery-making and create a zone in Ghana where, in addition to the Precious Minerals Marketing Company (PMMC), which produces a lot of jewellery, everybody who comes to Ghana as a tourist can go and buy Ghanaian-designed and Ghanaian trademark gold items, using Ghanaian gold. That would bring a lot of revenue to the country.

When you think of manganese, that too needs a lot of power to turn it into what maybe a steel industry would use, but, again, if we mean to do it, we should link it up to the iron deposits that we have. We have iron deposits in Upper West, as well as at Oppong Manso. We should link the mining of manganese with the mining of iron, and then that also becomes an integrated industry. Steel is still being produced by China in great quantities, so we could do a joint venture there. That would help a great deal. We have a lot of other industrial minerals: we have kaolin, we have silica, we have what we call feldspar, we have dimension stones, we have a lot of clay throughout the country; we have isolated diamonds, we have limestone. It would be very important for us, if we want to get into manufacturing and industrialisation, to also begin to focus on some of these known industrial minerals, which will then readily dovetail into the kind of economic development we want. I really think we should do that.

IA-D: So why haven't we been able to do this over the years?

JA: It is one of the questions I keep asking. I really think – and I must apologise if what I'm saying is perhaps exaggerating things – that governments have focused more on the revenue that they will get from Mining, rather than using Mining as a catalyst for development. These are some of the advocacy issues that we are raising from the Chamber: we really need to make Mining a catalyst for development. We should mine our minerals with the sole aim of using them to develop our country. If we have that kind of policy, then everything we do will have a future in mind. For example, before you give a lease for a mine in a community, you must first think of how you perceive or envision the community's development, the region's development, the district's development in the next 20–25 years. That would enable us as a country to really plan for the sort of things that will expand the development of that area. But if by the establishment of a mine all we are thinking is that we are going to get revenue, then we are really short-changing ourselves as a country.

IA-D: From what you are saying, it seems like we have minerals everywhere!

JA: We do have mineral deposits. In fact, there probably are some minerals that we do not know of. Thankfully, the EU has a project and they are doing an aerial survey of the Volta basin. I am sure we are going to have a lot of surprises, that there are far more minerals in Ghana than what we know. The Western Region actually has shown a lot of minerals, preponderantly gold but the other things as well. You wouldn't even believe that there are some bitumen sands areas in the Western Region, and we have discovered oil.

IA-D: What does the discovery of oil mean?

JA: We have discovered oil and there is a lot of gas. If we plan, the way I'm talking about, to use the oil as a catalyst for development, then we will be looking again at the backwards integration, as well as the forwards integration. We will be thinking of industries that will feed into the oil industry, and other industries that would benefit from the oil. That is what we should do, and also do maybe what the Norwegians are doing. They have a special fund called the Oil for Development Fund. We should set up something like that, and I know that the Minister for Finance is very busy talking to the Norwegians about that, so I'm sure it will happen. There's also the Extractive Industries Transparency Initiative, which we are members of, and which enjoins us to transparently indicate how much money we will be getting from oil.

I would also look forward to us getting into the gas immediately. Even though the oil will give us gas, we also have large gas deposits. I don't know whether they are the same fields, but whatever it is I think we should take full advantage of what we have and make it an *integrated industry*. We shouldn't just think of the oil. Everything that is required to make an oil industry work, we should think of, and provide the environment for people to come and establish industries that will do that. Then we should think of what we call forward integration, that is adding value. For the products that may be needed, as much as possible we should try and create conditions for them to be produced here. Then comes the value addition. It must be a package. We have missed it in Mining but we shouldn't miss it in oil, and we shouldn't think that in Mining we have missed it completely. This is the time for us to make that kind of decision so that both minerals can really change Ghana's economic development fundamentally and positively.

IA-D: There are people who also look at the environmental aspects of it and perform environmental impact assessments. Do you think that sometimes it is more dangerous to have these things than not?

JA: Technology has moved a lot, and environmental protection has advanced a great deal. Right now, there are much better ways of doing things, and so the danger can be significantly minimised. Once you know that what you're doing has repercussions on the environment, and you know that there is knowledge, there is technology, there is information for you to mitigate the dangers then, that is what you do. People forget that, until the late-1960s, the whole world thought that the earth's resources were infinite, and therefore everyone used them the way they wanted. It was only in the late-1960s that we all woke up and realised that the earth's resources are finite and that we must really protect them and make sure that they are available. That is why we talk about sustainable development: you use the resources in such a way that the generations after you will also be able to use them. Since that awakening, a lot of knowledge has come.

Even in Mining, where you would say that it is a wasting resource in the sense that what you dig out you cannot replace, the thing is that you cannot dig out everything. Some time ago, the technology for gold mining was underground. That was the only technology. With time it was recognised that wherever there is gold underground, there is also gold on the surface, even though the surface grades are lower than the underground grades. The underground grades are usually very good. So, surface mining for gold became an option, but with that option has also come a way in which you actually backfill your pits and replant. When you are doing surface mining, when you strip the land, you scoop the topsoil and put it away for re-use. Even the rocks that you blast, the ones that don't contain gold, you put them away for re-use. Later on, you backfill with some of the rocks and then you put the topsoil back on. Then you plant nitrogen-fixing plants to make sure that you enrich the soil before you do the replanting, and then the soil becomes, perhaps not as pristine as God created it, but definitely you get as close to it as possible with a human touch.

Let me say that every economic activity has an environmental impact and so environmental protection is not just for Mining and other industries; it is for everything we do. If we recognise it as such then we will make sure that we all take impact assessments seriously.

IA-D: You have worked extensively in the Private and Public sectors. Which side do you prefer to work in and why?

JA: Actually I don't mind. I think the Public Sector is good in the sense that it is a direct service to the nation. Contrary to what people think, I think that, depending on the way people work, you can make your service in the Public Sector also very exciting if you see it as *serving*, rather than just a way of getting money to make ends meet. There must be some motivation for you. Personally, I have always chosen to work in areas that interest me. I don't want to work somewhere I feel frustrated. If I feel frustrated, I'll change. I'll change and go and work elsewhere, because you must be interested in what you're doing so that you can give your best. You must also get personal fulfilment from the work you do. It is not because somebody has employed you; it is because you have *offered* yourself to be employed. Employment is a choice, so once you choose to go and work somewhere, you must give it your best. You must show interest in it, and that has been my philosophy for work. I have really enjoyed everywhere I have worked.

IA-D: Do you think that is why the general public is in love with everything you do?

JA: Maybe I exude so much enthusiasm! I think that we should be enthusiastic about what we do. I also have great faith in people. I think everybody has something to offer, and I truly believe in the human spirit. I think there is so much we can do, and that sort of defines the way I relate to people and I relate to my work.

IA-D: You have been recognised nationally.

JA: That came as a surprise. I was pleasantly surprised, and grateful to President Kufuor for recognising me with the Order of the Volta.

IA-D: Thank you very much.

JA: Thank you also.

December 2007

Dr Richard Anane

Dr. Richard Anane is the current Minister for Transportation, Member of Parliament for the Nhyiaeso Constituency in the Ashanti Region, and serving member of the Parliamentary Committees on Privileges and Health. As Minister for Transportation, a position he has held since March 2008, and previously from February 2005 – October 2006, he has overseen the expansion of the national road network from 38,000 km in 2001 to 63,000 km in 2008 and established Metro Mass Transit Ltd., advocated for free school bus-rides. From February – November 2001, he served as Minister for Health, during which time he called for under-18 free care under the National Health Insurance Scheme and appointed the first Rector to kick-start the College of Physicians and Surgeons, among other initiatives. Before the New Patriotic Party (NPP) came to power, Dr. Anane was Parliamentary Minority Spokesman for Food and Agriculture and a Ranking Member of the Parliamentary Select Committee on Food and Agriculture, both from January 1997 – January 2001.

A Medical Practitioner by training, Dr Anane has attended several academic conferences on issues of Health. He has also represented Ghana in a political capacity at a number of international events, including the WHO Ministerial Conference in Geneva, the International Maritime Organisation in London (where he led the Ghana Team to win a seat on the IMO Council in November 2002), the Public Private Partnership Conference in Infrastructure Development in Berlin (2003) and in London (2005), and the International Civil Aviation Organisation (where, in Montreal in 2004, he led the Ghana Team to secure a seat on the ICAO Council). He recently participated in the preparation of the *Handbook on the Control of Corruption* for parliamentarians and civil society as part of the Laurentian Seminar on the Control of Corruption.

Dr Anane attended the University of Science and Technology (now the Kwame Nkrumah University of Science and Technology) in Kumasi, where he earned a BSc in Human Biology. He also holds a Bachelor of Medicine and Surgery degree (MB ChB) and several Post-Graduate Certificates and Diplomas, among them: Radiation Protection and Quality Assurance in Diagnostic Radiology, Reproductive Health, Minilaparotomy, Manual Vacuum Aspiration (IPAS), and Obstetrics and Gynaecology. He completed an Obstetrics and Gynaecology attachment at St. Bartholomew's Hospital, London.

Ivor Agyeman-Duah: Dr Anane, what is the structure of the Ministry of Roads and Transport, and what is it now?

Dr Richard Anane: Initially, the Ministry of Roads and Transport covered the areas of aviation; maritime; and the ground or road sector, including rails. That means that that Ministry had to deal with the development of our road infrastructure, the management and development as far as the policy decisions and policy directions for transportation in general were concerned. It also had to do with managing the rail infrastructure, as well as rail services. It had to do with maritime services and everything encompassed in maritime issues. It also dealt with the Aviation Sector. In the Aviation Sector, we had Aviation transport and services. We also had the Civil Aviation Authority, which also ensured that our airspace was regulated. So these were the areas that the ministry was catering for.

Currently, even though it is still called the Ministry of Transportation, the main focus of the Ministry is on the development of road infrastructure and then the management of transportation, especially on ground – vehicular transportation and access to the various areas.

IA-D: Has it always been like this?

RA: Well, some time past in previous governments there was the Ministry for Roads and Highways, but that was also basically focused on the development of road infrastructure, and not so much the management of transportation – road, aviation, or maritime – because that fell under the Ministry for Transport and Communications. However, before the New Patriotic Party (NPP) government came in, the Ministry of Roads and Transport had been created.

IA-D: Some of the sectors within the remit of the Ministry – the railway sector for instance –collapsed some time ago. Does this mean that they were not relevant to the economic development of the country?

RA: It is sad, because if you take rail transportation in particular, it is over a century since we started it in Ghana and one would have expected that over the years conditions would have been improving rather than deteriorating, but on the assumption of office in 2001, the entire rail infrastructure had collapsed. In Ghana we have a triangular rail network, from Accra to Takoradi, from Takoradi to Kumasi, and from Kumasi to Accra. The eastern line from Accra to Kumasi had virtually collapsed. The central line – from Accra to Takoradi – had also collapsed. It was only the line from Takoradi to Kumasi that appeared to be functional, and then only at a minimum level because a lot of the infrastructure had broken down. Part was being maintained with the support of some of the mining companies because they also had been using them. However, the NPP government thought it necessary to pay a little more attention to these sectors. We even started passenger transportation from Nsawam to Accra and as we speak now, the line from Tema to Accra is actually rehabilitated and passenger transport is in progress. The line from Accra to Takoradi is yet to be rehabilitated, but virtually all the lines would eventually be rehabilitated because government has prioritised the revamping of the rail infrastructure and even to extend it up to Paga so that we can link the Southern sector to the Northern sector. The major results we hope we can get are: first, to equalise prices of goods and food, and second, to improve on the location of industries up North.

IA-D: What about the Aviation Industry?

RA: The Aviation Industry had over the years also gone down. Indeed, the passengers through the Kotoka International Airport had not been anything to write home about. Our airports needed rehabilitation. Our national airline, as you must have been aware, had also been run down, and at the time the present government took over the airline was running at about a $1 million loss per month. These were not tenable issues. Government felt the need to do what was right. Over the years there have been a few decisions taken – some have not been pleasant but they were necessary. If you do not take such measures now, they will need to be taken later and it is better that they are taken sooner than later.

There are still many challenges in the industry, but we hope that with a few measures such as liberalisation and increased participation of the Private Sector, we should be able to get our Aviation Sector on keel. Currently the airports are all being rehabilitated, and we hope that soon we will get even brand new airports put in place. We hope that with these, and with the re-focusing of the Civil Aviation Authority into its current regulatory function and the creation of an airport company, the Aviation Sector will be put on the right keel.

IA-D: It looks like the bulk of the Ministry's work is in the road development sector. How important is this in terms of economic development?

RA: First and foremost, transportation is about the creation of access – the movement of people from one point to the other in order to facilitate socio-economic activity. It also has to do with the movement of goods and services from one point to another, again in the socio-economic milieu. If you are in a country where about 95 per cent of passenger traffic is by the Road Sector, and 97 per cent of the haulage of goods is by the Road Sector, you appreciate that there is a very major need to focus on the Road Sector so that these actions could facilitate the transport of the people in their socio-economic needs, as well as the transport of the goods.

IA-D: When the NPP came to power, what was the state of infra-structure in this respect?

RA: Perhaps a reference to the road condition mix would be helpful. Let me cite one example: the Road Condition Mix of our trunk road network as at 2001. In 2001, only 23 per cent of the trunk road network was in good condition; a further 27 per cent could have been said to be in fair condition; but 51 per cent was in very bad condition. Over the years, from 2001-2004, this changed from 23 per cent good to 40 per cent good, and then from 27 per cent fair to 30 per cent fair, and from 51 per cent poor to 30 per cent poor. As at September 2007, the Road Condition Mix for our trunk roads showed a very marked change: 57 per cent good, as compared with the 23 per cent in 2001;

26 per cent fair, as compared with 27 per cent in 2001; to 17 per cent poor, as compared with 51 per cent in 2001. If you can appreciate what I have just told you, it will give you some idea as to how our road network was when government took over and how it is now.

That was in relation to the trunk road network. If you were to take the national mix – that is, trunk roads, feeder roads, urban roads, and all the others – in 2001, when this government came in, 27 per cent of the roads were in good condition nationally, 17 per cent were in fair condition, and 56 per cent were in poor condition. By 2004, 40 per cent of these roads were in good condition, 30 per cent were in fairly good condition, and the remaining 30 per cent were in poor condition. By the end of 2006, 45 per cent had been raised to very good condition, 28 per cent in fair condition, and just 27 per cent were in poor condition. If we were to take the results of last year – that is 2007 – which are currently being collated and should be available by March 2008, we will find that there has been a marked improvement in the National Road Condition Mix. If you appreciate the Road Condition Mix that will tell you how the roads looked when the government came in, and how they are now. That shows the kind of input and investment the government has made in improving the roads, and in so doing, increasing and improving on access to facilitate the socio-economic activities of people and the movement of goods and services.

IA-D: What about the development of feeder roads?

RA: Feeder road development has also been part of the entire Road Development Scheme. Maybe to go back a little bit: the changes that I just talked about have not been done without investment or funding. Between 2002 and 2006/7 about $1.2 billion has had to be invested in the entire road network to ensure that these changes which we just talked about occurred. Indeed, in the feeder road network too we have similar changes. Perhaps you may want to measure improvements in the Feeder Road Network by improvements in food prices because it is creating access for the rural areas and the farm gates. By opening access to the farm gates, it makes it possible for food to be easily accessible on the market. One of the things we should notice is that over the years, the price of food has been quite stable on the market. This has contributed significantly to the stability of our inflation rates, because food is one of the major factors in inflation creation.

Feeder roads have also seen a major improvement. Indeed, when you look at feeder roads, what is most significant is that they constitute about 72 per cent of the total road network in the country – that is about 41,000 km. Out of this, only 11,800 km are engineered. When an engineer talks about a road being engineered, he means that this road can be used virtually year-round. The only way that roads can be used year-round is when he has put in a few improvements – putting in some culverts, drains and other things to make sure that these roads are generally not flooded or do not permit water to form on them so that it makes accessibility difficult. Some of these roads have also been properly gravelled so that it is easier to move on them, and some have also been tarred. Over the last few years, you will notice that between 2001 and 2007, about 12,000 more kilometres of road had been engineered. Now, government met 11,800 km of road engineered over the years, but from 2001-2007 about 12,000 more kilometres had been put under engineered status so that such corridors can be used year-round. That tells you the amount of work that has been done over the years. When I talk about expenditure of $1.2 billion, one can appreciate where some of these monies are going.

Before then, tarring of feeder roads did not seem to be very prominent. Government thought it necessary, because when roads are gravelled but not tarred, especially in Western Region, part of Central Region, and part of Ashanti Region where there are a lot of rains, the rains tend to wash the roads away. So government also adopted a policy to ensure that a lot of our roads are tarred. Indeed, between 2001 and the present, about 450 km of roads have been tarred. This is against 874 km of tarred roads throughout the country that were there before the government came to power. This means that since independence, only 874 km of feeder roads had been tarred but from 2001-2007, 450 km of road had been tarred and an extra 200 km are in the process of being tarred. If they are finished, then it means the total will almost equal the length of roads that had been tarred before the government came in.

Again, if you look at the interventions that have been made over the years, you can also look at it from the point of view of the Road Condition Mix of the feeder roads. I will always want to use 2001 as a reference point because that is when the government took over. In 2001, 29 per cent of all feeder roads in the country were in good condition, 13 per cent were in fair condition, and the remaining 58 per cent were in poor condition. Even at that time the inventories of feeder roads in the country approximated 32,600 km. Out of this, I am saying that 29 per cent were in good condition. Now, if you talk about feeder roads at the end of 2006, 40 per cent were in good condition, 26 per cent of the roads were in fair condition, and just 34 per cent were in poor condition. The difference here is that, as at the end of 2006, the Feeder Road Network had risen from 32,600 km to 41,000 km, and it is the 41,000 km of which we had 40 per cent in good condition and then 26 per cent in fair condition and 34 per cent in poor condition.

You see that in addition to expanding the Feeder Road Network, there has also been a marked improvement in the condition mix within the same period of time. This can be shown in graph form here [making reference to graphical presentation], where in 2001, 29 per cent were in good condition, 13 per cent in fair condition, and 58 per cent in poor condition. In 2004, 41 per cent were in good condition, but even then the quantum of the road network had increased; 31 per cent in fair condition; and 28 per cent in poor condition. There was a slump in 2005–6 because by 2005, 43 per cent were in good condition, 33 per cent in fair condition, and 24 per cent in poor condition. There was a little slump which led the network to deteriorate, because as I said the length had increased; the road network had expanded. Because of the expansion, the poor ones were added in the evaluation of the condition mix, making it look poorer than before. Even then, 40 per cent were in good condition, 26 per cent in fair condition, and 34 per cent in poor condition.

If this is what has been happening, then one can easily tell how the road network has improved over the years with the interventions that government has been able to make. These were all funded through the national Budget, the development partners, and the Road Fund.

IA-D: What about the issue of maintenance of roads?

RA: The maintenance of our roads is basically done through the Road Fund. We get funding for the Road Fund through a fuel levy–raising of the levy on consumption of fuel – road tolls, and payments from drivers through the Vehicle Licensing Authority which are used for maintaining the road network. But that can never be enough. As at last year, this amount was expected to be about 1 trillion old cedis, the equivalent of about $100 million. That will not be enough to maintain the road network, so occasionally government might have to come in to support the maintenance of such vital infrastructure which creates access for all of us.

IA-D: What is the role of the multilateral institutions in all of this?

RA: They are generally more interested in development, especially in the Feeder Road Network. The European Union have been supporting under the STABEX, the DfID in the UK also supports, and then DANIDA also occasionally supports, but currently the European Union is the major supporter of Feeder Road Development and Maintenance. We have to learn to depend upon ourselves, and that is why the Road Fund had been formed and that is why we have to find ways and means of getting more money into the Road Fund in order to maintain not just feeder roads, but urban roads and the major trunk roads where we have problems with them.

IA-D: We have a problem with fatalities on the roads. These roads are supposed to serve an economic purpose, but at the same time they have become a sort of albatross around the neck of government.

RA: Do I call it an albatross? For every good thing, there is always a bad point. Vehicles are machines; whenever they move they may have some faults. The operator may also not be able to manage the way it should be, and therefore may tend to have what we call accidents. Indeed, the road traffic accident fatality rate in this country used to be very high. In the 1990s it was in the region of 73 deaths per 10,000 vehicles, but as at the end of 2006 this had come down to 22.1 deaths per 10,000 vehicles. I am hoping that when the records are collated, as at the end of 2007 it may even be better. The reason I am hopeful is that our road network has been improved, and there has been some very major collaboration among the various agencies such as the Road Fund Secretariat, Road Safety, the Vehicle Licensing Authority, and the MTT of the Police Service to make sure that drivers who use vehicles on the roads use them appropriately. This has helped to diminish the rate of accidents in the country, and I am very hopeful as I said that the end of 2007 may see another improvement in our road traffic accident fatality rate.

Indeed, if I still go back to 2001 – because I said that in the 1990s the road traffic accident fatality rate was about 73 – it had come down to 31 deaths per 10,000 vehicles. Then in 2004 it had come down to 23.6 deaths per 10,000 vehicles. At the end of 2006, it was 22.1. That is why I am saying that we are expecting it to even go down more. With these developments, and the necessary interventions that government is making, one: we are making accessibility quite easy; two: we are facilitating the movement of goods and services and three: we are collaborating to improve on safety on the roads. This is through inter-agency and inter-sector collaboration.

IA-D: What are your hopes for the economic development of Ghana in the coming years, whatever political direction the country takes?

RA: If you can make a judgement out of the interventions and the results of the interventions even in the road and transport sector, one can see that if there are such major and positive changes in this sector, one expects all the other sectors to be showing such major improvements. The end result of positive changes in the various sectors is positive change in the nation. I believe that this nation should rather be going forward; it cannot come down.

IA-D: Thank you very much.

RA: Thank you very much.

September 2007

PART THREE

Crossing the Jordan: Stimulation and Innovation in the Economy

Professor E. Gyimah-Boadi

Professor E. Gyimah-Boadi is the founder and Executive Director of the Ghana Centre for Democratic Development, (CDD-Ghana), an independent research think-tank examining Democracy and Governance in Ghana and Africa. He is also Executive Director of the Afrobarometer, a survey research project tracking public opinion on democratic, social, and economic developments in 20 African countries. Specialising in the politics of economic reform, good governance, corruption, and democratic development in Africa, Professor Gyimah-Boadi has undertaken consultancy assignments for such institutions as the World Bank, the UK Department for International Development (DfID), the United Nations Development Programme (UNDP), Transparency International, and the African Development Bank. He serves on the Governing Council of the Ghana Integrity Initiative (the Ghana chapter of Transparency International) and on the Board of the International Centre for Transitional Justice (New York).

Professor Gyimah-Boadi has taught at a number of American and African universities, including Dartmouth College, the School of International Service at American University, the School of Advanced International Studies at Johns Hopkins University, and the University of Swaziland. He has held Visiting Fellowships at the Woodrow Wilson International Centre for Scholars; the International Forum for Democratic Studies of the National Endowment for Democracy; and the Centre for Democracy, the Rule of Law and Development at Stanford University. He is currently a Professor in the Department of Political Science at the University of Ghana, Legon.

He is a member of the Research Council of the International Forum for Democratic Studies, the Editorial Board of the *Journal of Democracy*, the International Advisory Board of *Development Policy Review* (UK), the Editorial Advisory Board of *Columbia International Affairs Online*

(USA), and the *International Journal for Transitional Justice* (South Africa). He is also a Fellow of both the Ghana Academy of Arts and Sciences and the World Academy of Arts and Sciences (USA). Recent published works include: "Political Parties, Elections and Patronage: Random Thoughts on Neo-Patrimonialism and African Democratization" in Matthias Basedau et al eds., *Votes, Money and Violence: Political Parties and Elections in Sub-Saharan Africa* (2007); "Ghana and South Africa, Assessing the Quality of Democracy" (with Robert Mattes) in Larry Diamond and Leonardo Morlino eds., *Assessing the Quality of Democracy* (2005); *Public Opinion, Democracy and Market Reform in Africa* (with Mike Bratton and Robert Mattes, 2005); and *Democratic Reform in Africa: The Quality of Progress* (2004).

Professor Gyimah-Boadi holds a BA from the University of Ghana and an MA and PhD in Political Science from the University of California, Davis. He is married with two children.

Ivor Agyeman-Duah: Professor Gyimah-Boadi, can you tell us the pur-- pose for the establishment of the Ghana Centre for Democratic Development?

Professor E. Gyimah-Boadi: We were first of all inspired by the democratic opening of Ghana and Africa in the 1990s. We saw a need in 1998 to use research as a basis for diagnosing, as a basis for documenting, and as a basis for conducting advocacy towards the promotion of democracy and good governance in Ghana and Africa.

IA-D: What was absent when you got in?

EG-B: Well, a number of NGOs and think-tanks had begun to emerge in Ghana from the early 1990s, but none was focusing exclusively on governance and democracy, and therefore the political side of Ghana's political liberalisation and democratic experiment. In addition, none was using research to support advocacy in the area of democratic governance

IA-D: What were some of the core areas that you worked in? How were these related to development in terms of politics and economics?

EG-B: Well, starting in the late 1990s when we came in, we realised that Ghana was heading towards a major political transition – because the Presidency of Jerry John Rawlings was coming to an end – and that Ghana was going to have a government and an administration in this Fourth Republic that did not have antecedents in the military. Whether it was the National Democratic Congress (NDC) under then Vice-President Mills, or it was the New Patriotic Party (NPP) under Kufuor, it was clear that Ghana was going to go through a change that it had not experienced before: an elected government would be handing over to another elected government.

IA-D: It is obvious that politics has affected the way the economy has been run. To what extent would you say that this has affected it negatively?

EG-B: First, that political successions in Ghana had not been smooth and/or peaceful in the past was unnecessarily disruptive of national progress. The idea that policies started by one administration would have to be completely terminated by the next one, and the general sense that in our political system there was no possibility for or experience with regular political succession, was one which was bad for investment. Investors looked at Ghana and concluded that this was a country where investment may prosper under one regime at best, but could not be guaranteed under the next one.

One of the major areas of progress in Ghana, and one that is not well recognised by most commentators, is the kind of progress you see both in terms of policy continuity and also in terms of the continuous development of infrastructure programmes from one government or administration to the other. If you go back to the previous era (before the Fourth Republic), you would see cranes and scaffolding on construction sites that had been up since the last *coup d'état* or a change of government, and never to be revisited under subsequent administrations. That has changed, happily, in our current setting. I think that the previous state of affairs was a deterrent to progress on the economic front, a deterrent to investment; the current state of affairs is a boost to progress on the economic side.

IA-D: What are your research findings in terms of institutions, in terms of electoral attitudes? I know you usually go into the field to observe how elections are conducted, and you also do opinion polls to gauge attitudes of people to politicians, etc.

EG-B: Well first let me make a distinction between the types of research that we do. First, we do the opinion surveys within the Afrobarometer and also as part of diagnostic research we undertake. When we do that kind of research, the findings reflect what the people say, what they see, and what they think. On that score, I think there is a general sense among Ghanaians that democracy is good for Ghana, democracy is the most preferred form of government for Ghanaians, and that dictatorial or military rule is overwhelmingly rejected. In fact, Ghana comes up very high on the list of African countries polled about rejection of authoritarian rule, rejection of non-democratic forms of rule, and support for democracy. Also, we find that Ghanaians register very high scores in terms of demanding and expressing a wish for democratic rule. When it comes to actual satisfaction with democratic rule, or what democratic rule has been able to deliver to Ghanaians and for Ghanaians, the achievements fall short of expectations. But even so, Ghana scores quite well on the scale with other African countries in terms of satisfaction with democracy. Ghanaians are generally fairly satisfied with the way democracy works in Ghana and, most importantly, they are quite willing to wait for democracy and the democratic experiment to work out. We call that "patience for democracy" and Ghanaian respondents are far more patient than respondents in other countries polled in the Afrobarometer.

In terms of our analytical work, especially in the kind of research we have done subjecting the 1992 constitution and the practices that have evolved in the last 15 years or so to a democratic test, we find that there are still major deficits in terms of creating a process and building institutions for sustained democratic governance. The greatest area of concern has been Executive Branch hegemony. We get a strong sense in our analysis that the distribution of power in our Constitution and the political system is over-loaded in favour of the Executive Branch. This also has implications for what we see as over-centralisation of political and administrative power in the country. In our view that is part of the reason why decentralisation reforms have been much slower than expected. It is also a big reason why we still have so much political patronage in our system, and why corruption remains persistent.

The other area of reform where we find deficits in our system is on the political culture side. As Ghanaians, on the one hand, we are quite supportive of democracy; we seem to have a great deal of tolerance among ourselves, though not nearly enough. On the other hand, there is still a tendency for public support to gravitate towards whoever has the most power, and so typically businesses, for instance, do not feel that they should show openly that they are supporters of an opposition party. This is abating somewhat – it used to be worse – but it is still the case that most people feel that they cannot afford to offend the State and power-holders. This we take to be a limitation on people's sense of freedom and people's sense of efficacy.

Let me give you an example: we were observing the run-off in the 2000 election and we found that, prior to that election, most of the vehicles in Accra that bothered to display party paraphernalia had NDC flags. Almost as soon as the NPP won and President Kufuor was sworn in, all the NDC paraphernalia disappeared from the windows and windshields of all vehicles and were replaced by NPP ones. We know that this was not organised; it was not done on the basis of instructions by the ruling party or by the government. People did that voluntarily, and that clearly shows that people have a certain understanding of politics in the country: you do not dare offend whoever has the highest position of political power, no matter what party is in government. We are waiting to see how that will work in the 2008 election. We expect that maybe it will not be as one-sided as on previous occasions and in previous elections, but you will still see that those who support the ruling party will feel much freer to display their affection for the party than those who support the opposition party, and that is a measure of a remaining gap in people's sense of freedom.

From an economic development point of view too, it suggests a certain limitation because a whole lot of people are making economic decisions based on partisan considerations as opposed to strict economic considerations. Having said that, we must acknowledge one other positive thing our cross-country research shows. When you do a comparative analysis of Ghana and other African countries, Ghana definitely comes out very well. On scores of democracy, even anti-corruption, Ghana does reasonably well. For me, the challenge for Ghanaians should therefore be: should we really be satisfied and patting ourselves on the shoulders because we score so well on African rankings – the African Peer Review Mechanism, the Mo Ibrahim Index, Afrobarometer and so on? Is that all? Shouldn't we set higher standards for ourselves, especially if we see ourselves competing not just in Africa, but competing on a global scale?

IA-D: These are interesting findings, but is the Centre able to influence government policy in some of these areas, or even the political parties themselves, or the Private Sector?

EG-B: It is a complex matter, but your good-self, as a purveyor of Akan proverbs, would appreciate the meaning of the proverb we have in Ghana that says: "If you want to speak to God you speak into thin air". So one way in which we seek to influence the policy process is to do these analyses painstakingly and to publicise and disseminate the findings widely. For instance, Afrobarometer results are often publicly released, both in Ghana and outside. We go to the extent of putting them on CD-ROMs and circulating them to Social Science Departments in the universities in Ghana. We also put out a quarterly called *Democracy Watch*, which is the Centre's mouthpiece, expressing its well thought-out views on various developments occurring within the quarter on the political front, on the economic front, with respect to elections, or anything else that needs to be commented on.

In addition, we do quite a lot of quiet work with Parliament. We work closely with the Constitutional and Legal Affairs Committee of Parliament and with the Subsidiary Legislation Committee of Parliament, to help them mobilise public input, inputs from independent sources, from scholars, and also international best practices into the policy process. We also help them to mobilise public opinion into the policy process. Our methods of influencing public policies are highly indirect. It is not our role to directly make policy; we can only make suggestions, put them out there, and hope that some of them are accepted.

IA-D: There was an interesting contribution that the Centre was said to have made during the work on the Ghana side of the African Peer Review Mechanism (APRM). I am told the Centre was involved in trying to shape understanding of the policy process.

EG-B: Well, first of all the African Peer Review Mechanism fitted well into our purposes. The instrument was one that combined all the tools we use in our analysis and diagnostics of governance and democracy and democratic development in Ghana and elsewhere. We were privileged to have been selected as the technical team to lead and undertake the Political Governance and Democracy component of the assessment. The other components of the Ghana APRM report are Corporate Governance, Economic Governance, and Social Development. We were also able to help in shaping the original draft instrument for the APRM study because Ghana was the first country to go through the process. We provided inputs into the instrument which had been developed by the APRM together with the ECA and others outside of Ghana, and helped them to shape it appropriately.

We also got the opportunity to work with a number of Ghanaian institutions. With our deep knowledge of the local terrain and available local expertise, we could easily recognise that, for instance, when it came to analysing the progress of women in Ghana, we were not the best placed to do it and that there were other institutions that were better placed to do it. So we deferred to those institutions and/or experts and relied on them to provide us with the inputs. On the civil-military side, we also relied on expert institutions. In addition, we brought some of these national experts together to form an internal Advisory Group – a Peer Review group to the CDD-Ghana study. This was not a requirement for the African Peer Review Mechanism country assessment protocol at all, but we felt that we could not make ourselves experts over everything, and that it was important to get the findings of our study validated by our own peers within the NGO community, within the think-tank community, and within the advocacy community even before sharing them with the general public.

The Centre has also been trying to help with monitoring the implementation of the program of actions that Ghana has committed itself to undertake to address the gaps and deficiencies in governance captured in the Country Report. After all, the national Peer Review was done under the auspices of the National African Peer Review Mechanism Council, which is an independent body. It is supposed to be doing this on behalf of the Ghanaian public. Part of our role was to monitor and determine the extent to which the final report the National Peer Review Council submitted to the Peer Review Secretariat and the Eminent Persons Group reflected the inputs of the CDD-Ghana study. We were happy to note that, in the case of Ghana, the National Peer Review Council largely adopted the findings of our study and presented them without undue adulteration, which gives us a lot of confidence in the Ghana report.

The other role we had to play came about because we were intimately involved in the compilation of the Ghana country assessment, and also because we live, unfortunately, in a politically polarised society. We felt compelled on several occasions to come out and clarify certain misconceptions and misperceptions that certain political players and constituencies had about the APRM. For instance, there was some controversy about whether or not the APRM findings exclusively reflected the good things that have occurred under the John Kufuor government. We came out to explain that the APRM of Ghana covered a period that overlapped the latter years of the NDC Rawlings government and the first term of the NPP Kufuor administration, and that both the credit and the blame in the report should be shared by both regimes, rather than anybody handing all the credit to Kufuor or to the NDC, with the other party taking all the blame.

Secondly, we also felt compelled to point out that the NPP government and Kufuor should be given a lot of credit for taking a hands-off approach to the Peer Review process – not interfering in the process, allowing a fairly independent Ghana Peer Review Council to steer the process, and leaving the Council to appoint technical teams to undertake the job based on technical criteria. I think this is what makes the Ghana Peer Review report stand head and shoulders above all of the country assessments undertaken so far. It was one that was done with complete independence and autonomy on the part of the agencies that undertook the assessment. This probably made the Ghana report the most detailed and most credible of all the reports that have been submitted so far, capturing both the good things that are going on with democracy and governance, economic and social development in Ghana, and also the bad things. We thought the government took a lot of courage, and that people should notice that.

IA-D: We have been having continuity of democratic practice for 15 years or more. If this continuity should be seen over the next decade, what does the future hold for Ghana?

EG-B: Well first, speaking as a Ghanaian, it is great to see the progress the country has made, and it is particularly great to see that Ghana, especially over the past 15 years or so and in this Republic is moving up and is doing reasonably well on the economic development front, including the poverty-reduction front, and then also on the democratic governance front. That is unprecedented in many ways. In the past, we either got a little bit of political freedom, but a lot of economic mismanagement, or we got economic mismanagement and political repression at the same time. Now we are in an era where even if things are not moving as quickly as they should and as we expect, they are in general trending upwards. Political and economic developments in Ghana are trending upwards, and that is good. I expect progress to continue, partly because Ghanaians continue to care about having good governance. The public has also become increasingly empowered to demand accountability, responsibility, and responsiveness from our government. We may not be getting enough of it, but at least the opportunity is there and it has stayed open so far.

To answer directly your question, I would say: if the democratic space continues to stay open; if the media regime continues to stay liberal; if civil society continues to be so empowered and active; and especially if elections continue to be competitive, generally free and peaceful, then Ghana will continue to make progress on the economic, political, and social fronts. Having said that, I think there are some areas where we can do more and do better. Also, there are some things we have to do in order to protect this process and to prevent a reversal. One of them has to do with the persistent inequality, and especially North-South inequality in Ghana. It is not fair to expect that the progress we are making will continue or can be sustained unless we bridge the North-South inequality, or bridge inequality altogether. What we have now, which is good, is that we are reducing poverty. We may succeed in reducing poverty and we are likely to meet some of the Millennium Development Goals, but we will do even better if we also begin to bridge spatial inequality. I also believe we have to do something about decentralisation. Much of the progress we are making on the economic front gets eroded by migration from the rural areas to the urban areas, especially of young people/school-leavers who really have no chance of making it in the city but also cannot accept their lot staying in the rural areas. I think rural development would do much better if we were more decentralised politically and administratively.

IA-D: Thank you very much.

EG-B: You are most welcome.

December 2007

Mr Ken Ofori-Atta

Mr Ken Ofori-Atta is the Executive Chairman and Co-founder of the Databank Financial Services Limited, the leading investment banking firm in Ghana. In 2007, Databank won the first ever Most Respected Company in Ghana Award, while Mr Ofori-Atta was voted the second Most Respected CEO in Ghana, in a poll organised by Pricewater-houseCoopers (Ghana) Limited in association with Business and Financial Times.

Mr Ofori-Atta has over twenty years' experience in the finance and investment banking industry in both the United States and Ghana. He has worked with Salomon Brothers and Morgan Stanley, both in New York, on debt and equity issues and financing for a variety of industries. Upon returning to Ghana, he co-founded Databank in 1990, a company which has since developed into a full-service investment banking firm offering stock brokerage, corporate finance, asset management, equity research and private equity services. In particular, Databank has played a very significant role in the development of capital markets and mobilisation of offshore funds to the Ghana Stock Exchange. It currently manages the most successful Pan African Equity Mutual Fund, the $80 million EPACK. Mr. Ofori-Atta is also on the Boards of Trust Bank Limited of The Gambia, and Enterprise Insurance Company (EIC).

His contributions to the financial system and commitment to excellence have earned Mr Ofori-Atta a nomination as the only Black African in the world's top fifty financial managers for the 21st century and recognition as Marketing Man of the Year for 1996 by the Chartered Institute of Marketing, Ghana. He is the first African fellow of the Aspen Institute's Henry Crown Leadership programme and Co-founder and Chairman of the African Leadership Initiative.

Mr Ofori-Atta attended Achimota School in Ghana, before

proceeding to Columbia University in New York, where he earned a BA in Economics. He also holds an MBA from the Yale School of Management. He is married with three children.

Ivor Agyeman-Duah: Many years after independence, why would you say that it took so long for people of your generation – Ghanaians who have acquired international skills – to come back to Ghana and contribute to economic development?

Ken Ofori-Atta: Actually, that is interesting, because at least my recollection of the time we were growing up was that our parents were going and coming back, and then there seemed to have been a change in that sociology, that in the 1980s a lot of us after secondary school took awhile longer to come back. I think there was a dislocation in the society; the advent of the military coup, especially the Rawlings era, kept considerable numbers of us out. It wasn't until the 1990s, when there seemed to be a shift back to democracy and rule of law that you had people beginning to trickle in, to come back to support the development of the economy.

IA-D: Would you say it was a critical mass, in terms of the return of people of your generation?

KO-A: It took awhile. We came in 1990-91 to start this enterprise, but I think the real flow had been somewhere after 2000, when we saw a lot more critical mass of people coming in, and for the new generation, people graduating after their first degree and coming back because they saw opportunities at home. So there has been a sea change in these past seven years.

IA-D: Before decolonisation, it took Kwame Nkrumah, J. B. Danquah, Joe Appiah, William Ofori-Atta and others awhile – between 10 to 15 years – to finish their studies and acquire some knowledge. They then came back and started the decolonisation period – in terms of the actual struggle to free the Gold Coast from colonial rule. That was one class of people. In your generation, some of you were away for about the same length of time – 10 to 15 years. What was the mission of your generation of "returnees"?

KO-A: I've never really thought about it that way. It's so difficult to compare your generation to the generation that literally founded the country, but clearly it's a different "army of patriots", I would say. Ours has been a return to continue with the skill set that we have acquired, towards the economic evolution of this country. I daresay it's been a struggle, because it has not been a society, at least in the past 30-40 years that revered entrepreneurship and success. That has always been a challenge, even though we know for sure that the successes of cocoa farmers who became very rich and powerful was once upon a time something taken for granted, until Nkrumah's rules took more of the capital into a centralised system, as opposed to an individual basis. But I guess since we have been back, we have penetrated that consciousness to let people begin to appreciate that individuals do matter, that people are assets, and allowing people's creative energies to be exploited actually goes to promoting the total development of the economy. But I think these are fights that would take another decade or so to be re-institutionalised.

IA-D: What were the skills that your generation of people in the "Diaspora" brought to the table?

KO-A: I suspect the difference was that our fathers went, got educated, and came back primarily to get into Public Service – universities, hospitals, politics, education, etc – and therefore more often than not, they had not acquired any working experience in the West. This new armada of returnees were more people who went to school, found means of getting employment on all levels – from cleaning homes to working on Wall Street, in the best financial firms and law firms and also in the hospitals – and so it's an incredible kaleidoscope of skill set, which is necessary for the development of a modern society. I think it also counts to transform the dogma that it is politics only that develops the country into more of an economic paradigm which says, "Let's look at the skills relevant on the Private-Sector level to push this economy into a modern state". That is what we bring. It challenges the existing appreciation of individual versus the political regime or elite, and we are still trying to adjust as a society to these sorts of new forces that we have to deal with and acknowledge if we are to develop.

IA-D: Talking specifically about your own experiences, what kind of

skills did you acquire after your education in the United States, and where did you acquire these skills?

KO-A: Well I was really blessed with my decade or so in the States. In Ghana, I went to Achimota School for secondary school, then I got into Columbia undergrad in New York, and by the time I graduated in 1984, it was really the Reagan era, which was a break in terms of Wall Street being recognised again as a powerhouse of development. So we were all swept into the City as graduates, and got involved in corporate finance and mergers and acquisitions in the heat of that period. I managed to save some money and then went to graduate school at Yale for an MBA and came back to the Street to work at Salomon Brothers. So really, one got "in the ring" of the highest order of financial engineering that was happening in the States in a very charged period of major transactions and development of the US financial system. So that was the type of exposure one obtained between the skill set and between also demystifying Wall Street for an African, and having the confidence that such things could be replicated and that, with a good education and a clarity of purpose, our nations could also be transformed. Because not only did you get close to the entrepreneurs whom you were looking to finance, but you were also working in the trenches to find solutions.

During that period, you also got to appreciate the financial economic history of the States and the role of the Vanderbilts and the J. P. Morgans in terms of development of the country: how the railroad system was financed, how major infrastructure deals were done, which all seemed to be clear collaboration between Wall Street and Washington, but with the titans of Wall Street driving it. Now there's a very different sense in Ghana, where one believes that government should be the one doing all of these. Once you break and change that paradigm, you realise your relevance to the modernisation of your society, and therefore the confidence to challenge existing dogma, to say that there are various parties to this development enterprise that we are going forward with.

IA-D: Did it make you think that you wanted to do a similar thing, or at least engage in a similar activity in Ghana on your return?

KO-A: But the return was not as choreographed as it might seem. I left in August 1980 to go to the States and then the Rawlings coup happened in 1981 – the "Second Coming" as they call it – and therefore my family had left. Dad (Dr. Jones Ofori-Atta) was in Parliament then, but he left and became Advisor to the Central Bank in Uganda. So before I knew it, from 1980 to 1990 I had not been back in the country. I came to visit for the first time in April 1990 and just felt a tug to come back home. I wasn't too clear on what I was coming home to do, except that there was skill set that made one comfortable in the sense that if it didn't work, one could go back to continue with what one wanted to do. Even without that clarity, there was, however, a confidence in the limitlessness of what one could achieve if one decided on a course of action. That was really it – breaking that bound of limits and saying to oneself that you are a citizen and determining, even though one was not clear what one wanted to do, that "I'm coming back to stay and nothing is going to drag me out anymore". And so, as an educated person with this skill set, one could find a way to apply it to the benefit of the country.

IA-D: What was the economic atmosphere, and especially public policy orientation in terms of what role the Private Sector was to play in economic development?

KO-A: When I returned, the nation had determined that it wanted to return to democratic rule; they had been through the country and that was clearly being stated. The Botchway-Rawlings regime had also embraced the Economic Recovery Programme and the Structural Adjustment Programme of the World Bank and IMF, so clearly one was working in an environment in which market prices were the determinants of how things worked. The currency was free-floating and interest rates were also market-determined, so there was beginning to be a space for both the Private Sector economically and the rule of law and the sense of democracy, which then in a sense gave you room to operate, whether you had different political sheen or not. The challenge then was whether you were ready to take that risk of a transition period, but the trend was clearly towards the Private Sector as the "engine of growth", as they used to say, and democracy coming in.

When do you plant your flag? Most people thought it was rather early to take the bet in 1990.

IA-D: How was Databank Financial Services set up in the midst of this?

KO-A: In the midst of this, my cousin, Danny, was a contractor, who passed recently. Then there was another colleague from Yale who graduated a year after me, James Akpo, and then a childhood friend, Keli Gadzekpo, who was working in Washington D.C. at Peat Marwick. So as I thought through the idea of coming back, I solicited collaboration with them and we set up this company called Databank, primarily to organise and analyse data and support foreign investors in making decisions to invest in the country. We found out that people just don't pay for such consultancy work, and fortunately that Ghana Stock Exchange was then going to be opened in November, so we re-oriented our skill set to look at the Exchange as a means for which our company would be functioning.

I think that was just a break in industry that did not exist, that had very little understanding with family pressures which said, "What are you doing back home, because there is really nothing for you here"; given the level of development of the financial system and the uncertainties of the political environment. But we were challenged and loved what we were doing and were confident, I suppose, that we had a skill set that was universally transferable and so taking that risk or that challenge was not as overwhelming as one would have thought. Clearly, one was not looking to make fortunes, so it made life a lot easier.

IA-D: So with a weak financial sector, as you were saying, at that time were you able to make any impact in terms of the financial growth of the industry?

KO-A: Well I think that can clearly be assessed by where we are today, but when we started the stock market had 11 companies, the market cap was about $75 million, and the index which we created – the Databank Stock Index – was pegged at 100 and by the end of the first year – that's November/December – it had come down to 85. Today it is $16 billion it is over 12,000 in terms of the index, 33 companies listed. An incredible amount of money has come through, from a market cap which was maybe 0.1 per cent of the GDP to something that is equal to the GDP of the country today. It has been slow in happening, but I don't see a modern state that should not have a capital market, a stock exchange, and the successes such as Ashanti Goldfields, the recent sovereign bond, etc. all indicate the impact that we have made in the financial landscape.

IA-D: Would you say that the collaboration between the Ghana Stock Exchange and Databank was one of the most successful Public-Private sector collaborations we've had in contemporary financial history?

KO-A: You know, it was informal, however we had one of the great leaders as the MD of the Stock Exchange at that time, Dr Yeboa Amoa, who realised the importance of the Stock Exchange, realised the skill set that we brought in terms of modern financial skills, and a way in which he could legitimise the Stock Exchange not as a Mickey Mouse operation but as a Stock Exchange which had Wall Street alumni participating in it. So, unlike quite a number of leaders here, he was very willing to share that space and promote us, and in that vein, our skill set was also accepted, encouraged, and we've built something that has become enduring.

IA-D: Apart from people sometimes resenting people like you with skills from outside, the confidence in the economy itself was also low at the time; so how were Ghanaians prepared to buy into some of these stocks, some of these companies, whose reliability in terms of profit were not assured?

KO-A: Ghana has sometimes quite a psychotic character because in the 1970s, Acheampong nationalised quite a number of the multinationals, or insisted that at least 40 per cent of those companies should be Ghanaian-owned, so clearly he created a set of investors who were invested in UAC, PZ, but had sort of gone and put to bed their share certificates. So there was something there that was going to be built on and inasmuch as people were nervous or unclear, there was also a remembrance that they owned these shares and therefore something better could be done about them. The decline in the economy made financial instruments quite worthless so it was only when the Exchange was established in 1990 that people began to dig up their certificates and saw a certain worth in them.

So you had a group of people for whom it was in their interests to protect this, whilst you also had another group who were unsure as to what this would lead to and what it was that we were doing. It also was a challenge to the existing banking infrastructure, which had been the only means through which we all transacted all financial transactions. So this alternative proved a challenge for even those in the financial industry.

IA-D: Acheampong and others nationalised private businesses, but we also saw Databank engaged in the privatisation of Ashanti Goldfields; this also created arguments in the financial and political circles – so what actually happened?

KO-A: Well, there was Ashanti Goldfields I, II, and III. Ashanti Goldfields I, post-Acheampong being able to secure substantial holdings for Ghana by re-ordering what Lonrho had, was what gave Ghana the opportunity in 1994 to put the company on the various stock markets – Ghana, London, and Australia. That created the normal privatisation argument, as to whether a company should be privatised or not, and we were part of the slew of brokers who evangelised this privatisation and sold the shares, etc., etc.

I don't think that was as controversial as Ashanti Goldfields II, which was in the 1998-99 era, where the group Lonmin was looking to buy the company from the government and the government felt that it was being ambushed and that the pricing was not what they would otherwise have gotten. But it was also peppered by the whole hedging crisis, and that created a situation which was clearly, in my mind, management's responsibility. We did not feel, as we were mandated by government as Databank and CAL Bank to represent government in this saga that the price that they were giving us was appropriate; we felt that our value in Geita – that is the mine in Tanzania – and the whole portfolio should command a higher price. However, the strength of character of the Head of State, Jerry John Rawlings, and the CEO of the company, Sam Jonah, created a whole different cacophony which clouded the issues that we as investment bankers had to deal with. Taking the two personalities aside, the question before us was to determine whether what was being put before us was good for Ghana or not, and we felt that it wasn't.

I think Ashanti Goldfields III, where Anglo American purchased it in this present regime a number of years later, goes to prove the difference in price that we eventually got at this juncture. So it was a difficult period for the firm, working for an unpopular government and therefore being seen, erroneously, as agents of government as opposed to investment bankers facing a transaction that had to be done. If we look at what transaction was eventually done in the NPP regime, I don't think anybody would now dispute that our analysis of the situation was right and it was a good time to let Ashanti go. then.

IA-D: Did this increase your own personality and that of Databank in terms of high profile, internationally? I also understand that your father, Jones Ofori-Atta, who is a distinguished economist in his own right, was against the privatisation.

KO-A: Dad was against the privatisation, and he, if you realise, in 1968 was also against the famous Abbot privatisation. I don't think there is ever sort of a right or a wrong. I mean, I thought that privatisation was something that should go ahead but they had genuine concerns about the privatisation including a lack of clarity on the use of the proceeds. I guess history will bear them out; we still can't quite say what we did with the proceeds. So those were warnings that maybe Parliament should have taken seriously and therefore circumscribed exactly how these proceeds should be used. Today, we are not sure what occurred.

IA-D: What is the standing of Databank now in terms of work profile, in terms of your equity standings in Ghana and beyond?

KO-A: We've had quite a blessed period in terms of where we are. As you know, we started from one room in Kantamanto in 1990-91, borrowed $25,000 in 1992 from CAL Bank and STC, which was short-term money between five of us, and we currently are about 100 people. We have four offices in Ghana – Takoradi, Kumasi, Tema, and Accra; we've opened up in The Gambia and Liberia; and we have quite a commanding presence on the Stock Market. So the whole spread of the Mutual Fund Industry has been spearheaded by us. Currently we have one mutual fund called EPACK, which is not only invested on the Ghana Stock Exchange, but is Pan-African with branches on 14 exchanges out of 23 on the continent. Our Research Team last year won the Best Research House on the continent and our Institutional

Investor Group also won the Best Institutional Investor Group. We were co-managers in the recent Sovereign Bond Floatation that occurred for $750 million for the country. So we are doing quite a bit, and more significantly, sort of evangelising the issue of savings and investment culture, which is critical if we are going to develop because the level of investment is somehow tied to the savings culture of the people, outside of what you can bring in.

We are pleased with where we are but there is a lot more to do. Our challenge is to operate on the Stock Exchanges of all countries in Africa, to be managing accounts for two million Ghanaians by 2010, and to be managing about $2 billion as an Asset Management Enterprise, and then to go public so that the company will take on a much more profound and lasting image. So there is still a way to go yet. It has been 17 years of some sober reflections, lots of successes, and a deep feeling that we have, at least in a small way, opened a certain vista of development which otherwise might have been some-what stunted.

IA-D: What would you say has been the biggest impact on the Ghanaian economy – of your operations I mean?

KO-A: Um...

IA-D: Are there so many?

KO-A: It's difficult to quantify unless one sort of can translate the transactions one has been involved in as impacting the Ghanaian psyche, which are the work in Ashanti, bringing companies to the Stock Market, our work in privatisations, and culminating this year in the company being voted by peer CEOs as the Most Respected Company in the country. That came as somewhat of a surprise, but we felt that once again what we were doing was in the right direction, and our values and our unapologetic recognition of God in what we do as an institution was a lasting paradigm that we should continue to pursue.

IA-D: Religious belief defines what you do here; it's even on the building, it's in the people who work here I'm told.

KO-A: Yes, as a student of our history, to see where we came from in 1990, with an industry that did not exist, in a political environment that was choppy; to have not only survived that but to have been successful and moved on to significantly impact people's lives and the psyche of the country, makes you clearly feel that it's beyond your hard work and your skill set, but due to a certain Divine Support. And so, after much grappling with the issues of our success, we as a firm came to the determination that God has a big part in this and, in recognising that, we would steward the skill sets we have and be proper custodians to give.

IA-D: The Banking Sector was dominated by a few British banks – Barclays, Standard Chartered – and a few Ghanaian ones like SSB and CAL Bank. Would you say that this limited operation affected businesses in terms of savings and credit accessibility for entrepreneurs?

KO-A: Oh clearly, but even beyond that was really the state of the economy; an economy that was dominated by the Public Sector, such that the Private Sector was literally crowded out. When government paper was offering 40-50 per cent, really the banks were making an economic decision which supported their financing of the Public Sector. So I'm not even sure whether this was because of the dominance of the multinational banks or whether really rational economics would lead any CEO who wanted to bring profits to his shareholders to respond to the market environment. Of course there were certain legislative tools that also helped because recently, by the Bank of Ghana becoming more autonomous, it then cut down political clout to a certain degree from the Ministry of Finance, and therefore Monetary Policy was quite distinct from Fiscal Policy. It has gone ahead to eliminate the Secondary Reserve, reduce the Primary Reserve, which in itself injected a new capital into the system. Also by opening up Licensing, now you have a plethora of banks competing pretty aggressively to support the Private Sector.

But the Private Sector was also not that strong, and the ethics and ways of operation were not as formalised; we had a much larger informal system of operation than we currently have, even though it's still dominant. But you are also beginning to see a more formal entrepreneurial class emerging and the banks are responding to this new breed of entrepreneurs that are coming. You know, for most people we now have an economic environment which enables them to measure their risk much better than the way it used to be. So in a sense, one does not want to saddle the blame on the manner in which multinational banks operated, but more so, how *we* operated our economy and therefore led to decisions that all banks made. But, needless to say, with the expansion in the banking industries, both Barclays and Standard Chartered Bank are having to compete a lot harder than they used to before and that is a breath of fresh air.

IA-D: What are the pan-African dimensions of it? We now have Nigerian banks in Ghana, and you are operating in Liberia and The Gambia and I'm sure in the coming years this would be expanded. When we talk of Pan-Africanism, what are the economic dimensions?

KO-A: I think it's really a new period that we must recognise. In the same way in which Ghana is beginning to acknowledge the space that they should give the Private Sector, we should acknowledge the space we ought to give to international banks in our environment. Our traditional relationship with Nigeria is something we should cultivate more because they, by changing the rules in their banking system, have now created mega-banks capable of competing anywhere in the world. The question for us as a nation is: how do we create the environment for a banking industry that would rival any in the world and with Ghana being the gateway for that? That really should be something that should be a focus or challenge, and I think the challenge for companies like us, and the new ones that have come in, is appreciating that, and lobbying or creating the platform for that to happen, as opposed to waiting for government to lead that. We can see how the creation of these banking powerhouses in the United States in the 1800s and early-1900s led to the development of the economy. It was not because Washington prescribed it; it was because titans of industry appreciated how their country should develop and what they needed to do to attract the type of capital required to open up society.

IA-D: Structures were set up by your generation of businesses, and those who returned to West Africa from abroad. How did this translate into political influence – over Obasanjo in Nigeria, Johnson-Sirleaf in Liberia, Kufuor in Ghana, and others?

KO-A: I think it's a new order, and it's more of an economic paradigm I might say, which essentially is acknowledging that a bigger market in the sub-region is good for everyone. In particular, Ghana stands to gain tremendously if we can create this market because there is something about this country that makes people comfortable. How do you then translate these relationships with the other Heads of State to create a comfort level where we export skill sets, or create an environment which can export capital because this is a place to reside your capital?

Certainly with Nigeria, with the blessing of the Head of State, at the beginning of 2000 we were clearly in a crisis for the supply of fuel and President Kufuor was gracious enough in selecting me to join his group to negotiate for better terms for oil to be delivered into the country at favourable rates. That stabilised the early beginnings of the Kufuor regime, and then with his own good policies, led to a more stable place. With Liberia, for example, it's interesting because with that, President Johnson-Sirleaf had determined that there would be electricity in Monrovia for the first time within 100 days of her Presidency, and, working with President Kufuor again, we were able to arrange financing, and worked with Volta River Authority (VRA) to switch on the lights at the right time. There is quite a tremendous amount of good will, therefore, being built by economic agents or bankers.

I think eventually it all leads to creating this environment as a country which is modernising fast, which is acknowledging the Private Sector as partners in this intense commitment to creating a modern society. So it has been helpful, and our challenge is to use it to the benefit of this country. We have a destiny of greatness as a country and the challenge is how to marshal the various resources we have, especially people resources, to be able to get to where we should be.

IA-D: As usual, you are being very modest. I'm told you have real influence on some of the top leaders in Africa, apart from what you say.

KO-A: I don't know. It's honest friendships, and if it benefits Ghana we do what we have to do.

IA-D: You are a member of the Kufuor government's Advisory Group on the Economy and Business. What specific role did your group, which is made up of other equally respected persons, play beyond giving advice that you can say has led to growth in the economy?

KO-A: This was the President's Ghana Investors Advisory Group, and I was of course in the Finance Committee. One thing that we focused on was the whole issue of Ghana as a Financial Services Hub, and therefore we were very instrumental in proposing the whole concept of Ghana being a Centre for Finance, which Barclays then moved on to create this Offshore Banking Act that is being proposed. There are the sort of hard manufacturing things that we must do, but I think we also recognise that with the nature of our people we could also do very well in the services-oriented area – providing Education to Africa, providing Healthcare services, and providing Financial services. We took the opportunity in that group to then look at the whole concept of Ghana as an offshore banking site, and began to put the pillars in place for that to occur. So that is one thing we have done that is very material to how we develop. Right now, the issue of development and investment capital cannot be linked and we need to do that.

IA-D: What are your own opinions on Ghana's economic development in the coming years?

KO-A: I am very bullish about the future, and I think this is really resided in the fact that we have an incredible store of human capital. We do have about 3 million Ghanaians outside. These people have all sorts of skill sets and they are currently bringing in over $1.5 billion a year. That clearly is a resource equivalent to or greater than cocoa, and more than gold. If we combine that with the natural resources of gold, cocoa, and now oil, I believe you have a powerful formula for development. And that under-girded by an enlightened civil society and an entrenched democracy, gives us just limitless potential. If ever there is going to be a first modern Black African state, I am unequivocal in my belief that it will be Ghana.

IA-D: Do you hope to play a major role in the process, post-today, in the Public Sector for instance?

KO-A: You know, I still feel very strongly about the Public-Private Sector partnership, because I think it's beyond the fact that you combine various skill sets to get a project done. It's also breaking the sociology that entrepreneurship is negative to one that is positive. We did talk about the Morgans and Vanderbilts, who never necessarily got into politics, but from the citadel of where they sat, and the skill set that they had, propelled growth within the country. I hope that I can remain in the financial industry but be more aggressive about the need for collaboration and change, and be instrumental in that type of transformation.

IA-D: Thank you very much.

KO-A: Thanks.

June 2008

Mr Tony Oteng-Gyasi

Mr Tony Oteng-Gyasi is the Founder and Managing Director of Tropical Cable and Conductor Limited, a manufacturing company of electric and telecommunication cables, and the only wholly-owned Ghanaian firm of its kind. He has other companies in the aluminium and garment industries. Mr Oteng-Gyasi also serves as the President of the Association of Ghana Industries (AGI), Chairman of the Council of the University of Ghana, and a Member of the Advisory Board of the African Centre for Economic Transformation (ACET), founded by former Head of the Economic Commission for Africa, Dr K.Y. Amoako, and chaired by Nobel laureate, Professor Joseph E. Stiglitz. He is a past Member of the Council of the Ghana Stock Exchange and has served for two terms as Vice- President of the Ghana Furniture Producers' Association (now the Furniture and Wood Products' Association of Ghana – FAWAG). In 2008, he was decorated with the National Award, Order of the Volta (Officer Division), by the President of Ghana, His Excellency John Agyekum Kufuor.

After one year of National Service with the Research Department of the Bank of Ghana (1975-76), Mr Oteng-Gyasi's career began at the Ghana Operation of British Petroleum, where he rose rapidly but resigned after nine years to pursue his entrepreneurial instincts. His first company, Tropical Products Limited, became the largest manufacturer of wooden crates and pallets in Ghana. He founded Tropical Cable and Conductor Limited in 1997, after concerns arose about the environmental impacts of wood products.

In 2000, Mr. Oteng-Gyasi earned the EMPRETEC Star Award for Entrepreneurial Achievement. The following year, his company was judged the fastest growing EMPRETEC Client Company and was short-listed for the Shell Award for Sustainable Development by the

Worldaware Institute, the UK charity with Her Majesty the Queen as Patron. In 2005, he was named Marketing Man of the Year at an awards ceremony held by the Chartered Institute of Marketing Ghana, and was also considered the INDUTECH Outstanding Personality in the Electrical Sector at the Ghana Industry and Technology Exhibition (INDUTECH 05) organised by the Association of Ghana Industries (AGI). Under his tenure at AGI, the Association has been appointed by the World Economic Forum as Ghana's partner in the compilation of the Global Competitiveness Index, which serves as a basis for comparison of business environments across countries.

Mr Oteng-Gyasi attended the University of Ghana, Legon, where he earned a BA in Economics in 1975. He also holds a Diploma in Marketing from the Chartered Institute of Marketing, UK. In 1987, he obtained a Qualifying Certificate in Law from the University of Ghana, and was called to the Ghana Bar in 1989, after a further two years at the Ghana Law School. He is married with five children.

I

Ivor Agyeman-Duah: Ghana's postcolonial dream was an industrialised state in sub-Saharan Africa. From the perspective of the business community, what do you think went right and what do you think went wrong?

Tony Oteng-Gyasi: Well, you're right, at independence we had very high hopes, and I believe that, as far as sub-Saharan Africa was concerned, we were one of the countries with the most potential. Whilst we have not fully realised our potential, I would not say that something went wrong. What I would say is: why haven't we done as well as we could have, especially in relation to our peer countries in Asia? I would attribute that to the peculiar problems of African countries, African economies. Military intervention has obviously not helped any of our colleague countries, nor has it helped Ghana at the times it came. A lack of leadership primarily – whether of the military or civilian type – has also been an issue here, particularly so if we remember that whenever we talk about military intervention, invariably the reason given for the intervention has been some failure of leadership. Whether that is true or not, it has been used as an excuse and we see that the military people who have intervened have themselves not done as well as they thought they could, which leads me to think that without leadership qualities, good intentions are not enough. So Ghana hasn't done as well as we could have, but compared with other countries in our sub-region, we are clearly ahead.

IA-D: The State in the 1960s was supposed to lead in the Industrialisation of the economy. What was the role of the Private Sector then, when the State was dominant in terms of direction, in terms of policy?

TO-G: I think that the so-called "dominance" of the State is a little overstated. Of course, we had the state-owned companies, and because they were state-owned they were dotted all around and they became prominent. But at the same time, if you look at an economic directory of Ghana in 1960, you find many non-state-owned manufacturing enterprises. I mean, the very founder of the Association of Ghana Industries (AGI), Dr (Mrs) Esther Ocloo is an example of a non-state-owned company which has fortunately survived up to this day. We had industries by people like Philips of Wiseway, the Peprahs and many others – all these people had manufacturing concerns which were not state-owned. They did not have the benefit of the publicity that the state-owned ones had but in terms of numbers and variety of products, there were many more private companies than the state-owned. So we have always run, in my opinion, a mixed economy, but I think the Private Sector – the privately-owned portion – has always been larger than the state-owned portion.

IA-D: Some of them have also had a short life-span in the Private Sector; in some of the family-based businesses, for instance, when the founder is gone, the business collapses and things like that.

TO-G: You are right, almost all of them have had a relatively short life-span, but that is more to do with the state of two things: one, our own management capabilities; and two, the economic environment in which we have all had to operate. It is not only the privately-owned firms which have gone under, or have not survived beyond the founder's generation; the state-owned firms have also had similar problems. Many of them have not survived, or have been propped up to appear to have survived. So really it is more a function of the management and then the economic environment in which the whole Private Sector has had to operate.

IA-D: With modern ways of doing business, like the operations of the Stock Exchange where companies can sell shares, do you think this will change the dynamics as they used to be in the 1960s and 70s?

TO-G: Definitely. Modern methods – you mentioned the Stock Exchange yes, venture capital funds are also coming in, yes – are changing the dynamics of doing business, but there is something more fundamental at stake. We are beginning to realise that as a nation the State's role in ensuring a certain kind of economic stability is not enough. I think that the worst failure of the State in previous times was to assume its role is limited to macro-stability. Where you allow inflation to hit hyper-inflation levels like we have seen in this country before; you have an exchange rate that is depreciating by the day, sometimes by the hour; you have interest rates which have been known in this country to have gone as high as almost 50 per cent it is obviously not good. But the State must go beyond that. The lessons we have learned from this is that, no matter the kind of management you have in place, it is very difficult to run a successful enterprise in such an unstable economic environment. As a nation, I believe we have reached the stage where we have realised that Government's role at the very minimum should be to keep a stable macroeconomic environment and allow actors to operate within it. In addition, the State must also make policy at the micro or sector level to achieve sustained accelerated growth.

IA-D: Your predecessors, including the distinguished Dr (Mrs) Esther Ocloo set up the Association of Ghana Industries. What were the intentions at the time?

TO-G: At the time, they felt that indigenous industrialists, indigenous businesspeople did not really have a chance against the might of the large multinationals, the large foreign-owned companies who dominated the economic landscape. So really the original vision of the founding fathers was to have an indigenous business grouping as against the then-Ghana National Chamber of Commerce, which had all the big trading names and industries in there. I am glad to say that, with the passage of time, we have evolved beyond this vision; we have reached a stage where now we realise that the ownership of the enterprise is not as important as the environment and the possibilities such as employment generation that an enterprise has in that environment. So now we are not an association of *Ghanaian* industries, we are the Association of *Ghana* Industries, and our membership includes the largest multinationals to the smallest SMEs.

IA-D: Definitely the objectives of that period were different to those of today. The economy has expanded, there is acquisition of finance capital, the population has increased, the entrepreneurial class has also increased – definitely the objectives cannot be the same.

TO-G: No, they are not the same; we are looking ahead. This year is our 50th Anniversary when AGI celebrates its Golden Jubilee, and the theme for that celebration is "Creating African Industrial Giants". So we have looked beyond starting up and being able to operate and surviving to the stage where we are thinking about creating industrial giants; we are thinking about companies from Ghana being able to compete globally, being able to compete with the best anywhere in the world, and this is the kind of vision which underlies our efforts today.

IA-D: So what is the profile of the AGI? What companies, what firms make up the AGI?

TO-G: We have over 1000 companies, ranking from the biggest multinationals I mentioned – the Unilevers, the Nestlés, the Ghacems, the PZs – I mean, they are all there, and we go as low as some of the very small SMEs.

IA-D: How are these big ones able to relate to the small ones?

TO-G: They are divided along three lines. One, we have regional offices. Two, we have sector groupings. Three, we have categories of size, so you will find that categories 1, 2 and 3 are companies of a certain size and we go as low as a category 7 I believe, which has the smallest sizes. We seek to have the big ones give sub-contracts to the small ones and in the process nurture them to grow.

IA-D: When industrialists complain today of constraints within the industry, what are they really talking about?

TO-G: Several. Let me give you some of the findings of our latest business climate surveys. This is a survey we do annually to look at the challenges facing Industry in Ghana and I think it will be best to hear from what this survey says. In 2007, when we carried out the business climate survey to find the challenges to doing business in Ghana, this is a record of the ranking: number one at that time was the national load shedding programme – that is the electricity problem we had last year. I am glad to say that that is no longer relevant, but the next after that was competition from imported goods – we are talking about China, globalisation, competition from especially Asia – and then the cost of credit. So this should be an indication. Other challenges include access to finance, access to land, land ownership, bureaucracy, lack of transparency and things like that.

IA-D: Have you, as an Association been able to dialogue with people who are putting up these constraints, or who are connected with these constraints, in terms of how to generate more growth within the industry?

TO-G: Yes, that is the purpose of doing this climate survey in the first place, so that we have basis for the kind of engagements that we have with policymakers. Once we have this survey done, we then move to the next stage of engaging policymakers on solutions to these problems for Industry. I think, like I said, the national load shedding programme was the number one problem in 2007. Thankfully, that is almost all but over. As at now, we are talking actively to the Ministry of Trade, Industry, PSD & PSI, the inspection agencies, various people, about competition from imported goods.

IA-D: Have these problems always existed?

TO-G: Have they always existed? Yes, they may have always existed, but the world in the last decade or so with globalisation has changed dramatically, to the extent now that you can have goods from China on your shelves in a matter of weeks. So though they may have always existed, in the past few years it has become a major problem.

And let me explain that we are not talking about fair competition here. When we talk about competition from imported goods, we are talking about imported goods that do not meet the quality standards which we as a nation have set for ourselves. That is the first thing. Local manufacturers are enjoined by Ghana law to manufacture goods which meet a certain standard, and because we are based here, you can have regular inspections from the relevant regulatory agencies – Ghana Standards Board (GSB), Food & Drugs Board (FDB), etc., etc. – so you have to produce to meet those standards. If you allow somebody to bring in goods which do not meet those standards and they undercut you on price and take the market from you; that is an unfair competition. So that is one kind.

There is also actual dumping: the goods may meet the quality standards, but you find that goods may end up on your market at just the cost of the raw materials which go into them and are sometimes sold cheaper than on their home markets. So that is another form of unfair competition, and these are real problems. Obviously, governments may be subsidising some of the industries in their countries; countries may have such huge production capacities that, beyond a certain level of production, they can virtually afford to give away the goods at below production cost. That is a kind of dumping and we need to look at it.

IA-D: Globalisation has also done some good things. Access to credit is not as it used to be, interest rates at the banks are not as they used to be, and even at the local level, rural banks have increased in terms of build-up by 30-40 per cent so people doing business at the local level, in villages, have access to credit. Is that not the case now? When you talk of problems with access to credit, is it not at least better than it used to be?

TO-G: There has been an improvement definitely in access to credit. The very fact that the banking industry has been opened up – you have more banks in the country – is a plus. The fact that banks are being asked to capitalise at a higher level than before, so that they become bigger and deeper and can lend more, is another plus. However, when you have a situation where government still borrows too much from the banks, there is always the tendency that the Private Sector does not get enough access to credit. That is one. There is also the situation where the banks have not grown big enough to be able to finance really big, in Ghana terms, Private Sector projects. For instance, there is a huge demand for cement in this country. If a Ghanaian wanted to set up another cement plant and needs $200-million, how many banks in Ghana would be able to do this? I doubt that any single bank in Ghana can do it, and even with a consortium of banks, some of these really big projects are difficult. But like I say, the Central Bank's effort at getting the banks to increase their capitalisation is a step in the right direction.

IA-D: So what is the profile of the industries? What do we manufacture in Ghana that you would say forms the bulk of AGI's profile?

TO-G: We have several sectors from automotive to leather and garments, electricals and electronics, building materials, pharmaceuticals, rubber and plastics, foods and beverages, telecommunications, service sectors, etc. And I think that there may not be many industries in Ghana, but in almost in every sector you have a few companies if you realise that our membership runs over 1000.

IA-D: What is the domestic consumption of what these industries produce and what percentage is for export?

TO-G: For the manufacturing sector, most of it is consumed locally. Apart from a few companies who produce goods like canned tuna and processed cocoa for export, you will find that for manufacturing, most consumption is local. But there are areas which are coming up very strongly on the export side. Virtually, all our pharmaceutical manufacturing industries have markets across the sub-region, and this is an area we, at AGI, are looking at very actively because we think that the West African sub-region is a natural export market for manufacturers in Ghana, and we have demonstrated this again and again. We do what we call "solo exhibitions" in countries around us and each time we have gone to an exhibition, there has been tremendous interest in manufactured products from Ghana. Some have led to businesses for many of our members, some have not, but the major problem when it hasn't led to business has been the mechanics of shipping and transport and intra-West African trade more than the quality or pricing of our goods.

IA-D: One of the areas that appear to be neglected is the creative industries – we are talking of traditional products, cultural products, like *kente*, *adinkra*, we are talking of beads and the Bolga baskets. These could form a whole composite of growth but it looks like over the years this area has been neglected. Is that the case?

TO-G: Yes, it is the case, but I wouldn't use the word "neglect". The problem with some of our creative industries has been that the very creativity which has enabled it to become an attractive product has also been a stumbling block in the sense that, to make many of these things marketable products, you have to increase the scale of production, you have to have a consistent quality, you have to be able to do it within a certain period of time. In other words, the modern methods of production must come into play. Where the creators of these articles are reluctant, due to some cultural inhibitions where they think they are the beneficiaries of some hidden knowledge or talent or skill which has been passed on to them from generations, to give out the information in order to commercialise it or use modern production methods for doing it, then it becomes an obstacle.

I think a lot of our creative industries have suffered in this regard. If you look at the *kente* industry for instance, for all the decades, if not centuries, that we have been involved in *kente* weaving, we have seen it as a woven product; *kente* is always woven. Why must it be so? All the Chinese did was look at it and print it. Initially, when printed *kente* started coming out of China, many in Ghana felt that it was inferior, that it wasn't the right thing, and wouldn't even consider it as competition. But for the outside world – the market where you want to get to – the impressions were different. So we need to find ways in which we can adapt some of these local products into international commodities.

IA-D: You're talking of China, and there was also the Vietnamese copying of the Bolga basket and then making it an international product now. We're talking of property rights internationally, copyrights. Do these things work in the business sense from what abusive practices that we see?

TO-G: What people don't know about the Bolga baskets and the reason why we seem to be losing the battle to Asia – Vietnam and

China – is the fact that, initially, many of the American companies who buy these for their chains started out placing orders in Ghana, and many of our producers – I wouldn't call them "manufacturers" – but the artisans who produced these things were unable to meet the demand. So here we have a product which we have not been able to commercialise. It is an absence of modern production methods, skills, techniques which is leading to us losing our creative advantage in this manner. So I would call for an in-depth look, a more, if you like, business-like, professional approach to the production and marketing of these goods. Intellectual property rights in some of these areas are not only difficult to prove, but also expensive to enforce. We should rather concentrate on commercial exploitation of our skills and knowledge in these areas.

IA-D: So you think in this particular instance that it's more to do with the traditional mentality of the artisans than, for instance, access to credit?

TO-G: Well, both. In many of these things you can't just take out one cause; it's normally a combination of factors. Access to credit you can always solve, but where the talent-possessors, the people with the skills, are not ready to help duplicate it, where he will take only five apprentices for one year and he does not want any more because he thinks he is $protecting himself and protecting his knowledge, then no amount of money and management will help. So it is a combination of factors, and we need to deal with these factors together. We need to go into programmes on a project-like approach, so if it is Bolga baskets, what are the problems in there? Finance? Skills? People to do it? The mentality of the people who first discovered how to do it? The approach should be as a whole and try to solve all the problems in order to say, "We want to move this product from a traditional scale to an international commodity".

IA-D: It looks like this needs to go down in terms of dissemination of what you were discussing and also backed by stronger government policy. Is AGI looking into possible collaboration with the Ministry of Finance & Economic Planning and the other related Ministries to ensure that people in the rural areas, where thousands and thousands of these people reside, understand these issues?

TO-G: One of the philosophical problems the Association of Ghana Industries has had with past and present governments is the free market. I mean, our policymakers – and I want to emphasise past and present – have been led to believe that if you create a certain economic environment, development and job creation and manufacturing and progress must necessarily follow. But experience of all countries who have managed to break out of poverty and under-development shows that it is not enough to create the so-called "enabling environment". You will need active intervention at various stages, because the market out there is not perfect. The information in the market, the theory underlying all the theories of economics has certain assumptions which do not exist. I think that gradually the realisation is coming, and I hope it does to all African Governments, that governments need to intervene in markets to encourage and to help their industry grow.

II

IA-D: We have you as Chairman of the Council of the University of Ghana, our premier University. What do you think necessitated the appointment of business executives? I understand you are not the first person from the business class to be so appointed.

TO-G: I think it's a very simple reason. The universities are not businesses; they are not for profit – that should be clear. But at the same time, they should be run like businesses: they should be run efficiently and they should be run in a way which is sustainable. I hope this is the fundamental reason why government has seen it fit at various times to appoint businesspeople as Chairmen of the University Council.

IA-D: As Chairman of the Council, you should have an idea as to what kind of training is being given to students, especially those who are interested in business, who are interested in coming out to set up enterprises and things like that. Do you think they are adequately prepared to face the world after school?

TO-G: You know, like many other universities across the world, the University of Ghana produces a wide range of students. We have some of the most brilliant, world-class students who can compete with any student anywhere. Sometimes people complain that some of our graduates are not good enough but that is a tiny minority which we are working to address. So we have that spectrum, but the important thing is to have the mass middle, where we are producing a consistent graduate of acceptable quality.

A university is not a vocational training institute; you are training minds, and you are training minds in a way in which they should be able to adapt to their place of work in as short a time as possible. You find that graduates from the University of Ghana, whether in History or Political Science or Classics, actually find their way sometimes into Banking and in Finance and Investment, which, I think, is an indication of the quality of people that we are producing. However, in recent times, there has been a lot of talk of producing graduates who are suited to the world of work, as in technical subjects, technical areas. Being a dynamic institution, this is an area which the University of Ghana is addressing itself. We've just opened an Engineering school and we are looking at adding a School of Pharmacy in a few months' time. All this is in order to continue to make our graduates relevant to the needs of our nation.

IA-D: But if University PhD holders, Lecturers, Senior Lecturers, Professors are trained outside with a set of models which may not be very relevant to the situation back home, and then train students who are supposed to come out and solve local problems, the models may cause problems. Have they not at the university?

TO-G: They shouldn't if whichever university that trained them is worth its own name. I mean, if you go to Harvard Business School, and like you said the Harvard MBA programme is based on case studies as is well known, when you come back to Ghana to teach, one would expect that you would develop case studies based on local companies, local conditions. Of course you can always have the international flavour there with the odd foreign case study, but if your training in Harvard has been worth it and you are coming to teach in Ghana, you need to be able to adapt.

Let me also add that Curriculum Development is something which we are doing, and doing regularly in Legon. As I talk now, we are in discussions with the Carnegie Institute for some help in looking at Curriculum Development. The strength of the university system is its ability to adapt to the changing needs of a nation, the society which the university is supposed to help and assist. While sometimes changing and adapting can be slow or even painful, the important thing is that it is possible and it is getting done, and I think that Legon is a very good example of an institution which is moving in the right direction.

IA-D: Thank you very much.

TO-G: You're welcome.

July 2008

Dr Gobind Nankani

Dr Gobind Nankani is President of the Global Development Network (GDN) (an international non-governmental agency with offices in Giza, Egypt; New Delhi; and Washington, DC), a position he has held since August 2007. Before GDN, he worked for the World Bank in various capacities for more than 30 years, most recently as Vice-President for the Africa region from 2004-2006. He has also served as an Economic Advisor to the government of Ghana, of which he is a national. In recognition of his contribution to Ghana and Africa's development, and his promotion over the years of Social Development Policy and Financing, Dr Nankani was awarded the Order of the Volta by President J.A. Kufuor in July 2008.

Dr Nankani joined the World Bank in 1976 as a young professional and has since held management positions in various regions and sectors across the Bank. He has, for instance, served as Country Director for Brazil (1997-2001), Country Director for Argentina, Brazil, Chile, Paraguay, and Uruguay (1994-97), and Chief Economist for the South Asia region (1991-94). As Vice-President of the Poverty Reduction and Economic Management Network (PREM) from 2001-4, he oversaw the Bank-wide work on poverty reduction, growth, governance, trade, gender, and debt issues, including the Highly Indebted Poor Country (HIPC) programme. From 2004-6, Dr Nankani worked as Vice-President of the Africa region, in which role he was responsible for the overall strategy and management of the Bank's programme of financial knowledge and client relationships with all 47 Sub-Saharan African countries. He was also in charge of design and implementation of the World Bank's Africa Action Plan.

Dr Nankani provided overall direction to the 2004 work, *Economic Growth in the 1990s: Learning from a Decade of Reform*. He has a number of other publications to his credit, including: "Acting

Strategically and Building Trust: Reflections from Brazil", in I. Gill et al. *At the Frontlines of Development: Reflections from the World Bank* (2005), to which he also contributed the Foreword.

After earning a BSc from the University of Ghana, Legon, Dr Nankani proceeded to Harvard University, where he earned a Masters and PhD in Economics (1976).

I

Ivor Agyeman-Duah: When John Maynard Keynes led the British negotiation team, with his counterparts – Harry White and others – for the establishment of the World Bank and the International Monetary Fund, do you think that the post-World War II reconstruction they were setting up would increasingly serve the needs of the developing countries, developing economies, than the reconstruction of Europe?

Dr Gobind Nankani: I think the motivation behind the setting up of the World Bank and the IMF after the Second World War was in part to ensure a more stable global trading payments system and in part to help with the reconstruction of Europe. The word "development" did appear in the name International Bank for Reconstruction and Development (IBRD), but it was there simply as a cloak: there wasn't really any serious prediction that the Bank would be supporting development programmes in developing countries. But very soon after – certainly in 1947, when India got its independence, in the early 1950s with other countries in North Africa, and then in 1957, Ghana – that role quickly transformed. There was also a bit of surprise about how quickly Europe re-emerged from the Second World War, with the Marshall Plan and other activities. So very quickly the Bank and the Fund, in effect, had the time and opportunity to work with developing countries.

IA-D: In what ways does the sharing of big power – that is the Presidency of the Bank going to the Americans and the IMF to European countries – affect the way the Bank is run, especially in relation to Africa and its development?

GN: The nature of the leadership of the Bank and the Fund has been controversial for quite awhile, but in today's world it has really come to head. It is controversial because when we look at where the bulk of global growth today is taking place, it's in emerging and developing economies: India, China, Russia, and Brazil together are really the engines of growth of the global economy. We have a situation, therefore, of complete disconnect between the governance of the Bank, both in terms of representation of countries on the Board as well as the leadership at the Presidency, and global economic power. My feeling is that change is coming slowly; it has already begun on the IMF's board and it is likely to pick up speed. We've seen it also in discussions relating to the G8, which now increasingly invite developing and emerging economies to their meetings, and I think it's only a matter of time.

As to whether this has affected the Bank, it certainly has affected the perception of it. The governance of the Board, as well as the leadership of the Board, has affected perceptions. The quality of intellect and the experience that there is at the staff of the Bank is tremendous. There is no place else in the world with that concentration of talent and experience. My feeling is that the perception of the governance of the Bank being somewhat lopsided has affected its ability to advise governments: government's feel, perhaps – just perhaps – that the advice is not completely thought of from their point of view. So there's a de-leveraging of this advice and talent and experience that takes place because of this disconnect in governance, which is unfortunate.

Now I have to say very quickly that, at the end of the day, every government owes it to itself and its people to develop its own respect and point of view and to negotiate hard for this perspective with the Bank or the Fund. When countries do that, most of the time they succeed, so we should not let governance of the Bank be an excuse for everything that we fail to do.

IA-D: James Wolfenson, former President of the Bank, is credited by some as having made major reforms. Since you worked during his tenure, what were some of the things he did, particularly to change the perception that the institution has always been dictatorial?

GN: I think James Wolfenson's greatest contribution when you look at it with the benefit of hindsight was what he called his "comprehensive development programme", which then became a recommendation to countries to develop their own poverty reduction strategies. The biggest input he had there was in making it very clear that strategies had to be home-grown. Strategies had to be developed by the country; they needed to be developed in consultation with stakeholders in the country, including the NGOs, the Private Sector and the Churches. And this has now become so much a part of the way of thinking on development that people have even forgotten where the idea originally came from.

That said, James Wolfenson's legacy is really an excellent one because, if you'll remember, the period preceding Wolfenson's was a period in which, certainly on the African continent and in Ghana, there was a lot of talk about the Structural Adjustment Programme and its conditionalities and a sense that these policies were not fully developed at home. A lot of this has certainly changed as a result of James Wolfenson's contribution. Now, having said that, I think there is a long way for many countries to go. Ghana's Economic Recovery Programme (ERP) is much more focused and driven by Ghana's needs than, for example, an ERP in a country where domestic talent and experience are not as great as they are here, so countries are not taking equal advantage of this opening. That was certainly his biggest contribution.

IA-D: Why did it take so long for such major reforms to take place at the Bank?

GN: Well, everyone was caught unawares by the post-1979 global crisis. Oil prices, which are rising again today to phenomenal levels, went up in 1972 and then again in 79. In 1979, there was a tripling of prices. Until then, countries had been able to borrow or had good prices for their commodities and were able to make ends meet. In 1992, after the Mexican debt crisis, there was a realisation that the global economy had changed. There was almost a sense of panic that unless major reforms were undertaken, and were undertaken by all countries almost overnight, the situation would just go from bad to worse and poverty would increase and so on.

And so change began to work, with governments really under this kind of pressure to turn things around with policies that were well-intentioned, based on first principles, but not adapted really to countries. When you look back at the history of the Bank's advice on Marketing Boards, for example, all over Africa and in other countries, you cannot but say that the decision to induce governments to shut down Marketing Boards was actually wrong. It was wrong because it didn't take account of the fact that, when you shut down Marketing Boards, the Private Sector responds to fill the needs that the Marketing Boards were filling earlier. So advice always needs to be adapted to the conditions of a country and I think it was unfortunate, I think it was regrettable, but I can say that it was well-intentioned.

Certainly the learning of the 1990s has been good. I want to mention a particular study in which we looked at the lessons of growth in the 90s and the fundamental conclusion was that all the countries that had succeeded in the 90s were countries in which the growth and equity strategies were developed at home, taking account obviously of some general principles. Those principles are three: one, you have to have macroeconomic stability – you cannot have rising or volatile inflation; two, you have to take advantage of the global economy, not act as if the global economy is not there; and three, while you have to take advantage of markets, the State has a very critical role to play.

IA-D: Would you say that Ghana has always had the capacity in these negotiations with the Bank, especially from 1983 onwards, or has it just followed the instructions given by the Bank in terms of how to work on the economy?

GN: I would say that Ghana, certainly on the African continent, has had a lot more of a give-and-take relationship with the Bretton Woods institutions. Certainly the 1983 Economic Recovery Programme without a doubt developed here in Ghana, and I think over the years with the kind of international standing that Ghana has gained because of its reforms in the 1980s and 90s; it is also seen as a bit of a role model for the rest of the African continent. Having said that, obviously leadership is a problem; over time I think there has sometimes been a lapse of some bounds, but in general the average for Ghana is going up.

IA-D: In any case, there are many professionals from the developing world working at the Bank. Ghana, for instance, has around 100 people working between the World Bank and the IMF. Is it still reasonable to say that the leadership of the Bank is being hijacked by others and that we are being dictated to by the top if we have this calibre of economists coming from developing countries?

GN: Well, first it is true that there are a large number of Ghanaians at the Bank, much more in proportion to our population – certainly in the top two or three countries in proportion to our population. This is much less true in the IMF, not just for Ghana but for Africans in general; the Bank is much better represented. We have staff in all sectors and at various levels. The Bank is a very technocratic institution, where good technical work finds its voice. When we talked earlier about the governance structure of the Board, I emphasised perception much more than the reality. I'm sure there are issues on which all sensitivities do have an influence on staff country. It's hard to pinpoint, but I wouldn't say that never happens. But the big issue is much more on perception, and that will never be addressed until the governance structure changes. We should be happy that there are so many of us at the Bank, and I think we have voice. But it's a technocratic institution.

IA-D: Does it strike you in any way that after 50 years of its existence it is Britain under Gordon Brown that is leading the Commonwealth countries, including Ghana, in calls for reform of the Bank and how the Bank and the IMF could monitor and help evaluate the economies of Europe and America?

GN: It's not surprising that there is a call for reform of the Bank and the Fund at this time. If one looks at the last 50 years, whenever there was a global crisis – whether in 1972 or 79, or more recently in 98 after the Russian and Brazilian crises – there was always a call for reform of the Bretton Woods institutions. Gordon Brown is to be complimented for taking the bull by the horns using the mantle of the Commonwealth Group of Nations in pushing for this. He certainly has, both as Chancellor of the Exchequer and now as Prime Minister, played a very important role in championing the cause of African countries and particularly for increasing Aid to African countries. So for both reasons I'm not surprised and I think it's a good thing. I do know that, increasingly, the leadership on these issues has to be taken by developing countries, including Ghana.

IA-D: What is the set up of the African division of the Bank, which you once headed?

GN: I held the Vice-Presidency. It is divided into twelve country departments, so the 44 sub-Saharan African countries that come under the Africa Vice-Presidency had, if you like, twelve Country Directors. And then there is also a structure of technical specialists, grouped under four different areas: Private Sector Development, Sustainable Development, Poverty and Health Management, and Human Development. This is a matrix organisation and Country Directors play a very important role in the dialogue with country authorities, and the technical staff in the four divisions or departments that support the country teams. I think it is a good structure; we have been able to attract some of the best people – certainly some of the most noted people in the Bank – to come and work in the African Vice -Presidency.

I do think there are challenges that countries face which the Bank has to do better to support, and I would say that in each of the four areas there is at least one challenge that needs even more attention. In Human Development, it is Education. Emphasis on Primary Education is appropriate, but it is not sufficient. If one looks at Secondary Education, access to Secondary Education, let alone Tertiary Education, is very low, but if you look at the experience of East Asia, Education is fundamental. If you look at the Sustainable Development department, Agriculture needs a revolution on the continent; we're not there yet. Infrastructure is a big stumbling block. In the area of Private Sector and Finance, there is the beginning of growth in the Private Sector in African countries but the access to Finance issue is severe and creative methods have to be found to do even better. In Poverty and Health Management, the biggest challenge for African countries, including Ghana, is how best to manage the revenues that are coming from mineral and petroleum resources that countries have, to get the best out of those for their people.

IA-D: Apart from being the Vice-President for Africa at the World Bank, you have also been an Advisor to the government of Ghana. What has been the trend of Ghana's relationship with the Bank since 1957? What have been the major landmarks?

GN: Well there was a big hiatus in 1962-3 when the Bank and Ghana disagreed over the construction of the Akosombo Dam. That was one big point at which relations were strained. From 1967 through about 72 the relationship was a very strong one, but then again between 1972 and 79 under the Acheampong regime, there were strains and stresses – lots and lots of attempts to find common ground. Then you have the period between 1983 and around 1991, which was the Economic Recovery Programme era, which is seen as really the beginning of a turnaround on the continent with Ghana taking the lead in the approach to its development. I think the relationship was extremely strong then.

Since then, the relationship has basically attained a very high level and is on a bit of a plateau, at a high level, with a lot of give-and-take, a lot of mutual respect, a lot of mutual accountability. I would say that it's a very mature relationship, so much so that Ghana was seriously considering, and had discussed with the IMF for example, going on what they call a PSI, which is a kind of supervised IMF monitoring of a government programme without any cash resources with respect to the Fund. That would mean that the Bank would be the major interlocutor with Ghana in that scenario. How much the current fuel and food price crisis may have affected this desire on the part of the government or not I'm not sure.

IA-D: People talk of the first major reform – that is the 1983 Structural Adjustment Programme – and then sort of label Ghana as the "star pupil" of the World Bank and the IMF. What did it mean at the time?

GN: Well, it certainly meant that Ghana enjoyed access to some of the best staff within the Bank, who were the people made available to work on the Programme in Ghana? It certainly made a difference in access to the finance that Ghana was able to get. Remember the Bank's financing is not just significant because of its own level, but also because it triggers a lot of financing from other partners – from the bi-laterals, from the UN agencies and so on. So for those reasons Ghana did benefit, and of course once Ghana got the reputation of being a star performer, other benefits began to flow – I mean particularly in the form of access to short-term financing; access to investment financing for mining companies; and you saw most recently something that was attained by Ghana which was supported in a broad sense by the Bank, when Ghana was able to float and have its sovereign bond over-subscribed by a factor of four.

IA-D: As Economic Advisor to the government of Ghana, what was your role?

GN: Well, there was an Economic Management Team – a handful of us – working very closely trying to diagnose the problems as we saw them.

IA-D: When was this?

GN: This was in 1982-83. There was the Corporate Sector, where the share of the corporate farmer was miniscule; the Timber Sector; the Gold Sector. A few of the mining companies were not confident enough to invest in Ghana at that time. As for the pricing of imports, essentially it was an exchange rate issue, which had been compounded by a very severe drought so there was a food crisis as well. I think that what's important was that there was recognition that you basically had to raise prices on imports in some way in order to finance higher returns to exporters, and when that was explained to stakeholders, it was crystal clear right from the word go. It was only later that people made the connection and saw that really that wasn't very different from exchange rate adjustment. But what was important was being able to convince our external partners that this was something that the then-government was going to implement. But once that hurdle was over, the financing to make the Programme succeed became available. So that was then.

Then in 1985, when this was behind us, there was a need to go beyond immediate macroeconomic challenges and to start thinking about reforms and sectors – Public Enterprise Reform, Agricultural Sector Reform and Private Sector Reform. So in 1985, the fully-fledged Economic Recovery Programme was put together, and I led the technical team that did that. And then that was presented to a Consultative Group meeting in Paris in 1985.

I should also mention that I was home in 1981 also as an Advisor to the Hilla Limann government (1979-81), and initially the help that was sought from me was to be the technical leader to pull together a Five-Year Development Plan, which had to be presented to Parliament by a certain deadline. Once that was done – and it was done successfully and on time – I was invited then to the Ministry of Finance to lead the technical team in the negotiations with the IMF, which was very interesting. I hadn't worked in the IMF, but I knew enough about their operations and of course I had been home for several months and I had a much deeper understanding of the situation then. That was when we actually got very close to an agreement with the IMF, again based on an analysis done by a technical team at home, of our own situation. And this whole scheme of paying exporters higher prices on the basis of import duties was actually developed also at that time, in 1981. In the end, Limann's government didn't go for it, but a lot of the work that was done then was picked up by me and some others in 1982-83, which finally led to an agreement.

IA-D: After the Structural Adjustment Programme, we transited to the Ghana Poverty Reduction Programme and then we also went to the HIPC, in which you played a very critical role. What were the stages we went through up to HIPC?

GN: I was back from Brazil – I was the Country Director for Brazil for the World Bank – and returned to Washington in 2001 when the HIPC programme was very much at its implementation stage. I knew that Ghana had debated during the 1990s whether or not to accept the HIPC programme and from my point of view, looking at the financial gains to Ghana, found it hard to understand why any country would not grab it as quickly as possible. But I understood that there were some important bilateral partners of Ghana – who I'd rather not mention – who felt that that would make it impossible for them to extend further credits or grants to Ghana. I think it was excellent that, in 2001, the debate was joined again – 2002, I think it was, the Ghana government decided to accept the HIPC programme.

My own role as the Vice-President for Poverty Reduction and Economic Management Network was to oversee the HIPC contract design and implementation. It was really to be sure that the debt sustainability analysis was robust, and I certainly felt that most African countries had onerous debt burdens and the HIPC programme would be of benefit to Ghana and other African countries in a major way to allow development financing for investment projects to take precedence over repayment of debt. We have to credit again Gordon Brown for his leadership on this issue, but certainly also a lot of the NGOs based in Ghana and abroad who fought very hard for this to happen. My own sense is HIPC gains really were gains that would come to countries over a 20-40 year period, so we are still enjoying the benefits of that.

What is most important is to ensure that our public investment decision-making machinery about what to invest in is really robust so that the gains from HIPC actually make a difference to the standard of living of the poorest Ghanaian. I'm not aware of any evaluation of this – I know the government has been very keen on earmarking HIPC funds for specific projects all over the country, which is good, but we really need to be sure that the funds are being used in the best possible way.

IA-D: One of the difficulties of HIPC as a concept or as a strategy was that policymakers of some countries in Africa didn't fully understand the implications of what they were supposed to go through and so decision-making on whether to join or not was a problem. Does the Bank normally in situations like this take the time to go down to grassroots level, to domestic policymakers who don't understand some of these issues, before implementation is carried out?

GN: Yes, very much so. You could argue that the Bank could have done even more, but very much so. I remember, for example, attending a HIPC meeting in Malawi at which there were representatives from all African countries – not just government representatives, but NGO representatives and academics – to discuss the HIPC programme, to add inputs to the design of the debt sustainability framework. Similar to that, there were many meetings held across the continent, and all over the world in fact, including many meetings in Washington D.C., again to which NGOs, academics, and government officials were invited in the design stages to comment on and help shape the HIPC programme. So the Bank certainly did that. The problem with the HIPC programme was that many countries like Ghana who are proud of their achievements didn't want to be stigmatised as having to be forgiven their debts, in the fear that that could possibly jeopardise their access to future commercial finance. Well, we know what happened when we launched the Sovereign Bond last year, so certainly history has gone the decision-makers' way in this sense.

IA-D: Do you think it has been worth it?

GN: Absolutely. There has been a tremendous gain. I'm trying to recall some numbers, but I know that certainly for Africa as a continent, the HIPC programme has delivered somewhere in the neighbourhood of –

if my memory serves me right – $35-40 billion, so maybe $4 billion of that was for Ghana in net present value terms. And I don't see what the loss was; in fact we are more credit-worthy now because of HIPC and free of any possible stigma HIPC could have given. The only thing is, now that our debt capacity is low and we're able to borrow in fact well under the financial crisis of today is another complication. We have to be absolutely sure that we don't get into that trap again.

IA-D: Apart from the Bank, finance capital and technical assistance can today be accessed from international markets and private investment banks like JP Morgan and others. How is this going to affect Ghana's relationship with the Bank?

GN: Well, we are seeing a test of that right now, with the increase in the prices of oil and food. Many countries all over the world – Asia, Africa and Latin-America – are less under strain and stress. Why? Well first of all, these price increases for importing countries are raising inflationary pressures which means that the government has to tighten its monetary policy. That is happening; the Bank of Ghana has been raising interest rates. There's a need also to protect your people from some of the worst effects of these price increases, so the government has to find ways of subsidising some of these items, and I think President Kufuor's recent package in June 2008, which is estimated to have cost about $100 million, was a good package overall in that direction. So countries are under strain. I'm not sure what our level of reserves is, but I think in most countries including Ghana, reserves certainly are much lower than they were a year back.

Under these circumstances, it's going to be harder and harder to repeat the sovereign bond issue of last year. It's not impossible; I think there are still corporates in the emerging world that are raising funds, but less than a year back. It wouldn't be wise even for Ghana to try and raise funds now because it would probably, if it succeeded, have to pay a much higher interest rate, and you just don't want that to be a benchmark for future issues. Under these circumstances, as rightful members of the Bank and the Fund, my advice would be to take full advantage of the facilities we have there, to borrow if we need the resources. If we don't need them, we should manage without them.

IA-D: Were the food crisis and the oil/petroleum crisis that we have now expected, they seemed to have come so suddenly? Were there any indicators that it would come to this?

GN: You have to separate the food and oil crises because the underlying dynamics are different. The food crisis was accentuated by a number of things being added to what is essentially a growth in demand for food coming out of very high growth rates in Asia. Some of these things were not foreseen – the drought in Australia, which is a major supplier of wheat. Australia has had a seven to eight year drought and it has become worse every year – that was not foreseen. I think also the price of oil affected the price of fertiliser, which affected the price of food. The price of oil was not foreseen. And you also have other things that are happening. The price of oil itself has generated a policy in some countries to favour bio-fuels and so there is an increasing demand for food caused by the price of oil. But the main thing about food is its demand is very inelastic: with a sudden shortage of food, prices rise because everybody has to eat. So some degree of surprise is always there, but no one expected it to go this high. It went this high also because there were a series of events which affected it.

With the price of oil, it's hard to say. I suspect that what is happening is because of the financial crisis in global confidence. People are making portfolio choices and shifting their funds around and finding that the only two places they can park their funds without risking losing even more money are either in cash or in commodities. So again, demand is rising because of the growth in demand from Asia, but the need for some to invest their funds in commodities has raised demand even more and thus raised prices. There is a structural increase in commodities because of China, India, and other countries, but that, in my personal view – there is a lot of debate about this – explains about 70 per cent of what we've seen. There is a 30 per cent element that is more a consequence of the financial crisis.

II

IA-D: You've been Chief Economist of the World Bank for South Asia. There are often comparisons between Ghana's growth performance and those of Malaysia or Korea. What went right in Malaysia or Korea that didn't happen in Ghana? We had the same characteristics after colonial rule.

GN: The East Asian "miracle" was studied in the early-1990s, and now a few months back there was a Growth Commission Report which also looked at the countries that have grown at 7 per cent a year or more in the last 25 years. They found 13 countries, of which I believe nine were in East Asia, so your question is very pertinent.

You know, Joe Stiglitz was in Ghana a few weeks back and when he was asked this – I wasn't around but I read about it – he said the single most important explanatory factor was probably Education. I visited Malaysia recently with some African Finance Ministers in 2006 to get a better understanding of what they could have done differently. The Deputy Prime Minister said the same thing: Education. It has to be said that, while we are doing a lot in Education today, it does not compare very favourably with what Asian countries were able to do 30-40 years back for their educational systems, in terms of Secondary Education, in terms of Science and Technology. Today, the number of papers published in journals by Chinese and Korean scientists is way above any one of those countries and way above all of the African continent, including North Africa. So Education in a very systematic way is critical.

The other thing is: East Asian governments experimented with policies as we have, but somehow they were able when those policies went wrong to pull back and not keep going. Whether that has to do with the governance system, whether that has to do with some kind of Asian way of getting things done I'm not sure, but we have to say that the institutional ability of East Asian countries – whether it's Singapore, Korea, or Malaysia – to correct decisions is something that we have found much more difficult; "we" meaning the rest of the world, the non-East Asian countries. So sometimes it's better not to experiment if you think you can't correct your mistakes. I would say that we should experiment still, but find ways to correct our mistakes. So these are two things I would stress.

IA-D: To what extent would you say the colonial experience contributed to this? Asia was the last continent to be colonised and by the time colonialism got to Asia, some of these domestic institutions that you were talking about had been developed already. Don't you think that the impact of colonial rule in Africa was far more extensive than in Asia?

GN: It's a very debatable point. Certainly colonial rule had its strong negatives, in particular the extraction of raw materials with very little processing and very little payoff for the rest of the economy, but then if I look at the difficulties faced by a country like Ethiopia, which for all practical purposes was not colonised, it's not easy to dismiss that example. If you look at countries in Asia – look at Thailand which was not colonised – it is doing very well today. Malaysia, which was, is also doing very well. I would say that you have to look at the country context and make a judgement as to whether the net effect was negative or neutral or positive. Certainly countries have found ways of working around some of the constraints that colonial institutions may have put on them.

IA-D: Ghana's relationship with China, India, and to some extent Japan, is unprecedented. Some say that this sort of relationship is one of exploitation – extraction of African raw materials for the growth of Asia. Others think that this will also give Africa some level of growth. What is the nature of these relationships and what benefit will they be to Ghana?

GN: I think that, in a way, Ghana and other African countries have a second chance: the natural resource boom we're seeing today is a tremendous opportunity for African countries. The world is back at our door looking for something that they need and we have. But we also need to make sure that we get in return what we need. I was at the Beijing summit in November 2006 – most impressive. It was Chinese economic diplomacy at its best. Fifteen Heads of State were represented, and what struck me the most was that each one of our countries was negotiating bilaterally with China. China is an 800-pound gorilla compared with any one of us. I think we need to make sure we get the best possible deal, and we're not there yet.

What do I mean? Two things: First of all, China, and India also, have said that exports from the least developed countries in Africa to their countries – to India and China – can be tariff- and quota-free. The problem is; these developing countries don't have the capacity to export much. Countries like Ghana, Kenya, and Tanzania, which do, don't have this benefit. We should not accept that. Really the benefit has to be given to all African countries, but we have not negotiated this as yet. When China invited investors from the US to try and develop its economy, it insisted on joint ventures, it insisted on technological transfers, skills adaptation – all of those things. We should do the same when Chinese firms invest here. Why should they bring their own labour? I could go on – there's a lot that we can do.

So I see it as a tremendous opportunity but we need to do a few things. We need first of all to negotiate, either as the AU or as ECOWAS, and if not then as groups of like-minded countries, but not alone, because that will increase our powers of negotiation. Secondly, we need to get duty- and quota-free access for all African countries. Thirdly, we need investment codes agreed with China and India which ensure that the benefits are shared much better. Fourthly, we need a lot of exchanges and training programmes so that we use the highest skills that they have to upgrade our own skills in the shortest possible time. So I see it as a tremendous opportunity. I've just seen a study which looked at the impact of Chinese investment in African countries in terms of growth and in terms of other variables. A statistical study has its limitations, but by and large, even under current conditions, it seems that the net impact is positive. It could be much more positive, but the onus is on us.

IA-D: But do you not think the sudden flooding of Chinese goods on the Ghanaian market is, to some extent, destabilising local industry?

GN: Well, let's think again. As long as they're not breaking patents; as long as they're producing goods which don't have patents, and are able to produce them very cost-effectively, certainly Ghanaian consumers benefit. It's the manufacturers who are having a hard time. So it's not an open-and-shut case, and my own feeling is that there are things that could be done. The first country in Africa that has struck a good deal with China is South Africa. South Africa has joint ventures, technological transfer agreements; they even have voluntary restraints on exports of manufactured goods to South Africa from China, so they have struck a good arrangement. I think we can do some of that, but let's not penalise the Ghanaian consumer by having her or him buy local goods at higher prices and lower quality. What we need to do is ask ourselves whether there are things Ghanaians can produce which others can't, which somehow we're not able to now. There are a lot of things like that, including particularly in Agriculture, in Information Technology, services – there are all sorts of problems that businessmen in these sectors face in trying to make a success of these ventures. We can do more by supporting them and not keeping out high-quality, cost-effective Chinese imports for our consumers.

IA-D: I've checked the records and over the last couple of years, the Tokyo International Conference on African Development (TICAD) process has recorded much more investment in Ghana than previously in the struggle for natural resources. From even China and India, it's up. Is there a trend that the competition between India and China will lead to some form of growth in Ghana itself?

GN: I think it's terrific for Africa, for African countries, for Ghana that China, India, and Japan are competing with each other to try and have access to the kinds of products that we have and they need. And it's primarily natural resources. So that's terrific, and the competition has certainly helped. But it will not help as much as if we also, as I said earlier, try to ask ourselves: what is Africa's China policy? What is Africa's India policy, or Japan? In short: what is Africa's Asia policy, and how can we get a fairer deal? I call it a "grand bargain". We have the natural resources, they need the natural resources – let's have a grand bargain. We need access to their markets, we need investment codes so that the investment they make here will be win-win, and we need to take advantage of their knowledge and skills to upgrade our own skills as quickly as possible.

IA-D: Final question: what are the potential areas for growth in the Ghanaian economy in the coming years? Of course, we have oil now and there is a huge debate about what it could do for the economy of Ghana and what it cannot do. Apart from oil, are there other potential areas for growth?

GN: One of the countries we should look at and adapt to our own situation – but look at – is Malaysia. Why Malaysia? Malaysia started out with natural resources like ours – agricultural resources; oil palm, which they borrowed from Nigeria. Malaysia invested in oil palm and has developed a slew of downstream products relating to oil palm, which it exports; it has the patents for these – body lotion, all kinds of things. It did the same in other agricultural products. And then it found oil and it managed the oil wealth very well. For Malaysia, oil wealth has been a blessing, not a curse: it has used a lot of the oil wealth for Education. So it added Education and Technology to its Agriculture and to its Oil resources, and then, when the time was right, it also went into manufacturing. It started assembling electronic goods and so forth. So it combined its natural resources with Education and Technology and then to Manufacturing. I think that's what our vision could be, adapted for us. It can't be the same; we have to do it ourselves.

And this is where sometimes we get a little misdirected when we think that we should go straight to Manufacturing. We will get there, but what the world needs from us is natural resources, and what we need to make sure is that we use these resources to educate ourselves; to get the right technology; to develop new products based on those natural resources, in addition to the exports that we are already doing, which will help us to have a niche of our own. And the Manufacturing will come when we get the Education. Right now, wages are rising very fast in China; the exchange rate is also appreciating very fast in China. Things that China was producing five years back, five years from now, it will not be able to. Some of those things will then be niches that we can move into, but we need to get the sequence right.

IA-D: Thank you very much.

GN: Thank you.

July 2008

Epilogue

This anthology of reflections certainly does not say everything about the economic history of Ghana from the postcolonial period to the early or first decade of the twenty-first century. Many books have been written on sectors of the economy such as banking and investment, finance and capital markets, even the recent "birth" of the Ghana Stock Exchange, commodities – cocoa, timber, cotton; minerals – gold, bauxite, and others. If these are big issues, some of which have been central to arguments or reflections in this book, there are "mundane" areas of the rural economy, mainly cultural, that were not the direct target here (except briefly with Oteng-Gyasi). These include the role of tourism and the textile industry, such as the *Kente* and *Adinkra* cloth weaving (in Bonwire in the Ejisu-Juaben and Kwabre districts of the Ashanti region and also the Ewe *Kente* industry in the Volta region), art works such as sculpture, beads, pottery, weaving (especially the famous Bolgatanga baskets in the upper parts of Ghana, whose export values the Ghana Export and Promotion Council estimated in 2007 as part of the $1.2 billion of the non-traditional export market. This was from its 2006 value of $892 million, thus a 30.5 per cent increase), which create sources of revenue for hundreds of thousands of rural dwellers who are not in the main agricultural sector. In fact, if the United Nations Education, Scientific and Cultural Organisation (UNESCO) figure of the global creative economy of $2.4 trillion or 7 per cent of Global Gross Domestic Product for 2001 is used, it means that the global cultural economy or creative industry is growing at 14 per cent. Ghana has still not fully run its cultural capital. The cultural sector has been ignored for a long time in its economic calculation. It will surprise many to know that the third largest source of revenue for the Asanteman Council (by far the biggest traditional one in Ghana) apart from land and gold royalties is the Manhyia Palace Museum, which receives an average of 65,000 visitors a year, in addition to its merchandise sales. Before the late King of Asante, Otumfuo Opoku Ware II, established it on the 25th anniversary of his kingship (in 1995), there were some local critics including even some apparently enlightened people. Fifteen years later, his successor is contemplating another, bigger museum.

It is a sector worth looking at. I deliberately decided not to include the cultural economy in this discussion because I am engaged in a full-scale work on it. Indeed, no single book or work can claim authority on any particular sector of the economy: there will always be the traditional view; there will always be new evidence to challenge or endorse the traditional understanding, taking it into the realm of what is called revisionist point, and some could even say, of post-revisionist arguments. What this book is offering, however, is an opportunity for people who are interested in doing extensive work in specific areas of the Ghanaian economy to understand certain views that have prevailed and also engage with some of the people who have through their scholarship, professional career, or otherwise shaped them.

Certain questions deliberately run through, like the role of multilateral institutions, and the oil find in Ghana and its consequences for the economy, because for years to come the multilateral institutions will help to define the contours of our development through finance and technical assistance. The oil economy that Ghana is about to enter into will change the equation or strategy for good or ill, though hopefully for good. And in such an anthology you cannot escape the opinions of some of the policy makers.

About the Book

The postcolonial Ghanaian economy is half a century old. It was managed from the beginning by its famous independence leader, Kwame Nkrumah, and his Convention People's Party from March 1957. It has undergone periods of serious decline, near collapse, structural reforms, and sometimes hopes of revival between the eight regimes – military and constitutional – during the post-Nkrumah years from 1966. Consensus as to what went wrong and what went right is difficult to attain. Notwithstanding this "great divergence", there are still points of convergence and hope for the future.

In this economic anthology, twenty distinguished individuals – researchers and scholars on the Ghanaian economy, bureaucrats, ministers and former ministers of state, university dons, civil society leaders, Ghanaians and some non-Ghanaians – reflect on a half-century of transformation. They include from the "outside" eminent economists such as Jeffrey D. Sachs of The Earth Institute at Columbia University and Advisor to the UN Secretary-General; Dirk-Jan Omtzigt, a Dutch scholar who has taught at Oxford University and was recently an Adam Smith International Fellow in Africa; and Gareth Austin of the London School of Economics and Political Science, all of whom, apart from being scholars, have at different levels and times been associated with the Ghanaian economy.

Their views cut across the three themes of the book: Structures and Institutions in a Postcolonial Economy; A Vampire Economy with a Silver Lining (which looks at the role of Public Policy) and Stimulation and Innovation in the Economy. They are not alone in this as local Ghanaian economists of equally good standing and some with open ideological disposition are participants: former Vice-President Professor John Evans Atta Mills; former Vice-President of the World Bank for Africa, Dr Gobind Nankani; Professor Ernest Aryeetey of the

Institute of Statistical, Social and Economic Research at the University of Ghana; Dr Nii Moi Thompson of the Development Policy Institute and of the Convention People's Party; Dr Anthony Akoto-Osei, Minister of State at the Ministry of Finance and Economic Planning of the New Patriotic Party; and Moses Asaga, former National Democratic Congress Deputy Minister of Finance and Economic Planning, and others. There are of course bureaucrats who have had much to do with economic development over the years and they include here: Mary Chinery-Hesse, the first Woman Deputy Director of the International Labour Organisation and Chief Advisor to the President; and Ambassadors Annan Cato and D. K. Osei.

Others are: Social Policy Specialist Dr Ellen Bortei-Doku Aryeetey; Energy Expert Dr Charles Wereko-Brobby; in Mining, Joyce Aryee; Roads and Transport, Dr Richard Anane; in Governance, Professor E. Gyimah-Boadi; and in commodities, Isaac Osei.

Also included are some operators and eminent representatives of the financial markets and the manufacturing industry: Ken Ofori-Atta of the pre-eminent Databank Financial Services and Tony Oteng-Gyasi, President of the Association of Ghana Industries.

The reflections were conducted over a year by Ivor Agyeman-Duah, himself a trained Economic Historian and the main editor of this book. It is also the basis of a television series of the same title, the first ever attempts to use multi-media and in a bi-partisan spirit, to present, through multiple voices, a reflection on Ghana's economic history.

OTHER BOOKS BY
Ivor Agyeman-Duah

Political Reflections on the Motherland, co-author (UST Publishers, Kumasi, 1991).

Antiochus Lives Again: Political Essays of Joe Appiah, Editor (Catholic Press, Kumasi, 1992).

Some African Voices of Our Time (Anansesem Publication, Accra, 1992).

Asante Monarchy in Exile (Tri-Force, Kumasi, 1997).

Kyerematen and Culture – The Kyerematen Memorial Lectures, Editor (Glade Digital, Accra, Ghana 2001).

Bu Me Be: Akan Proverbs, with Peggy Appiah and Kwame Anthony Appiah (Glade Digital, Accra 2001).

Between Faith and History: A Biography of J. A. Kufuor (Africa World Press: New Jersey, 2002).

Africa in a Renaissance Mood – Ghana in the Early Years of the Twenty-First Century (Washington Times, Washington, DC, 2004).

Between Faith and History: A Biography of J. A. Kufuor (2nd edition, Ayebia Press Ltd., Oxfordshire, 2007).

Bu Me Be: Proverbs of the Akans, with Peggy Appiah and Kwame Anthony Appiah (2nd edition, Ayebia Press Ltd., Oxfordshire, 2007).

Pan-Africanism Caribbean Connections, co-author (Universe New York, 2007).

Index